Volume I:
THE FOUNDATIONS OF THE ARAB STATE

NATION, STATE AND INTEGRATION IN THE ARAB WORLD

Project Director and Series Editor: Giacomo Luciani,
Istituto Affari Internazionali, Rome

Volume I: THE FOUNDATIONS OF THE ARAB STATE
Edited by Ghassan Salamé

Volume II: THE RENTIER STATE
Edited by Hazem Beblawi and Giacomo Luciani

Volume III: BEYOND COERCION: THE DURABILITY OF
THE ARAB STATE
Edited by Adeed Dawisha and I. William Zartman

Volume IV: THE POLITICS OF ARAB INTEGRATION
Edited by Giacomo Luciani and Ghassan Salamé

Volume I:

The Foundations of the Arab State

Edited by
Ghassan Salamé

CROOM HELM
London • New York • Sydney

© 1987 Istituto Affari Internazionali
Croom Helm Ltd, Provident House, Burrell Row,
Beckenham, Kent BR3 1AT
Croom Helm Australia, 44-50 Waterloo Road, North Ryde,
2113, New South Wales

Published in the USA by
Croom Helm
in association with Methuen, Inc.
29 West 35th Street
New York, NY 10001

British Library Cataloguing in Publication Data

The Foundations of the Arab State. —
    (Nation, state and integration in the
    Arab world; v. 1)
    1. State. The 2. Arab countries —
    Politics and government — 1945-
    I. Salamé, Ghassan   II. Series
    320.1′0917′4927   JQ1850.A2
    ISBN 0-7099-4143-9

Library of Congress Cataloging-in-Publication Data
ISBN 0-7099-4143-9

Typeset in Times Roman by Leaper & Gard Ltd, Bristol, England
Printed and bound in Great Britain
by Billing & Sons Limited, Worcester.

Contents

Foreword
Introduction *Ghassan Salamé*   1

Part One

1. The Origins of the Arab State System
   Iliya Harik   19

2. Alien and Besieged Yet Here to Stay: the Contradictions
   of the Arab Territorial State
   Bahgat Korany   47

3. State-building and Regime Performance in the
   Greater Maghreb
   Elbaki Hermassi   75

Part Two

4. State and Authority in Arabic Political Thought
   Charles E. Butterworth   91

5. Notions of the State in Contemporary Arab-Islamic
   Writings
   Fahmi Jadaane   112

6. *Al-Watan* and *Al-Umma* in Contemporary Arab Use
   Said Bensaid   149

Part Three

7. Changing Perceptions of State Authority:
   Morocco, Egypt and Oman
   Dale F. Eickelman   177

8. 'Strong' and 'Weak' States, a Qualified Return to the
   Muqaddimah
   Ghassan Salamé   205

References   241

List of Contributors   253

Index   255

Foreword

The Arab State is a series of four collective volumes exploring
the origins, foundations, impact and stability of Arab states.
This volume is the first in the series; it is devoted to an analysis
of the historical and cultural foundations of the state in the
Arab region and a discussion of their peculiarity. It is indeed
often stated that Arab states are different because of their
specific historical origins or because of constraints imposed by
Islam or by Arab culture, and that they suffer from the tension
of an ill-defined national identity. The purpose of this volume is
to offer a fresh look at the question and to propose alternative
opinions as to the importance of this difference.

The series is the result of a collective research effort
organised by the Istituto Affari Internazionali over a period of
three years, under the general title of 'State, Nation, Integration
in the Arab World'. This undertaking was made possible by a
generous main grant from the Ford Foundation, and an equally
generous additional grant from the International Development
Research Centre (IDRC) of Canada. The latter was specifically
devoted to supporting the work of Arab scholars writing on
economic issues. Further financial support was received from
the Italian Ministry of Foreign Affairs, and from the Commission for Cultural Exchanges between Italy and the United
States.

The Istituto Affari Internazionali worked in co-operation
with the Panteios School of Political Science in Athens, which
was responsible for the organisation of two international gather-
ings, allowing authors of different chapters to come together
and discuss their ideas in depth. As a result, while these are
collective volumes, we believe that they have reached a degree
of homogeneity which is not normally found in these undertakings. The Panteios School also supported one of the meetings
with its own funds, decisively contributing to the success of the
project.

Help was also received from the Gustav E. von Grunebaum
Centre for Near Eastern Studies at the University of California,
Los Angeles, which entertained me in February and March
1984 and again in the Autumn of 1986.

The project was directed by an international steering

committee in which the following participated:
Roberto Aliboni, Director, Istituto Affari Internazionali
Hazem Beblawi, Chairman, Egyptian Export Development
  Bank
Ursula Braun, Consultant, Stiftung Wissenschaft und Politik
Marwan Buheiry, Professor, American University of Beirut
Alexander Cudsi, Professor, Panteios School of Political
  Science
Adeed Dawisha, Professor, George Mason University
Omaymah Dahhan, Professor, University of Jordan
Georges Sabagh, Director, the Gustav E. von Grunebaum
  Center for Near Eastern Studies, UCLA
Ghassan Salamé, Professor, American University of Beirut
I. William Zartman, Director, Africa Program, School for
  Advanced International Studies, Johns Hopkins University
  The committee played a major role, and I as director of the
project am very substantially indebted to its members for their
advice in planning the research effort and selecting contributors.
Some of the members also served as editors for a volume, thus
exercising closer responsibility on the material included in it:
this first volume was edited by Ghassan Salamé.

I received substantial help and advice also from other friends.
Ali-Eddine Hilal Dessouki was expected to be on the committee, but a variety of circumstances prevented him from partici-
pating in its deliberations. I did, nevertheless, greatly benefit
from his generous advice and detailed comments, during
numerous interviews in Cairo. My debt to him is indeed
substantial. I also greatly benefited from the friendly advice that
I received from Judy Barsalou of the Ford Foundation in Cairo,
Ann Lesch of the American Field Staff in Cairo, Andrew
Watson of the IDRC in Cairo, and Gary Sick of the Ford
Foundation in New York.

My personal thanks are also due to the staff of the Istituto
Affari Internazionali who contributed with sympathy and
dedication to the complex organisation of this undertaking.

The shape of this project was deeply influenced by the advice
of two friends who unfortunately did not live to see its conclusion. The steering committee decided to dedicate the four
volumes to their memory.

I had met Malcolm Kerr in Los Angeles when the project was
still in its planning stage, and he gave me valuable advice at that

time. I asked him to be a member of the committee, but he was then expecting to be appointed President of the American University of Beirut. He insisted, however, that he wanted to be associated with the project, so much so that the first meeting of the steering committee was hosted by him at Marquand House in June 1983. He participated in our deliberations then, and contributed to the formation of the basic decisions which shaped the project. His assassination was a tragedy for us personally and professionally, and has marked a disastrous turning point in West Beirut's struggle to remain one of the intellectual centres of the world.

The same negative turn of events finally drove Marwan Buheiry out of Beirut. Marwan was, personally and intellectually, a living example of West Beirut's intellectual curiosity and non-sectarian spirit. He participated intensely in the work of the steering committee and in the meetings connected with this project, until death struck unexpectedly, in exile.

It has been an honour and an educational experience for me to serve as the director of this project, and I wish to thank all contributors for the very many things I have learned. I hope that the reader will find these volumes as instructive as preparing them was for me. Any shortcoming, as usual, should be ascribed to my responsibility only.

Giacomo Luciani
Director of Studies
Istituto Affari Internazionali

Introduction

Ghassan Salamé

I

This volume, the first in the collection on the Arab state, deals with the conceptual, historical, and cultural environment in which the contemporary Arab state system was established and has evolved. As noted by one of this book's contributors, 'if the 1980s brought the state back into political analysis, the systematic study of the Arab state is still nascent'. Though not really 'systematic', this volume and, indeed, the whole series addresses the major issues posed by the emergence of contemporary Arab states, by their consolidation, the role played by foreign powers in their creation and/or their final shaping, their present strength, and their future in a region of the world that is historically not familiar with the European model of national states.

If the term 'state' was rarely used in American political sociology, this was not the case everywhere. As noted by Alfred Stepan, 'Society-centered views of political and economic transformation have never held the unchallenged sway in Latin America that they have in North America' (Evans, Rueschemeyer and Skocpol, 1985:317). Organic-state models of society prevailed there as well as in certain European countries, notably in France where 'l'idée d'Etat' has largely dominated the work of experts in constitutional law (Hauriou, Burdeau) and later of political sociologists (Bertrand Badie, C. Buci-Glucksman).

Hence when Skocpol notes that 'a paradigmatic shift seems to be underway in the macroscopic social sciences, a shift that involves a fundamental rethinking of the role of states in relation to economies and societies' (Evans, Rueschemeyer and Skocpol, 1985: 7), the judgement should be qualified. If 'state

1

power in the twentieth-century United States is fragmented, dispersed and everywhere permeated by the organised societal interests' (ibid: 12), and if 'the state was considered to be an old-fashioned concept, associated with dry and dusty legal-formalist studies of nationally particular constitutional principles' (ibid: 4), this lack of interest was not equally observed outside North America. It is, however, true that, as far as the Arab world is concerned, comprehensive analyses of the pivotal relation between states and civil societies remained under-developed, in comparison, for example, with Western Europe or Latin America.

Many newly established countries in the region (Kuwait, Qatar, Israel) retain the word 'state' in their official name, as if their statehood was too vulnerable not to be systematically reasserted. This also indicates that the debate has centred more on the viability of states as international, autonomous, 'sovereign', units than on states as actors shaping the societies they pretend to control. It also explains the Palestinians' emotional investment in a state of their own (a flag, a passport, a national anthem) without a detailed view of this potential state in relation to the Palestinians as a people, while M. Heller has tried to see what would be the implications for Israel if such a state were to be created. On the other hand, one is struck by the fact that Arab socialist trends in the 1960s and the 1970s were squeezed into a rather narrow view of what the 'public sector' should or should not include (when this discussion was possible at all), while largely ignoring the very wide effects which the nationalisation movement had or could have on society. By the end of the 1960s, for example, one out of every four Egyptians was directly or indirectly on the government's payroll, but the discussion of this feature as a political phenomenon remained limited.

The 'oil era' has blurred the picture even more. It is indeed widely accepted that 'a state's means of raising and deploying financial resources tells us more than could any other single factor' (Evans, Rueschemeyer and Skocpol, 1985: 17) about its capabilities, autonomy, strength, and viability. But the huge amounts of external rent accruing to the oil-producing countries after 1973 and indirectly to the non-oil Arab countries (through aid and expatriates' remittances) have certainly delayed (and largely aborted) burgeoning questions about the contemporary Arab states' capabilities to continue the *dirigiste* policies

2

adopted in the 1960s, and equally importantly, the kind of transition that will take place towards potentially different policies.

The prevailing question was, however, posed with insistence by all kinds of local and pan-Arab nationalists. American writers tended to consider the post-World War II territorial *status quo* as permanent. Their attitude clearly entailed a preference for an order that was widely favourable to the expansion of American influence in the world. One could sense an almost equally strong territorial conservatism in the views of the other major beneficiary of World War II, the Soviet Union. Gradually, when it came to the Third World, the two super-powers (and their social scientists) have generally shifted the discussion from the state as such to the kind of political regime (strong or weak, capitalist or socialist, authoritarian or democratic) prevalent in each of these countries. World War II seemed to have abruptly closed a lively discussion in Europe on what states to give birth to, what territories to allocate to them, and what populations to involve in this process.

This particular debate, concerning the original sin of state creation, was never closed in the Arab world, and this book is certainly not going to avoid it. To what extent were these Arab states (the twenty-two members of the Arab League, including the Palestine Liberation Organisation (PLO), a non-territorial state apparatus) created by a foreign, alien, hostile will? A derivative question that is probably more important today is to know if and why these states are perceived as foreign-made creations. A third and even more nagging issue is to assess the extent to which these internationally recognised units have taken root, less in the present-day world state system than in the hearts and minds of their own inhabitants.

In the absence of democratic practices, public opinion is very hard to assess. Five or six surveys, probably overquoted in this series, give the impression that states as sovereign political units are much more accepted than classic integrationist Arab nationalists would like us to believe. At the same time, one is struck by the amount of dissatisfaction with the isolationist policies followed by almost all Arab regimes, whatever their public ideologies. These policies make it difficult to cross an inter-Arab border, to call another Arab city by telephone, to get a work permit here, an export licence there, and a travel visa to almost everywhere.

But the debate was never ended. Besides the old polemical diatribes against Mr Sykes and Monsieur Georges-Picot who drew new borders for Britain and France across Greater Syria while World War I was still raging or against that French *ministre des colonies* who reportedly gave the Sahara to France (and hence to Algeria, its successor in 1962), or against the British administrator who broke the 'natural unity' of the Nile valley, a new body of scientific research has been growing during the past two decades, offering a balanced, documented, convincing history of the moment, the ways, and the meanings of the birth of most of the Arab States.

One could mention many examples in this respect: on Lebanon, the books of Zeine N. Zeine, Kamal Salibi, or Meir Zamir; on Iraq, William Stivers' *Supremacy and Oil*; the two books by Rosemarie Said-Zahlan on Qatar and the United Arab Emirates; Ali al-Mahafdha's writings on the formation of modern Jordan; those by Christine Helms or Gary Troeller on Saudi Arabia. Equally informative, though clearly espousing a traditional Arab nationalist view, is the collection of books commissioned by the Center for Arab Unity Studies in Beirut on the attitude of the great powers toward Arab unity, a collection opened in 1985 by al-Mahafdha's book dealing with French, Italian, and German policies in this respect before World War II. Of related interest are books based on geopolitical, quasi-millenarist hypotheses, such as the impressive and debatable book by Gamal Hamdan on Egypt's 'personality'. One has also to welcome the beginnings of a critical epistemology of Arab historiography, such as Ahmad Beydoun's dissertation, inspired by Michel Foucault's 'archéologie du savoir', which demonstrates how most of Lebanon's historians have projected their confessional outlook in their writing.

If the debate remains in spite of these rational reappraisals, it is first because the publication of a book does not automatically lead to a substantial change in a political culture. One has also to bear in mind that if nationalism has rapidly 'invaded' the Arab mind, it has not been met with a clear definition of where the nation is. Take the example of a Maronite Lebanese who is told by the historians of his community (and modern warlords) that the Maronite nation has existed for ages. But those Maronites who have rallied round the 1920 French-defined 'Grand Liban' tell him that if the Maronites have ever constituted a nation, this nation has now been diluted in the wider Lebanese modern one. Then the proponents of Greater (or Natural) Syria tell him that Lebanon is a purely artificial creation of colonialist France and that his loyalty should go exclusively to a Syrian nation present since Sumer and the Akkadians. Arab nationalists will insist that the Arab nation is the only 'true' nation, either in Sati' al-Husri's rather assertive way or in 'Abd al-'Aziz ad-Duri's more subtle prose. The proponents of an Islamic *umma* overshadowing all these terri-torially, linguistically or ethnically defined *'asabiyyas* (group feelings), tend to view these loyalties as pre-Muhammedan and thus anti-Islamic *Jahiliyya* concepts, which should have dis-appeared since the emergence of the Muhammeddan *Da'wa* (Call).

Each of these schools is indeed equipped with its own read-ing of the region's history. Hence the interest of the first three chapters in this volume, which offer a dispassionate though different contribution to this ongoing debate. Iliya Harik and Bahgat Korany both try to capture the state building process in the Arab world, with examples drawn from all over the area. While Korany is concerned with the territorial definition of the contemporary Arab states, Harik tries to relate the state to the type of government with which it has been associated since its inception. Besides the different angle, these two authors' conclusions are not always similar.

Harik tends to credit Arab states with old, genuine found-ations. Challenging a well-established view, he thinks that Arab countries are not only old societies but also old states. With three exceptions, 'they all go back to the nineteenth century or a much earlier period'. This statement specifies what is old and what is new in Harik's view — but this will probably remain an open question.

Harik dismisses the economic factors in the emergence of the Arab state system, stating that 'the lack of change in the economy during earlier centuries rules out economic factors as an explanatory principle of the formation of the multifarious state system'. Tracing the origin of the various states, he identi-fies their structure, power base, legitimacy, and traditions, which allows him to propose five different types of states: the *imam*-chief system (North Yemen, Oman, Morocco, for instance); the alliance system of chiefs and imams, as in Saudi Arabia; the traditional secular system in which authority is invested in a dynasty free from religious attributes (Lebanon

5

and the smaller Gulf states); the bureaucratic-oligarchy type in which authority is basically in the hands of an urban caste of garrison commanders helped by an extensive administrative apparatus (Egypt and other North African states); and finally, the colonially created state system, comprising the Fertile Crescent states (with the exception of Lebanon) carved from the defunct Ottoman Empire by European colonial powers.

This classification clearly implies that the contemporary Arab state system (with the exception of the fifth type) was not a pure creation of foreign powers, as is often claimed by Arab nationalists and by some scholars. Here a heterodox sect, there an alliance between a tribal leader and an Islamic reformer, or an ambitious Amir entrenched in rugged mountains, have established the nucleus of a state that will be later recognised by the foreign powers in the nineteenth century. Harik's point is clearest when he asserts that 'colonialism affected the boundaries of Arab states, but it did not, with the exception of the Fertile Crescent cases, create them. Colonialism gave more definitive form to the indigenous states and introduced elements of modern administration to them.'

Korany's position is much closer to the overwhelming Arab nationalist view that, to quote him, 'external factors predominated in the territorial definition of Arab states'. As far as the mere delineation of the borders is concerned, it is difficult to disagree with him. Korany identifies a 'tension' in Arab nation-state formation, triggered by what he views as its hybrid nature and its present transitional stage.

The external forces are European. They have succeeded in integrating the Ottoman empire into their own nation-states' political ideology, then they have destroyed Bani 'Uthman's empire in order to establish a mandate where, 'beneath the paper-work, the system's reality was in the hands of those who held the mandate power'. Korany sees a similar result of this colonial experience everywhere in the Arab world, namely 'the institutionalisation and consolidation of territorial states in the image of the European pattern'.

These new states have yet to face internal strains as well as territorial conflicts with their similarly created, similarly evolving neighbours. Korany's examples are drawn from the Arabian peninsula as well as from North Africa. But these conflicts are not annihilating those states. Korany's conclusion is that 'the Arab territorial state is becoming increasingly implanted and naturalised. The rise of the state of Israel and the oil phenomenon are equally serving this purpose.' He leaves open the question whether the contradictions of the Arab territorial state are closely related to its foreign origin: does this foreign origin provide sufficient and necessary reasons to explain also its continuing consolidation and supremacy?

Elbaki Hermassi, writing more specifically on the Maghreb, would probably view Korany's hypothesis as more relevant in the Mashreq than in North Africa, since

> contrary to the Mashreq where the unionist ideology prevailed, the Maghreb saw the rise of the national state and of territorial nationalism ... Considering political entities as transient and temporary territorial units is not verified by the objective and personal experience of most Maghrebins.

This early acceptance of the concept of a nation-state is somehow strengthened in the Maghreb by the levels of expectations triggered by the state apparatus as the centre of the national integration and economic development processes. Hence the very wide 'étatisation' of the Maghrebi societies, which is, however, challenged today by what Hédi Béji calls '*le désenchantement national*' (disillusionment with nationalism). This disenchantment appears now as a national crisis, because it is no longer restricted to the elite. It does not automatically lead to a real criticism of the state structure but only to the policies followed by existing regimes. Hence the limited structural impact of fundamentalism or of unionist movements à la Qadhafi.

Reading Harik does not contradict Hermassi's views, but only Hermassi's implied idea that the features he is discussing are purely Maghrebi. The disenchantment he alludes to is also widely felt in the Mashreq, as so well illustrated by the very mute reaction, both official and within the population, to important events such as the Israeli invasion of Lebanon in 1982. Disenchantment is, however, too vague a diagnosis to be really descriptive of the various and different cases where interest in politics and more specifically in state-building has faltered.

The arguments used by Harik, Korany, and Hermassi show that one could easily fall into a reductionist view, if and when one did not notice that European-modelled state apparatuses were more often than not superimposed on local, internally created nuclei of political power. There is indeed some formalism in the sudden reduction of the state to a framework, as in Charles Tilly's view of 'state-certifying organisations such as the League of Nations and the United Nations [that] simply extended the European-based process to the world as a whole. Whether forced or voluntary, bloody or peaceful, decolonisation simply completed that process by which existing states leagued to create new ones' (Evans, Rueschemeyer and Skocpol, 1985: 185).

The world system had indeed to deal with sometimes centuries-old local authorities. France did not create Lebanon from scratch. It had to deal with the three or four centuries-old principality of Mount Lebanon. Britain did not really create the Sudan, and no European power could claim to have created Morocco or Egypt. These are, certainly, variations even if the twentieth-century world system seems to be obsessed with a wide process of 'étatisation'. There are no *terra nullius,* and the rules are established to regulate the competition between world powers and to placate local nationalism and other group loyalties.

One feature that does not appear clearly enough in this volume is the role played by these powers in defining local loyalties or in helping some of them to prevail over others. Sectarian feelings in Lebanon do not exist only because people organise themselves along these lines but also because regional hegemonic powers have systematically dealt with the Lebanese as members of one confessional community or the other. Shi'i Arabs need the Sunni majority's recognition as well as their own loyalty to their faith if they really want to establish their sect as a politically effective cleavage. Challenging Shils and Geertz in their distinction between 'primordial' and 'secondary' loyalties, David D. Laitin has demonstrated that the Nigerian Yorubas' strong and apparently genuine attachment to their 'ancestral cities' as a major political divide has been systematically encouraged by British colonialism. British administrators chose to strengthen a declining social cleavage, instead of recognising (and hence reinforcing) emerging loyalties (religious, geographic, or nationalist) that could be less easily controlled. Analysing the case of Arabs in Israel, Ian Lustick convincingly shows how Israel has systematically re-established old, largely impotent ethnic and confessional cleavages among the Arabs residing in Israel in order to weaken nationalist calls among them (Lustick, 1980). It is probably easy to see confirmed in many Arab countries Laitin's conclusion that 'an exogenous power interested in creating order in a weak state would find it attractive to seek out a set of elites that had high legitimacy in the society but declining resources with which to exert authority' (Evans, Rueschemeyer and Skocpol, 1985: 311).

II

If one has therefore to study 'the role of a hegemonic state in fashioning a cultural product' (ibid: 308), how could one avoid the ongoing discussion of orientalism, as well as many Arabs' contemporary adoption of a reinforced, basically religious identity to confront it? Orientalists have indeed played a major part in the manufacturing of this 'cultural product', elevating to the recognisable category or pushing into oblivion tribes, confessions, national states, or religious groups. Edward Said has eloquently shown the intimate links between this meticulous activity and the colonial powers' expansion and rule over foreign territories (Said, 1978). It is indeed hard to refute Bryan S. Turner's view that 'the existence of exploitative colonial relationships between societies has been of major significance for the theoretical development of anthropology and sociology' (Turner, 1984: 23).

But one could also feel that orientalists *and* religious fundamentalists easily join in a common adulation of the highly ambiguous concept of 'specificity'. Laitin's discussion of British policies in Yorubaland has indeed shown how ambiguous was the British preference for the 'authenticity' and 'specificity' of ancestral cities in the shaping of the Yorubas' political identity. Abdallah Laroui's studies on North Africa have demonstrated how French colonial administrators have positively dealt with the most ritualistic, superficially 'authentic' trends in North African Islam and how Westernised elites kept external symbols of this 'authenticity' in their living rooms. Orientalism as a mode of apprehension and of perception, and not one of knowledge, is as interested in 'specificity' as are its extremist proponents among the Arabs. Both are indeed looking with the same fervour to see the gap between 'East' and 'West' deepen every day. By so doing, the orientalist establishes his culture's superiority and the fundamentalist his exclusivist grip on his own country's political culture. Both systematically try to deny social sciences any universal value, and for both of them no trans-cultural science could really exist.

One important ingredient in this supposedly unbridgeable 'difference' is the orientalists' refusal to recognise the existence of a civil society in Islamic lands. As noted by Bryan Turner (1984: 26),

> The Orientalist view of Asiatic society can be encapsulated in the notion that the social structure of the Oriental World was characterised by the absence of a civil society, that is, by the absence of a network of institutions mediating between the individual and the state.

Orientalists tended to take for granted that society has been devoured by the state, hence their lack of interest in an absent or marginal relationship between the two. Durkheim, Marx, or Wittfogel do not really depart from this very debatable hypothesis that the Arab world is characterised by superficial and dynastic changes and economic immobilism. One could push the argument to the extreme to state that there is no need to study non-existent Arab politics.

This absence of civil society is central in Louis Dumont's distinction between 'holistic' and 'individualistic' civilisations. While the latter (Christian, Hindu) tend to recognise the individual's rights and interests, the former are almost obsessed with the interests of the community as a whole. A typical case in this category is, in Dumont's view, the Islamic societies (Dumont, 1983). But here again, Dumont concurs with a prevailing orientalist view according to which the individual is, with the civil society, another victim of the Arab state.

> The notion of civil society cannot be divorced from an equally potent theme in Western philosophy, namely the centrality of autonomous individuals within the network of social institutions. Western political philosophy has hinged on the importance of civil society in preserving the freedom of the individual from arbitrary control by the state ... In Orientalism, the absence of civil society in Islam entailed the absence of the autonomous individual exercising conscience and rejecting arbitrary interventions by the state (Turner, 1984: 39).

Charles Butterworth's chapter in this volume directly addresses this issue. He first states that 'with the exception of Lebanon, all contemporary Arab regimes are ruled by one or a few persons'. The acceptance of such regimes is based, he argues, 'not [on] any particular set of ideas in Arabic political thought but rather its absence'. Butterworth argues that 'there is no discussion of "state" and "authority" *per se* in Arabic writings until very recent times'. Discussing the ideas of al-Farabi, al-Mawardi, Ibn Rushd, Nizam al-Mulk and other writers of the medieval period, he concludes that all of them 'agreed on the principle that rule should be in the hands of one or a few'. Arab as well as European political thinkers took their bearings from Plato and Aristotle, but the European tradition soon came to discuss the fundamental differences between the demands of secular rule and those of divine rule. This distinction was to lead in Europe to a modern realistic approach towards politics by authors like Machiavelli, Bacon and Hobbes, and to the emergence of the Lockean-Rousseauist principle of popular sovereignty. A similar rupture with medieval philosophy did not occur in the Arab tradition. Butterworth relates this to the end of Arabic political philosophy with Ibn Khaldun, whose death (in 1406) was followed by 500 years during which jurists and theologians were the sole exponents of political thought. Butterworth concludes that 'the absence of an unquestioned, perhaps unquestionable belief in the fundamental need for popular sovereignty is what primarily explains why political life in the Arab World differs so markedly from political life in the West'. This absence also led, in Butterworth's view, to a 'quietistic acceptance' by the citizens in the Arabic countries of non-democratic governments.

This sharp, though qualified, view of Arab cultural history clearly emphasises what could be termed the freeze in Arab political thinking for five or six centuries. Fahmi Jadaane does not completely disagree with this view when he begins his investigation with the collapse of the Caliphate, viewed in philosophical terms at least, as a central event in Islamic thinking. 'Ali 'Abd al-Raziq would not shed a tear over it. But his 'secularist' views were condemned by Al-Azhar and a very large majority of *ulama*, with the exception of Khalid Muhammad Khalid and possibly of Shaykh 'Abd al-Hamid ibn Badis. The latter, though, does not go as far as confining Islam to pure spirituality, and like 'Abd al-Raziq, rejects the distorted Caliphate system. Jadaane also analyses the ideas of 'Abd al-Raziq's traditionalist critics, such as Shaykh Muhammad Bakhit, who also tried to reconcile, in a less stimulating vein, Islam and modernity.

A good number of pages in Jadaane's chapter are devoted to a discussion of the writings of radical religious intellectuals, in particular some who are not very well known in the West: 'Abd al-Qadir 'Awdah, Muhammad al-Mubarak and Taqi ad-Din an-Nabahani. The former's influence was considerably enhanced by his execution under Nasser, which made a martyr of him. Nabahani is particularly interesting because of his Palestinian-Jordanian origin. The detailed treatment that Jadaane offers of these authors is an important contribution, and we hope that the reader will be patient with the inevitable diffuseness and reiteration of concepts.

With An-Nabahani, Sayyid Qutb, and Ayatollah al-Khumayni, modern Islamic thinking, in avowedly different ways, offers radical answers to contemporary issues. These answers are, in a sense, a form of cultural nationalism, in which religion gives more substance to the rejection of Western domination. A Muslim certainly goes a step further when he refuses not only the other's influence, but also his model, his mental categories, and his political vocabulary. But contemporary religious fundamentalism could also be viewed as a potentially sterile reaction to the more subtle answers provided during a century of quest for a proper answer to the West's challenge, a quest opened by al-Afghani and at-Tahtawi, and represented today by Muhammad Ahmad Khalafallah or Husayn Ahmad Amin.

Said Bensaid's chapter complements Jadaane's in reviewing more secular Arab views of the state and more general views of political authority. By so doing, it reintroduces some of the trends so well presented in Albert Hourani's *Arabic Thought in a Liberal Age*, and in the book edited by Marwan Buheiry on the Mashreq's early twentieth-century politicised intellectuals, only with greater emphasis on Maghrebi illustrations. Bensaid distinguishes the fundamentalist outlook from the local patriotic (*watan*), and the Arab nationalist, one. Each of these three schools of thought has given a specific meaning to the *watan* and the *umma* — two central and heavily loaded concepts in modern Arab political thought.

These three contributions were needed in order to show how

this thought has approached the notion of the state. They certainly do not give an exhaustive view and they are not the only surveys available. Besides the authors and pamphleteers they quote, they are an illustration of the various ways by which political authority might be approached. It is hoped that these and other contributions will gradually fill the largely artificial gap between 'East' and 'West' or 'Islam' and 'non-Muslims', so that new curious and critical modern Tahtawis will try to understand the national state-making process in medieval Europe. On the other hand, one might hope that the contributions of Arab and Muslim thinkers will become a part of the universal body of knowledge on the state. As recently as 1984, a book (Carnoy, 1984) entitled *The State and Political Theory* could still ignore Arab and Muslim thought (indeed, the 'South' in general) as if the theory of the state is definitively imprisoned in West-centred, Marxist or not, political theory.

III

From Ibn Rushd to 'Allal al-Fasi, we are dealing with well-recognised thinkers. This intellectualist angle has been largely complemented in this volume, where the interest in political culture pervades more than one chapter. This interest stems from the important differences, already noted by J.P. Nettl in his seminal article, in the way 'stateness' is viewed, even in the limited Western context (Nettl, 1968). French centralism is already different from American federalism, to mention one example — all the more so when one moves to an even more different culture in which the modern state apparatus has been superimposed upon traditional, well-established, and widely recognised loci of authority. This volume could in fact be a qualified regionally and culturally distinct answer to Theda Skocpol's quest for historicity when she writes (Evans, Rueschemeyer and Skocpol, 1985: 28):

> As we bring the state back in to its proper central place in explanations of social change and politics, we shall be forced to respect the inherent historicity of sociopolitical structures, and we shall necessarily attend to the inescapable inter-twinings of national level developments with changing world historical contexts.

13

Hence the interest of Eickelman's chapter in this volume, which is based on examples drawn from the two extremities of the Arab world (Oman and Morocco) as well as from its — at least geographical — centre, Egypt. One strong idea in Eickelman's contribution is the relative similarity in the way authority is perceived beneath the different constitutional forms. Eickelman also observes the decline of secular nationalism, to be compared not with Islamic revivalism but with the 'increasing inability of the regime to find practical solutions to popular grievances'. He correctly reminds us that in Egypt, at least, 'Islamic groups have been the major political threat to the regime in every decade since the 1930s'.

Discussing the Saudi case, my contribution to this volume tends to demonstrate that the encounter with the West could be less of an original sin than a later inevitable and highly weakening (in terms of legitimacy) event. The Saudi case is interesting precisely for its relatively late encounter with foreign influence when its credentials as an 'authentic' Arabian power, established by genuine local forces, have been already recognised. Drawing largely from Ibn Khaldun's *Muqaddimah*, I have tried to show how the mixture of group feeling, religious call, geographic isolation, and ideological isolationism *vis-à-vis* extra-Arabian powers have led to a traditional Arabian nucleus of power which was later weakened by its expansion into a kingship (*mulk*).

Lebanon is another example, where one *'asabiyya* (the Maronites') was gradually eroded after the creation of the state. Here the authenticity factor is real, but it is somehow weakened as a legitimising factor because of the *'asabiyya*'s early alliance with foreign forces, notably France. The erosion of the prevailing *'asabiyya* transformed Lebanon into a field in which one *'asabiyya* would trigger the emergence of another through a mimetic process that ended in civil war.

The Saudi and the Lebanese cases also show how difficult it is to transfer traditional Khaldunian ideas on states' strengths and weaknesses to the modern state units which exist today. Besides the not-so-original idea that sees strength in unity, contemporary Arab political culture does not provide us with a clear view of what the foundations of a strong state are. Indifference to the economy is matched by doubts *vis-à-vis* the military, leaving today's leaders with a rather wide margin of manoeuvre to define state power by and for themselves, and therefore to impose their definition on their fellow countrymen.

These and other issues are now more deeply scrutinised. On the particular role of Islam in politics, books keep appearing using different angles and different examples, and reaching different conclusions. Without engaging here in any critical bibliography, one could at least observe the very uneven quality of these undertakings, ranging from the careful, well-documented country monograph to the vehement quasi-racist diatribe against 'radical', 'militant', or 'violent' Islam. If the political-culture perspective is still restricted to a very limited number of new books and articles, it is indirectly pervading most of the writings. One has to mention in this respect the project commissioned by the Center for Arab Unity Studies on the State, which treats the Arab World according to its four — by now — classic geographic areas: the Arabian peninsula, the Fertile Crescent, the Nile valley and the Maghreb.

IV

Arab and Arabist scholars do not actually have, like some of their colleagues, to 'bring the state back in'. They would do better to try to widen the scope of their investigation, which has up to now been largely restricted to narrow questions such as those concerning religious legitimacy, the economics of the nationalised sector, or the role played by colonialism in the shaping of the Arab state system. This volume discusses these and other questions. The remaining volumes in the series widen the perspective to discuss the state as an actor in the society, its autonomy *vis-à-vis* the various socio-economic forces, and its relationship with civil society and with foreign actors. Then, when the view becomes really comprehensive, with the last decades' sterile polemics on the topic shunted off far away, the pivotal question about the viability of these states can be asked in a proper way, even if it is not readily answered.

One is really impressed by the number of books focusing on the state which have been published recently. This series on the Arab state, and particularly this volume, are yet another illustration of this widespread movement in the social sciences. Other references are listed at the end of the volume. We are, however, fully aware that this interest should not be substituted for the better-established, society-centred studies, and that this interest in the state does not amount to the discovery of a new determinism. Arab and Arabist scholars should be even more aware of these pitfalls in view of the very limited number of quality studies on Arab society, and of their deep khaldunian belief in the inherent vulnerability of all states.

Beyond any ideologised specificity, one feature clearly emerges from this undertaking, namely that 'the social structural, economic, cultural, and geopolitical circumstances within which the original European modern states emerged and in many cases came to accommodate constitutional political arrangements, were not the same as those in which postcolonial and other emerging national states have operated in modern times' (Evans, Rueschemeyer and Skocpol: 1985 p.362). Consequently I deeply regret that the late Marwan Buheiry could not add to this volume the study he had promised on British and French policies and state-making in the Arab World. He was exceptionally qualified to do this, having written extensively on French policy in Algeria, US policies in the Gulf, and the history of foreign interventions in Lebanon since the eighteenth century. One has to acknowledge the lack of a direct treatment of this perspective in this volume and, more generally, the painful loss of Marwan's scholarship and friendship. One hopes that other historians will pick up his interest in the topic together with his uncompromising yet deeply tolerant way of approaching it.

Part One

1

The Origins of the Arab State System

Iliya Harik

THE PRE-COLONIAL ERA

Introduction

The Arab world today consists of twenty-one states, officially members of the Arab League. Three of them, Mauritania, Somalia and Djibouti, are peripheral, with the latter two more African than Arab. The remaining eighteen, to which this discussion will be limited, have gained their political independence only recently. The earliest Arab state to achieve independence was the Yemen (San'a) in 1918 and the most recent was the United Arab Emirates at the end of 1971. From the Atlantic to the Gulf, only the territory known as Najd, of what is today Saudi Arabia, has not known direct foreign rule in some form or another.

The Arab states manifest a considerable degree of diversity amongst themselves, more so than the diversity that exists amongst ethnically heterogeneous states as in Western Europe, for instance. Five of the Arab oil-producing countries enjoy a *per capita* income of over $10,000, while the poorest, such as the two Yemens, Oman, Egypt and the Sudan, all rank below $800 *per capita*. The mode of life varies from disintegrating tribalism, particularly in Arabia and the Fertile Crescent, to sophisticated urban life such as can be witnessed in the supermarkets and theatres of pre-1975 Beirut, Cairo and Tunis. Yet, despite these outstanding differences there is something important in common to these states, something of which they are strongly self-conscious. They speak the same language and

19

basically share the same religion.

Language and religion have, through the ages, generated a unified high culture which bequeathes to them a sense of collective identity. From their language present-day Arabs have drawn their sense of national identity and from Islam they have drawn a collective sense of unity that often overlaps with nationalism. Both nationalism and Islam generate a sense of identification that cuts across state boundaries and supersedes, on the ideological level, local considerations.

THE NATION-STATE PROBLEM

Herein lies the paradox in Arab politics and history. Eighteen Arab states find themselves formally independent and sovereign and yet hardly any of them unconditionally accepts the legitimacy of its own statehood. The fact of the matter is that these states have, for a good part of the twentieth century, been caught up in the pull and push of conflicting forces, some coming from domestic centrifugal sources such as ethnic and sectarian divisions and some from the universal forces of pan-Arabism and pan-Islam, both of which draw away from the legitimacy of statehood enjoyed by these countries.

Under the Wahhabis of Arabia, the idea of a state system was seriously challenged by the universal principle of pan-Islam. In the 1950s and 1960s, Arab nationalism under Nasser seriously challenged the state system from a nationalist perspective. Though no other universalist movement since the expansionist periods of Wahhabism and Nasserism has seriously threatened the state system, the growing strength of fundamentalist Islam at present is a continuous reminder of the precarious status of the state system and secularist trends.

Arab nationalism as an ideology, more so than Islam, denies legitimacy to the state system. The true and natural state is considered to be the national state whose authority is coterminous with the nation, the nation being defined as the people of one language and culture, i.e. the Arab people whose area of habitation extends from Morocco on the Atlantic to the Yemen on the Indian Ocean. Using this ideological yardstick, the eighteen states just alluded to are to be considered one nation-state. The term 'nation' (*umma*) has throughout the Islamic era referred to the universal Muslim community (Haim, 1962;

Sharabi 1966; Hourani, 1962).

Around the end of the nineteenth century, however, the term umma started to appear in the political literature of the time in reference to the universal Arab community, thus acquiring a preponderantly secular meaning. Though Arab Christians figured prominently in pursuing this course, the new terminology was not limited to them (Antonius, 1955; Zeine, 1958). Arab nationalists, overwhelmingly Muslim, insist on this usage and stubbornly resist applying the term to the people of a single one of the Arab states. Even in the constitutions of these states, the term umma is avoided, as it is also in official usage. The name of the state, say Syria, or the term 'people' (ash-sha'b) are used instead. It is because of these conventional Arab usages of the words that the term 'nation-state' was avoided in the title of this chapter, for many would question my terminology and some would dispute it outright. It would be pointless to quibble about terms, for words have conventional or given definitions and one gains nothing by violating this understanding. I shall accept therefore the objection that these countries are not nation-states and just refer to the whole set as the 'state system' for each of them is undeniably a state in the formal sense.

The Committee on New Nations at the University of Chicago published in the 1960s a book called *Old Societies and New States* (Geertz, 1963). While this nomenclature seems reasonable, it tends to be misleading. The illusion of state novelty in the Third World among students of development may be due to the disinclination of modernisation theory to delve into historical inquiry. Social scientists have a particularly significant role in re-examining history and relating it to the present.

A quick look at the history of the eighteen Arab countries clearly shows not only that they are old societies but also old states. Except for three of them — Iraq, Syria and Jordan — they all go back to the nineteenth century or a much earlier period. The traditional state should not be overlooked or dismissed because of a modern outlook or other biases. Those who ignore it do so because of a formalistic definition of the state, and/or because of their limited historical curiosity. Indeed, very few, if any, have engaged in a study of comparative history to assess the origins and records of the state structures of the Middle East and North Africa.

An attempt will be made in this discussion to show that the

states of the eighteen Arab countries under consideration are not only quite old (and in some cases extremely old) but also have within themselves the sources of their own legitimacy and that this fact cannot be brushed aside by nationalists or scholars. Arab nationalists have ignored and belittled the state system as baseless and as a creation of colonialism (Haim, 1962). They have done so at their own risk and have paid a high price for their historical misperceptions.

The contempt heaped by nationalist ideologues on the state system has discouraged a detached inquiry. It is, however, to the credit of Elbaki Hermassi (1972), that he has looked at three Maghrebi states in the light of comparative history and given the state system its proper credit. Curiously enough, he received help in his endeavour from another Tunisian, that great historian of the fourteenth century, Ibn Khaldun.

I shall maintain here that fifteen of the contemporary Arab states are the product of indigenous and regional forces mostly unrelated to European colonialism, and in most cases predate it. Moreover, almost all of the fifteen states mentioned have enjoyed legitimacy in terms of the values of their peoples and times. That we may have a different set of values at present in terms of which we judge the right to rule, should not deny other people of other eras the right to their own moral judgement and its worth. However, the strength and time-honoured legitimacy of these states in the eyes of their peoples are in no way to be construed as grounds for their continued survival. States may come and go, sometimes by the will of their own people, at other times through external forces or historical accident. The traditional state of the Hijaz, for instance, did disappear (Baker, 1979). Most traditional states, however, have survived to the present day, even though with much-changed political institutions.

TYPOLOGY OF THE ARAB STATE SYSTEM

I shall try here to present a typology of the traditional Arab states according to the bases of their authority, a step which will take us to periods earlier than the nineteenth century. Then I shall discuss the impact of European influences and colonialism on these states during the nineteenth century, taking into account another dimension, namely, the emergence of new social forces that by and large reinforced the state system.

The principles which explain the emergence of the Arab state system are ideology, traditions and dominion. While the forces of ideology, traditions and dominion overlap, one can still clearly argue a predominance of one or the other of these principles in different types of Arab states. This approach may seem to ignore economic factors in explaining political formations. That is not the case. The economy of Arab states which can be traced back to the medieval period was based on subsistence and a limited exchange of goods. The lack of change in the economy during earlier centuries rules out economic factors as an explanatory principle in the formation of the multifarious state system. Thus, in the first part of this discussion, economic factors will not be considered. In the second part, the money market economy will be considered as a fourth principle affecting state institutions. One can, of course, argue that the traditional economies of distant times invariably explain the authoritarian political structures that prevailed then. Nevertheless the traditional state system of the Arab world showed considerable structural diversity, as will be made clear below.

First, let me briefly indicate here that when I use the term state I am not bound by the formal definition that would qualify the designated body for membership of the United Nations. I simply mean to refer to an established authority which enjoys jurisdiction over a core territory and people for an extended period of time, stretching over at least several generations. The jurisdiction includes powers to implement the law, impose taxation, and demand military service, loyalty and allegiance to the established authority.

The traditional Arab states, viewed from this perspective, will be found to have differed in structure, power base, legitimacy and traditions. I have been able to identify the following types, classified in accordance with these criteria and with a view to their origins.

1. The imam-chief system. Authority is invested in a sanctified leader. In this group of countries we find two sub-types: (a) the dissenter communities and (b) the mainstream orthodox communities. The first includes the states of Yemen, (San'a), Oman, Cyrenaica (Libya), and the second is comprised of Hijaz and Morocco.

2. The alliance system of chiefs and imams. In this case authority is invested in a tribal chief supported and awarded a legitimate authority beyond the confines of his tribe by virtue of his identification and/or alliance with a prominent religious leader and his teachings. The main case in this category is Saudi Arabia.

In these two types, ideology plays a predominant role in state formation, while force and traditions come next in order of importance.

3. The traditional secular system. Here authority is invested in a dynasty free from religious attributes. This group includes Qatar, Bahrain, Kuwait, the United Arab Emirates, the People's Democratic Republic of the Yemen and Lebanon. The role of traditions in these cases is pre-eminent, while state hegemony is cemented further by the possession of coercive power in the hands of a cohesive group.

4. The bureaucratic-military oligarchy type. In this case, authority originates in urban-based garrison commanders, who in time develop an extensive bureaucratic apparatus. This group of countries includes Algeria, Tunisia, Tripolitania (Libya) and Egypt. Monopoly of the means of coercion in the hands of an administrative-military 'caste' is the major feature of this state type.

5. The colonially-created state system. Here we come to the modern era which will be discussed in detail in the second part of this chapter, and will only be identified briefly at this point. This category is distinctive in that it refers to states that have been carved out from the defunct Ottoman empire on the basis of foreign imperial interests and in the absence of any credible local base of authority upon which to erect the new structures. The group includes Iraq, Syria, Jordan and Palestine. (To the extent that Lebanon was radically changed by the same imperial powers, it may be included in this context as well.) Colonialism left a serious impact on most Arab states, but in only the above-mentioned cases can one maintain that the state system itself was created by the colonial powers.

Since it is not possible to discuss all fifteen cases in this limited essay, I shall focus on some archetypes and touch briefly on the others.

The imam–chief type

The state of the religious chief is mainly found in a dissenter type which seeks survival in rough mountain and desert terrains on the periphery of the Arab heartland, i.e. at a considerable distance from the centre of the empire. Oman and Yemen are examples *par excellence* of this type of state.

Oman (Phillips, 1967), the forgotten backwater of the Arab world that hardly ever figures in Arab nationalist literature, enjoys one of the longest continuous statehoods in the Arab world, rivalled only by Egypt. The state started in the eighth century (its first Ibadi imam was elected in 751 A.D.) by a radical dissident Muslim group (*al-Khawarij*), which broke away from the first Arab empire of the four pious Caliphs, Al-Rashidun.

The sect found refuge in the desert- and sea-protected mountains of Oman, and there sought to live the pious life in a commonwealth based on faith. This is not, as might be thought, a state by default, but rather the product of a conscious and determined effort to design a political system consistent with the religious beliefs of the Ibadi Muslim faith. The Ibadis broke away from the body of Islam over the very issue of proper government and the legitimate election of the head of state. They believed that the right to govern Muslims lies only in a pious Muslim who is elected by the people.

The electoral process consisted of two steps. First, the learned and notables in the community would meet at Nazwa, in the hinterland of Oman, and nominate a person; then in the second stage, they would present the nominee to the people who had the right to approve or reject the nomination. Should the imam prove unworthy of his office and unjust, the people had the right to depose him, a right that was used promptly to depose the first imam of the Ibadi state soon after he was elected.

The Ibadis, without any doubt, laid down the most free principles of elections to be found in the history of the Islamic theory of state. Curiously enough, they were completely dogmatic and very narrow, even more so than the Wahhabis. Moreover, once properly elected, the imam (the chosen of God) and his acts assumed a holy character, a principle accentuated in later years by resort to a dual system based on the hereditary principle in conjunction with elections.

25

Like the others ruled by religious chiefs, with time the Ibadi state incorporated the principle of hereditary rights to power along with that of election. By the time the Bousaʻd dynasty took over in the middle of the eighteenth century, the hereditary principle had gained ascendancy over election and a separation of the imamate from the office of sultan followed. The Bousaʻd dynasty, it is worth noting, under whom Oman reached the apex of its power, is the same dynasty which is still governing Oman today under Sultan Qaboos.

Oman was not a small, isolated state, but a great one whose ships dominated the seas in the latter part of the eighteenth and first half of the nineteenth century from Kenya, Zanzibar and enclaves on the Iranian and Baluchi coasts. Its merchant fleet was the most important in the region, until it was made obsolete by British steamships in the middle of the nineteenth century.

The Yemen (Abadha, 1975) is the second important case of a state whose origins lie in the imam-chief system. The state of Yemen was founded in 900 A.D. by a descendant of ʻAli ibn Abi Talib, the fourth Caliph of Islam. The founder, Yahya ibn al-Husayn, was a believer in the doctrine of Imam Zayd ibn ʻAli, which makes the Yemen state a Shiʻi one, though, unlike the Persian Shiʻa, who believe in the twelfth imam, the Zaydis believe in a continuing line of imams. Imam Yahya began proselytising in the city of Suʻda in the nothern part of the country, where he also established his state. Later the capital moved to Sanʻa.

The Zaydi doctrine is one of the more moderate versions of Shiʻi Islam and is closer to the Sunni doctrine than that of any other Shiʻi sect. Unlike extreme Shiʻa (al-ghulat), the Zaydis moderate the claim of sanctity attributed to ʻAli and his descendants. Also unlike the Ibadi doctrine of Oman where every Muslim is entitled to hold the office, authority in Yemen is vested in the descendants of ʻAli and Fatima, the daughter of the Prophet Muhammad.

The Zaydi state of Yemen is based on the principle that any one of the descendants of ʻAli and Fatima is a legitimate candidate for the throne, and furthermore, that two or more imams can legitimately rule provided there is sufficient distance between their domains, a principle that conflicts with the doctrine of the indivisibility of the community insisted upon by the pan-Islamists. The Zaydis specify a number of qualities that the candidate should possess before he is selected by the learned scholars and notables.

Two requirements for the imam had a far-reaching effect on the shape the Yemeni state took: he should be a 'warrior' and a 'just' ruler who implements the religious law. Should he fail to be one or other, his overthrow by a legitimate contender is permissible. As is to be expected, the history of the Yemen is full of unrest and infighting among the Zaydis over the office.

The Yemeni state has known periods of expansion and contraction, but its core territory remained in the mountain range, where the Zaydi doctrine was prevalent. The Yemen fell under Ottoman rule intermittently, first in the period between 1538 and 1635, and then from 1872 until 1918. The history of Yemeni-Ottoman relations may be characterised as one in which a state of war was the normal situation. Though subjected to the Ottomans, the Yemen never fell under any other foreign rule. Oman, on the other hand, was never dominated by Ottoman rule, but suffered a short-lived Portuguese occupation of its coastal towns in the sixteenth century.

Following their normal practice, the Ottomans ruled their Arabian possessions indirectly through confirmation of the local rulers, such as the Zaydi imams in the Yemen and the sharifs of Mecca in Hijaz. The sharifian state of Hijaz, which enjoyed a longevity comparable to that of Yemen and Oman, vanished from the political map in 1925 when it was taken over by the expanding Saudi state (Baker, 1979). Though it enjoyed state features similar to the others, it was always a dependency of whoever happened to be the dominant Islamic ruler in Cairo or Istanbul. Thus, during the Ottoman era, the sharifs ruled in the name of the Ottoman sultan. Though Sunni in a Sunni state, the sharif was a descendant of the Prophet, and thus enjoyed the legitimacy of a religious chief. The Hijaz is not the only state in the region that has disappeared for political and/or military reasons.

Another country whose political system is rooted in a religious base is Morocco (Abun-Nasr, 1975; Barbour, 1965; Zartman, 1964). Morocco's early history is tied up with the Muslim empires of the West and it cannot, therefore, be fully identified as a country with a political system roughly coterminous with its present territory until the sixteenth century. However, it is reasonable to say that the Murabitun (Almoravids) of the eleventh century and the Muwahhidun (Almohads) of the twelfth century were empires based in Morocco proper and originated by religious reformers. In the case of the latter, it was a reformer who later claimed to be a sharif (Ibn Tumart), i.e. a descendant of the Prophet. I shall limit this inquiry, however, to the modern history of Morocco, from the Sadian dynasty in the sixteenth century (1510-1603) to the present. The Sadian family claimed sharifian descent in addition to having been connected to a sufi order, the Jazuliyya, in much the same way as the succeeding dynasty, the 'Alawites (1668 to the present).

The founder of the 'Alawite dynasty was a sharif who was elected sultan by religious leaders of the Tafilalt oasis. It is interesting to note that the present King of Morocco, Hassan II, is a descendant of the founder of the dynasty, Moulay ash-Sharif, and refers to himself as the Prince of the Faithful, the attribute reserved to a Caliph.

Both the Sadians and the 'Alawites were of rural origin and sought additional support from the religious establishments of the urban centres. However, in no case thus far has religion been the sole base of power, but always a support of dominion established by the sword.

The alliance of chief and imam type

The second type of traditional state is that of the chief and imam alliance. Saudi Arabia is the main case in this category.

Saudi Arabia (Winder, 1965; Hopwood, 1972; Howarth, 1964; 'Abd ar-Rahim, 1975) emerged as a state in central Arabia for the first time in 1745, and its fortune lasted until 1818. It was defeated in war, then restored in 1842; it declined towards the end of the century to revive once again in full force in 1902 under 'Abd al-'Aziz II.

Central Arabia was then a region consisting of independent tribes and lacking central control. A local chief, Muhammad ibn Sa'ud of Dir'iyyah in Najd, struck up an alliance in 1745 with the fugitive reformer Muhammad ibn 'Abd al-Wahhab and expanded his domain over the other tribes in the area of Najd. By 1792, his son and successor, 'Abd al-'Aziz I, had expanded the boundaries of the Saudi state into northern Yemen, the Hasa region on the Persian Gulf and the southern borders of Ottoman lands in southern Syria and Iraq. By 1810, the Saudi state comprised all of Arabia, except for Oman, Yemen, Qatar, Kuwait, and Aden with its protectorate. The Saudis felt strong enough to try to extend their government over Syria and Iraq, thus compelling the Ottoman Sultan to check their threat through the military might of his Egyptian viceroy, Muhammad 'Ali. In a matter of seven years (1811-18), Muhammad 'Ali succeeded in destroying the Saudi state and sent its chief to be beheaded in Istanbul. It took the Saudis almost thirty years to recover from the blow.

The Saudi state was founded on the conservative Sunni doctrine of the Hanbalite school of jurisprudence. Its basic political principle is the responsibility of the ruler to implement the *Shari'ah*, and to spread and protect the orthodox faith. The Saudi princes accepted in good faith this requirement enunciated by the religious reformer Ibn 'Abd al-Wahhab, and carried it out fully. Their state spread the Saudi dominion and the revivalist doctrine at one and the same time.

As for the selection of the Muslim ruler, Ibn 'Abd al-Wahhab evidently accepted the hereditary law of succession in the established dynasty. Though this is not the best principle for selecting rulers in Islamic doctrine, the practice of hereditary rule was established early in the Muslim Arab state during the seventh century. With the decline of the first Saudi state, the sharifian state of Hijaz revived and shook off the tutelage of the Sa'uds. The Najd area fell once again into a state of tribal pluralism and independence in which the Sa'uds held partial authority.

Another Saudi state re-emerged at the beginning of the twentieth century at the hands of a Saudi prince, 'Abd al-'Aziz ibn Sa'ud (1880-1953), who in 1901 captured the former Saudi capital of Riyadh from its then ruler, Ibn Rashid, and set the course of his followers in seeking dominion and strict religious observance in Arabia. Long before his death in 1953, he had restored the first Saudi state to its former dominions in Arabia, creating this time a more centralised structure and eliminating local centres of authority.

The present Saudi state is made up of what was nominally the Ottoman territory of Najd and Hasa, and the defunct states of Hijaz and 'Asir. In so far as political unification in the Arab world is concerned, the Saudi state has been, along with the United Arab Emirates and Libya, the only successful endeavour. None of its leaders, however, professed Arab nationalist objectives.

It would be easy to leave Saudi Arabia as the only example of the chief and imam alliance type of state, but the fact is that in many ways Oman and Morocco followed the pattern in later years in which the rulers' main attribute became dominion in alliance with the religious men of their day. Invariably, however, the predominance belonged to the temporal chief, not the imam.

The traditional secular system of authority

Chronologically the emergence of the state of Saudi Arabia occurred during the middle of the eighteenth century, at the same time as many other states in the Arabian Peninsula that are still with us today, such as Kuwait, Qatar and Bahrain. These belong to the traditional secular state type and their emergence at that particular time must have had something to do with the decline of Ottoman power. In all three states, the chieftain principle was paramount and the ascendancy of the ruling dynasty has been on the increase continuously to the present. Nowhere did religious power manifest itself, nor was it associated with the ruler.

Kuwait was the first of these states to appear on the map and it could also be called the mother state of the three (Abu-Hakima 1967; Winder, 1965; Ismael, 1982). All three states come from the same clan of the 'Utub tribe which moved from Najd into the small village of Kuwait. In 1752 a certain shaykh of the clan, Sabbah, was selected by his fellow tribesmen to be chief of their city. The city flourished under the 'Utubs and became within a very short period of time a rival to the port city of Basra in southern Iraq. Kuwait was located on the border line between the Ottoman power in Iraq and the domain of the Banu Khalid rulers in al-Hasa. It was through the permission and protection of the Banu Khalid that the 'Utubs settled in Kuwait at the beginning of the eighteenth century. There seems to be no historical evidence for the claim that the Sabbah family established its government by seeking authorisation from the Ottoman Mutasallim of Basra. Rather, it pursued the independent line of its former masters, the Banu Khalid. Later, it is true that the shaykhs of Kuwait sought Ottoman confirmation, which became particularly significant under the reformer *wali* of Baghdad, Midhat Pasha (1869-72). This measure cost the

Sabbah dynasty nothing in terms of power, since Ottoman suzerainty was purely nominal. They did not pay the Ottomans tribute nor did they have to seek Ottoman instruction regarding the succession. In fact, it was the Ottomans who paid the shaykhs a subsidy, which started as protection money given in recognition of the sea power of Kuwait in order to protect Basra from pirate and other attacks. Moreover, the shaykhs received generous gifts from the Ottomans in the form of palm groves in the Basra and al-Fao areas (Dabbagh, 1962; Hopwood, 1972).

A branch of the 'Utub, known for their financial power and skills, left Kuwait to establish a city state in al-Zubara in the area of Qatar, apparently with the permission of the Sabbahs. These were the Khalifas, who established dominion in the second half of the eighteenth century in Qatar and Bahrain. Later, Bahrain and Qatar became two separate states under separate branches of the same Khalifa family.

The 'Utub governments in the three states were basically the same in that they were based on the pre-eminence of the Arab shaykh who ruled supreme over the rest. In the urban setting of Kuwait, Qatar and Bahrain, the 'Utub chiefs ruled with the aid of councils of notables.

While these chiefs were Muslims, they did not enjoy or claim religious attributes which set them apart from the rest of society. Moreover, they showed no particular religious zeal nor did they mix religion with politics. Even in the case of the implementation of justice, they resorted to secular law in addition to religious law, a practice common among the tribes. This was also the case in the emirate of Mount Lebanon (Harik, 1968; Spagnolo, 1977; Salibi, 1965).

The government of Mount Lebanon is the oldest in this category of traditional secular states. While its origin can be traced back to the Arab chiefs who settled in the south and were there under the Mamluks, the principality of Lebanon really begins with the ascendancy of the Ma'nid house which coincides with the Ottoman conquest of Syria in 1516 by Sultan Salim I, who also confirmed the Ma'nids in the rule of the Shuf district in return for the assistance they gave him against the Mamluks.

The Ma'nids expanded their domain towards the north and left to their direct successors, the Shihabi dynasty, a larger domain than the one they had received in 1516. Upon the death of the last male Ma'nid, a Shihabi Amir succeeded, being a descendant of the Ma'nids on the maternal side. Thus Shihabi rule may be considered a continuation of the same dynasty over the same territory.

The government of Mount Lebanon was more complex than the secular traditional governments of eastern Arabia. It was a pluralist political system based on hereditary title among a group of aristocratic families, who were bound to the Amir of the Mountain by loyalty, though enjoying prerogatives of direct government over their subjects and by interposition between the Amir and his subjects. The government of the Lebanon was under Ottoman sovereignty, but the Ottomans left the local leaders in charge. Thus, the Amirs of Lebanon enjoyed autonomy in their internal affairs and paid tribute to the Sultan through his walis in Sidon, Tripoli and/or Damascus. During the rule of a strong wali, some interference took place in the political struggles among the rival lords in Lebanon. On the other hand, when a strong Amir ruled in Lebanon next to a weak Ottoman wali, he interfered in the wali's affairs and gained power at his expense.

A major characteristic of the Lebanese traditional system was its pluralist and secular character. Pluralism was manifested in the autonomy enjoyed by the feudal lords from the Amir and from one another. But pluralism also extended to other aspects of society: the religious realm, for instance. Though very small, this territory comprised members of various Muslim sects, schismatic and orthodox, in addition to a plethora of Christian denominations. For instance, the Amir's religion was Sunni Muslim, but the main feudal lords and also a large majority of the population were Druze and Maronite Christians. The principality also included some Shi'a, Sunnis and Orthodox Christians. Thus, there were more religious communities concentrated there than in any other Ottoman territory.

The 'clericals' of these denominations hardly interfered at all with governmental relations before the nineteenth century. Political relations cut across sectarian lines. Druze lords had, in addition to their own subjects, non-Druze, both Christian and Muslim. Similarly, Maronite lords had non-Maronite subjects. Political coalitions were made up of lords of diverse religious affiliations.

In all these cases of secular governments, the rulers were very jealous of their prerogatives *vis-à-vis* the outside world and territorial jurisdiction was generally recognised without formal boundaries; territories coincided with jurisdiction over subjects.

There were numerous violations of these informal boundaries over the years, but they were in the form of challenges to the other's authority rather than denials of the other's traditional jurisdiction.

The bureaucratic-military oligarchy

The last type under consideration here is the bureaucratic-military oligarchy. The only claim to legitimate authority of the military oligarchic government is its representation of the Ottoman Sultan, for almost all the four states under consideration, with the exception of Egypt, originated under Ottoman rule by Ottoman officers. Appearing in the first part of the eighteenth century in Algeria, Tunisia, Tripolitania and Egypt, the bureaucratic-military oligarchic system was urban-based. Its emergence reflects the decline of Ottoman power over the outlying districts, leading local Ottoman garrisons in the main cities to seek autonomy from the Sultan.

The bureaucratic-military oligarchy in its purest form was to be seen in Algeria, where the *dey*, the 'officer-king', and his foreign troops governed without any participation of, or ties with the native population (Abun-Nasr, 1975). Tunisia and Egypt proved to be different. The first phase of the autonomous state of Tunisia witnessed the emergence of a short-lived dynasty (the Muradists), which nevertheless managed between 1637 and 1702 to consolidate its power independently of the Sultan and to replace the local Ottoman troops with local tribes as the main source of its power (ibid.) The Husaynids, who succeeded the Muradists in 1706, followed the same pattern of government, buttressing their power with local support. Tunisia enjoyed stability and prosperity under the Husaynids for the whole of the eighteenth century. Up to the first half of the nineteenth century, the Husaynids were virtually independent of the Ottoman Sultan, even more so than Egypt. They paid no tribute, sent no soldiers to fight in the Sultan's army, and sought no investiture. Moreover, they waged war, signed treaties and received foreign deputations in their own name.

One of the interesting features of this otherwise absolutist government is the Legal Council, which consisted of local *'ulama* and whose function it was to pass judgement on the conformity of governmental legislation and decrees with the

Shari'ah. With the shift in power balance away from the military and the distancing of Tunisia from the Ottoman Sultan, the Husaynid dynasty sought new sources of legitimacy for its authority in the practice of Islam and the implementation of religious law. Territorially, Tunisia under the Husaynids was almost identical with the present-day country, as was Algeria, for that matter, except for the expansion of its boundaries into the great Sahara by the French.

It is hard to think of any time in known history when Egypt did not have a central government of some sort or another (Holt, 1966; Vatikiotis, 1980). One can go as far back as one wishes, but here we shall limit ourselves to the military oligarchy which was the immediate precursor of the modern state and goes back to the Mamluk period before the Ottomans occupied Egypt in 1517. Having defeated the Mamluks, the Ottomans, in their time-honoured practice, entrusted the government to the vanquished to rule in the name of the Ottoman Sultan. So the Mamluks were reinstated. It was not until Muhammad 'Ali came to power in Egypt in the wake of Napoleon's departure that a virtually independent state emerged.

An Ottoman officer who succeeded in securing for himself the office of Pasha of Egypt in 1803, Muhammad 'Ali rapidly moved to consolidate his power and built an army of such strength that the Ottoman Sultan, his suzerain, had to seek his help as early as 1810 to recover Arabia from the Wahhabis. But before his long rule came to an end, Muhammad 'Ali was to challenge the authority of his suzerain and seek to take over his empire by invading Syria and part of Anatolia. Before he could reach the Ottoman capital, Britain and France intervened militarily on behalf of the Sultan to push the ambitious and powerful viceroy back into the confines of Egypt where he continued to rule independently with only nominal recognition of the Sultan's suzerainty. His descendants ruled after him until 1952.

Like the rest of the military oligarchic states of Ottoman origin mentioned thus far, the power of the Egyptian oligarchy rested on the Ottoman garrison of the Pasha. But like the Tunisians, Muhammad 'Ali quickly freed himself from such dependence and involved the local population in his undertaking, primarily by recruiting Egyptian soldiers and administrators into his large army and civil service. He involved Egyptians also in the economic enterprises which he established to support his growing military power. He opened schools and sent many

Egyptians to Europe for higher education.

The 'Alawid regime reduced its dependence on Ottoman soldiers by recruiting locally, but it did not seek legitimacy by increasing its ties with the people. The Egyptians were represented, if at all, by their religious men, who were the essence of Islamic learning and the custodians of the oldest continuously operating university of al-Azhar. Muhammad 'Ali respected the Shari'ah but there is no evidence that he sought legitimation from the 'ulama or the preaching of Islam beyond the conventional observation of the Islamic religion. If anything, he was, of necessity, more of a moderniser and advocate of European learning.

His descendants ruled after him as an oligarchy, but one that established increasing links with non-military influential people in the country. The 'Alawid dynasty, however, as was the case in most other Arab states, fell into a condition of dependence on European powers even before the British occupied the country in 1882.

TRANSITION TO THE MODERN STATE ERA

It has been shown in the preceding part that the origins of the Arab states are different and can be traced back, in most cases, to a period before the nineteenth century. Two points are worth underlining here: first, that most of these states were locally rooted and enjoyed legitimacy in the eyes of their people; and second, that they had recognisable boundaries, or at least a core territory where their authority endured through the vicissitudes of time. By the beginning of the twentieth century, we find the inhabitants of these states possessed of a sense of identity as people of a country and a state, regardless of whether the term nation-state applied to them or not. I shall return to this point again later.

Up to the first half of the nineteenth century, we encounter no foreign factor in the making of these states. Some Arabs may point to the Ottomans as an imperialist agent involved in the process, but this would be an untenable position, for in these pre-nationalistic periods, Arabs under Ottoman rule did not perceive themselves as subjects of foreign rulers. They identified with the Ottomans and looked upon the Sultan as the Muslim head of a Muslim commonwealth of which they were a part.

Colonialism and the state system

If, as we have seen, the seventeenth and eighteenth centuries were credited with the formation of new Arab states, the nineteenth century marked the era of colonialism and Arab subjugation by European powers. It was the period when Europeans challenged the minds of Arabs and Muslims in general, and undermined their sense of security and confidence. However, the subject of security is much too broad to be broached in this context. What I hope to do in a brief fashion here is point out the major ways in which the advent of colonialism and of intensified contacts with Europe affected the fortunes of the state system.

By the first half of the nineteenth century we can see two major forces acting on the Arab states: European penetration, on the one hand, and the reassertion of Ottoman power, on the other. The Ottomans, who had not themselves stemmed the tide of territorial losses especially in their European domains, were able to reassert their authority in Egypt after the departure of Napoleon, albeit temporarily. They restored their actual power in Tripolitania in 1835 by abolishing the military oligarchy of the Qaramanlis dynasty, and regained their nominal claims on Tunisia which, for its own reasons, sought to be reincorporated into the fold (Abun-Nasr, 1975). They succeeded in destroying the new Saudi state in Arabia, re-entered Yemen in 1872, reasserted their claims over Kuwait (Abu-Hakima, 1967), strengthened their position with the sharifs of Hijaz (Winder, 1965; Hopwood, 1972) and regained control of the Syrian provinces (Holt, 1966). Iraqi provinces were also brought under greater central control (Longrigg, 1956). Not all these successes can be attributed to a reformed central government in Istanbul. The opening of the Suez Canal and the Damascus-Hijaz railway both contributed to the reassertion of Ottoman power in Arabia.

At the same time, the Ottomans suffered major losses, just as the Arabs did, from the expansion of the European powers. Before the century was over, the Ottomans witnessed the French occupation of Algeria in 1830 and Tunisia in 1881. The British occupied Aden in 1839 and Egypt in 1882. Italy occupied Tripolitania in 1911. Earlier, seven European powers intervened in Lebanon in 1861 and served as the guarantors of its autonomy and constitution.

Other Arab states were also affected by this imperialism. Moroccan territory was whittled away by the Spanish and French and the whole country was brought under foreign rule by 1912. Oman started to come under British influence in the middle of the nineteenth century and virtually became a protectorate by the end of that century. Again before 1900, Qatar, Bahrain and Kuwait became tied to Britain by treaties which for all practical purposes reduced them to dependencies of the British Crown.

The colonial mandate system

The zenith of colonial power was reached with the conclusion of the First World War. Britain and France emerged as the superpowers of that brief era, and they reasserted and expanded their control over Arab lands. This was most visible in the remaining Arab territories under Ottoman rule, namely the Fertile Crescent, an area brought under British and French rule in its entirety. Though British influence increased in the Hijaz, it lasted for only a very short period and no additional gains by imperial interests were witnessed in Arabia.

In the Fertile Crescent, the British and French created five new states, all of which were technically put under the League of Nations' mandate bestowed on the two European powers. These states were Iraq, Syria, Lebanon, Transjordan, and Palestine. Of the five, only Lebanon then constituted an autonomous polity. The rest were ruled directly by the Ottoman Government from Istanbul in much the same fashion as the military oligarchies in other places. No nuclei of autonomous states were in existence in the region before that time. The territory of the Fertile Crescent was divided into administrative units under the Ottomans, none of which corresponded to present state boundaries.

During the decline of Ottoman power, especially in the eighteenth century, local chiefs or ambitious Pashas, such as Dhahir al-'Umar in northern Palestine and al-Jazzar Pasha of Acre, emerged as autonomous Ottoman walis over their provinces. What these chiefs failed to do was to establish hereditary power or to perpetuate a military oligarchy. Their rule vanished with them and Ottoman power was easily reasserted (Rafiq, 1974; Holt, 1966). Members of the al-'Azm family of

Syria managed to fill positions as walis in various provinces such as Damascus, Tripoli, Sidon and even Egypt, but only as representatives of the Sultan at the mercy of Ottoman garrisons. And they never claimed autonomy or established hereditary rule.

In effect, when the British and French occupied the Fertile Crescent, they found no local authority or state such as that of Tunisia, Morocco, Oman, Kuwait, or Qatar; only in Lebanon was there an indigenous system of government. In the rest of the area, they had no landmarks to guide their steps; they had to create new entities on the basis of traditional claims and zones of influence.

Claims by local populations were expressed by the Syrians aided by the Hashemite Sharif of Hijaz, in Jordan by a Hashemite prince who moved into Transjordan, and in Palestine by Arab nationalists and the World Zionist Organisation at one and the same time (Antonius, 1955; Zeine, 1958). While the British and French fashioned the map much to their own liking, they could not escape the pressure of the rising tide of anti-imperialism and nationalism. They had to grapple with Arab nationalism in its early stages in Syria, Palestine, Lebanon and Iraq. And though not effective in its first encounter, nationalism was the main cause of the short-lived stay of the two powers in the area.

Lebanon confirmed its autonomy under the French, and expanded its boundaries to include territories that were previously part of Beirut province to the west and Syria province to the east. For reasons which are not entirely clear, the origin of modern Lebanon is a source of misunderstanding. It is frequently stated that Lebanon was part of Syria and was created by the French. This is not true. It was not part of Syria, since there was no such state before 1920, whereas Lebanon enjoyed a political order all of its own. Nor was it created by the French, since it predated the French mandate. The French, indeed, affected its boundaries and remodelled its government. The Constitution of 1926 which the French introduced was based on the model of the Constitution of the French Third Republic, but the net result looked very different. The document took on an entirely local character and what was in the French Third Republic a secular cabinet system turned in Lebanon into a presidential sectarian system.

The point is, however, that a fifth type of state system emerged in the Fertile Crescent at the hands of the colonial powers, which was not the product of local historical forces. These are the states which conform to Arab nationalist theory about the emergence of the state system. That the Arab nationalist view, extrapolated from these limited cases, gained credence in other states is surprising, but perhaps it can be explained by the fact that Arab nationalist ideology emerged in the Fertile Crescent and spread from there to the rest of the Arab world. Arab nationalist ideology was at that time a clear expression of the feelings, perceptions and aspirations of the politically conscious Arabs in the Fertile Crescent countries, but it was not really applicable to the rest of the Arab lands.

In general, colonialism affected the boundaries of Arab states, but it did not, with the exception of the Fertile Crescent cases, create those states. Boundaries were by and large determined during the colonial period, but a few were left for the independent Arab states to settle later on. Colonial powers affected the structures of many governments, especially by creating a modern civil service and sometimes the nucleus of a modern standing army. They also left a major mark on the local political elites, as we shall show later on.

The economic impact of imperialism

Two major features of the legacy of colonialism — administrative centralisation and economics — must be pointed out. In the first part of this chapter we specified that the Arab state system may be explained in terms of ideology, traditions and power. By the nineteenth century we see new forces emerging, partly under the influence of colonialism. Economically, the emergence of the domestic market and social stratification contributed in no mean way to the emergence of a new ideology: nationalism. The colonial powers inadvertently contributed to the emergence of the nationalism of the state system by introducing a centralised system of administration in most countries under their control. The central administration, colonial or native, became the focus of political orientation and action by the emerging modern groups and classes, and contributed to the inception of a sense of identification with the state.

Colonialism markedly weakened the powers of regions such as the Maghreb, when, at the Congress of Aix-la-Chapelle in 1819, the European powers forced the Maghrebi states to remove trade barriers and end their practice of supporting piracy. Similarly, British insistence on ending the slave trade badly hurt the Omani economy and reduced the power of the Ibadi state. The region's intensified contacts with Europe, especially after the signing of the trade convention with the Ottoman Government in 1830, sowed the seeds of an economic revolution by stimulating trade and the use of cash. The initial effect on local industries was disastrous, but agriculture was stimulated. In other respects, the increasing conversion of the medium of exchange into cash had a tremendous effect on the creation of new social strata and caused havoc in the fiscal administration of the state. The traditional elites showed ineptitude and irresponsibility in reacting to the revolution in finance, and their floundering laid them open to rapacious creditors and foreign intrigues which proved detrimental to their independence. This was true as much of Persia and Turkey as of Ismail's Egypt and Ahmed Bey's Tunisia (Issawi, 1984; Brown, 1974).

Aside from the weakening of the traditional state structure, the economic revolution had some interesting and long-range effects on the state system. In the first place, it created a new class of landlords and merchants who later emerged as the champions of nationalism and independence. The rising tide of nationalism weakened the old guard, because of their association with colonial rule. Merchant, landlord and professional groups emerged as the major rivals to the ruling dynasties, which had to come to terms with imperialism to preserve their status at the head of their states.

Second, a domestic market was stimulated and exchanges increased to such an extent that new linkages between the countryside and the city were created. These links were the first in a chain integrating the periphery with the centre and leading to the creation of a national society. Most notable in this respect was the emergence of a number of provincial towns and domestic merchants that served as links between villages and the capital, and of port towns which served as links between the country and the outside world (Harik, 1968).

These developments had an integrative role domestically and in most cases buttressed the forces that made for a new society and state in the Arab world. The rise of nationalism in Arab countries is most often attributed to intellectuals and their increasing contacts with the West. However, the stimulation of the domestic market is just as important, if not more so, in giving rise to nationalism, especially state nationalism.

The intensified economic exchanges and communications links, however, cannot be compared in magnitude with similar integrative forces in the European states of the nineteenth century, since the economic growth of the Arab countries remained slow and in some cases declined. Interestingly enough, the forces which tied the Arab countries to the world economy in a colonial and dependent relationship also generated the seeds of the destruction of colonialism, that is, nationalism. Port towns, I stress, appeared not as an isolated phenomenon but in conjunction with provincial towns. The first linked the country with the colonial powers and the second linked the hinterland with the capital. It was in towns that nationalists emerged and agitated for national independence.

While colonialism tied the hands of the governments of the area by financial bondage, it also gave rise to a new class, the custodians of small economic enterprises whose interests and culture were antagonistic to imperialism. These groups led the fight against imperialism. That this so-called middle and upper-middle class is now so beleaguered and castigated by contemporary political ideologies should not distract from the fact that it was indeed the pioneer of nationalism.

Structurally, the colonial administration had a complex effect on the state system of the Arab world in the nineteenth century. It bolstered the authority of a number of small states in the Persian Gulf area, while it undermined the power of one of the strongest amongst them, Oman. In the Fertile Crescent, it created four new states and reshaped the destiny of a fifth. In Egypt, it weakened the power of the central authority, as it did in Tunisia. In Algeria, it abolished that authority altogether and created a new colonial structure made up of *colons*. In Morocco, the case has similarity to the states of the Arabian Peninsula on the Persian Gulf, where colonialism consolidated the authority of the central government of what was previously a disintegrating monarchy.

In brief, colonialism introduced some contradictory trends in the area. It generated economic forces which tied the Arab economies to the West in a dependency relationship, on the one hand, and made for the domestic integration of state and society, on the other. A new class of businessmen, landlords and professionals emerged and held high the torch of nationalist

41

resistance to imperialism. Finally, colonialism contributed to the weakening of the dynasties of bureaucratic oligarchies in the Maghreb states and Egypt, while it buttressed many of the traditional secular dynasties in the Gulf.

CONCLUSION

Conflict between a universal and a particular outlook in the political lives of Arab peoples has raged since the appearance of Islam, the most powerful force for universal identity that the Arabs have experienced in their entire history. It may be said that two conflicting impulses, one yearning to preserve and sharpen the particular identity of a community, and the other to submerge particularistic differences in a great and uniform whole, accompanied the very early formation stage of Islam and coexisted with it for the rest of its history. Ibadi and Shi'i particularisms appeared scarcely a generation after the death of the Prophet. States in Oman and Yemen were duly formed to embody these yearnings. Yet the force of universal political identity has always been stronger and more pervasive.

The most important and durable states in the Arab world, though their rulers were not, for the most part, ethnically Arab, were Muslim and multi-ethnically oriented states. They were based on the universal principle which binds the Muslim community.

Few states like Yemen and Oman tried explicitly to assert their particularistic identity in the face of a strident universalistic empire. The emergence of particularistic state structures in other Arab lands occurred much later, mostly in the seventeenth century in the Maghrebi states and in the eighteenth century in Arabia. This tendency coincided with the decline and, to a certain extent, breaking down of the vitality of the universal Ottoman state in the east and the religious revivalist Almohad state in the west.

In response to compelling necessity, Muslims adjusted to the inevitable diversity and started to perceive the universal as embodied in the particular. In other words, the universal principles of Islam were required to be embodied in the workings of the local state. Insistence that the ruler implement the Shari'ah and the resort of pretenders to seeking legitimacy from religious leaders are clear indications of the subscription by the small-time ruler to higher and more universal ideals.

This tendency was also manifested in another fashion: the acceptance by Muslims of the religious and temporal authority of learned scholars from other lands. It may be pointed out here that the Sanusi of Libya, whose teachings and authority were accepted by the Cyrenaican tribes, was an Algerian, and the Idrisis of 'Asir were Moroccans. Al-Mirghani was a Meccan whose following developed in the Sudan and became known as the Khatimiyah movement. The Iraqis and Jordanians accepted Hashemite kings from Hijaz who, though not learned scholars, were nevertheless sharifs.

The new state structures survived the inner strains of their locality and region for centuries; what they failed to do was to face up to the larger world that was rapidly encroaching upon them. The state system succumbed in the nineteenth century to an exogenous force coming from Europe. It failed to rejuvenate itself by promoting the science of 'umran, development, as Ibn Khaldun would have put it. Consequently, a chasm appeared between society and state. The needs of society were no longer served by the extractive policies of the state, which also failed to generate positive trends and growth. Eventually, the conflict between a no-growth society and an extractive state undermined both and opened the way for foreign intervention.

Invariably, colonial powers in the Arab countries left the outer layers of the state system intact, namely its core territory and dynasty. Only in Algeria was the ruling dynasty abolished and the boundaries expanded in an extreme way. The tendency on the part of the colonial powers to accept the state system as they found it had the effect of enforcing the particular nature of the one-country, one-state idea and provided the state with a more accomplished formal character. However, before the colonial powers had exhausted their use and potency, they had weakened the ruling dynasties beyond redemption in most of the Maghrebi states, though not in eastern Arabia where they have seen them through with a protective arm up to the present. Obviously, the impact of colonial rule, though in many ways pernicious, is more diverse than we generally credit it to be.

At any rate, the confirmation of the particularistic state by colonialism later encountered the revivalist universalistic forces of religion and of Arab nationalism. Colonialism was opposed for two reasons: for occupying Arab lands and for reinforcing the particularistic development of states, which were considered in the nationalist universalistic world-view as symptoms of decline.

In much the same way, in the memory of younger generations the association of the localistic states with the imperialist period earned them the contempt of nationalists and pan-Islamists alike. Nationalists who had hoped to create a universalistic state anyway found in the colonial association a good excuse to undermine and discredit the state system. They did not, however, undermine the legitimacy and staying power of that time-honoured arrangement. Not only nationalists, but also social scientists, often overlook the fact that the structure creates the myth. Once an organisation is set up, it develops forces of vested interests and generates among individuals, almost habitually, a sense of identification with the structure.

Traditional authority, Weber tells us, is the force of habitually accepting the ways of one's forebears as the right ways. It does not even take centuries to develop this habitual sense of identity with the structure. In Kuwait, for instance, where one social scientist refers to his country as a 'gas station', it was found that the inhabitants have repeatedly opted against mergers with neighbouring states and prefer the identity of a 'gas station'!

Not even in Lebanon, after years of brutal and violent civil war, has anyone sought unification with Syria or lost his/her sense of Lebanese identity, despite all the pull of centrifugal forces and early opposition by many Lebanese Muslims to becoming incorporated into the Lebanese state. Arab nationalists in particular, therefore, would be well advised seriously to consider that the state system is here to stay and for good reasons. They may also consider that the state system is not necessarily a negation of Arab nationalism but may well be the main pillar upon which a federated Arab state may develop.

Looking towards the future, it would seem clear that the state system has gained strength and endurance despite the instability of particular regimes. True, there has not been any marked effort to provide the state system with legitimacy through intellectual treatises as is the case in universalistic ideologies. What we witness, rather, is the almost involuntary inculcation in the people of a sense of identity with their own state gained through habit, vested interests, local peculiarities and sensitivities, and common experiences. These things should not be underestimated, for in some cases they have both confirmed and lent legitimacy to the existing system and also generated a new particularistic nationalism such as the Palestinian ideology which has in recent years distinguished itself clearly as a separate nationalism, complementary to, but separate from, Arab nationalism. Uniformities created by state policies which affect only the people of that state often increase their tendency to draw together and result in their having common characteristics distinct from those of their neighbours.

Power considerations have also tended to strengthen the local state system. One can observe this tendency in the emergence of autocratic regimes jealous of their power and willing to unite with others only on their own terms of hegemony and dominion. Such approaches have tended also to distance Arab states from one another. Growing bureaucracies and the power of governments, coupled with stringent centralisation, have strengthened the patterns set in the past. Thus, curiously enough, the principle of dominion is still effective in explaining the state system at present as at the time of its inception. Absence of democratic freedoms has discouraged the development of inter-Arab relations by private citizens outside official channels.

Similarly, one sees that social forces have also tended to favour the state system. Different Arab economic systems have been developed which often resist integration and manifest protectionist tendencies dictated by particular needs and peculiarities. More recently, the sudden wealth of some Arab oil producers has tended to encourage the particularistic sentiments of the 'going it alone and protecting our privileges' attitude. On the other hand, the pull of the universalistic principle of Arab nationalism is not entirely dead as is sometimes claimed, and may be working in conjunction with particularistic trends towards a new order, whereby the sovereign states permit the growth of supra-national institutions leading eventually to some sort of future confederation.

Evidence of some remaining vitality in the principle of Arab nationalism is demonstrated by growing Arab co-operation in economic development activities and continued co-ordination regarding security and national issues. There is still something called mutual Arab engagements generating constant action and constant attention. Universalistic principles do not fade easily, and this is the case with Arab nationalism which has been weakened but not defeated.

Finally, I cannot, as a social science historian, let slip the temptation of drawing some academic lessons from the preceding arguments. We are all familiar with Weber's types of legitimate authority. I have strived to perceive the indigenous states which I have sketched out here through Weberian spectacles, but I could not always see a clear picture. This led me to wonder whether Weber's general category of traditional legitimate authority is not a bit too general to be useful.

Two lines of thought call for further attention in this context. Should we, for instance, consider an authority which is drawn up deliberately in the name of a higher ideal, and a divine one too, for that matter, simply as traditional, as is the case with a tribal chieftain or a medieval monarch? If we take the imam-chief type, and considering the explicit design and creativity involved in the Islamic making of that state type, it becomes difficult to accept the idea that it is a traditional system of authority in the Weberian sense. The conceptualisation of the divine in rational terms, plus the legalistic procedures for the selection of a legitimate ruler, do not allow us to consider the imam as a charismatic leader either. The imam-chief type fits neither the traditional Weberian idea nor the charismatic one. This may suggest that a comparative study of the types of Arab states may serve to enrich and help differentiate further the Weberian categories of legitimate authority.

NOTES

1. I am indebted to L. Carl Brown for suggesting the term 'bureaucratic' in place of 'military', which I had originally used.

2

Alien and Besieged Yet Here to Stay: the Contradictions of the Arab Territorial State

Bahgat Korany

INTRODUCTION

If the 1980s brought the state back into political analysis (Evans *et al.*, 1985; Kazancigil, 1985), the systematic study of the Arab state is still nascent. A survey of the existing literature on an enlarged concept of the Arab state shows the domination of two approaches: political psychology (i.e. the personalisation of the state) and religion (i.e. the role of Islam). Thus political psychology, emphasising the role of the leader or the 'big man' (Khadduri, 1981; Vatikiotis, 1978), led to a romanticised version of events and the perception of history as the product of powerful individuals. As for the emphasis on the role of Islam, it is a part of the well-entrenched orientalist (Said, 1978; Hussain *et al.*, 1984) tradition, and has become at present a flourishing industry after Iran's establishment of the Government of God (Bernard and Khalilzad, 1984) through the reign of the Ayatollahs (Bakhash, 1984). Despite their many differences, what these two major approaches have in common is to slight and overlook — if not to exclude altogether — the role of external factors and outside forces.

Yet if dependence conditioned the historical evolution of the international periphery — i.e. Arab and Third World countries — is not the exclusion *a priori* of powerful external factors an anomaly in both method and substance? Consequently, rather than political psychology or orientalism this chapter's approach emphasises political economy (Hollist, 1985; Staniland, 1985; Strange, 1985) to attract attention to the close interconnectedness between the vagaries of the world system and the *territorialness* (as distinct from the nation-ness) of the contemporary

Arab state. Thus, in balancing the literature's 'skewedness' in favour of psychological and orientalist approaches, it is hypothesised here that external factors predominated in the territorial definition of Arab states.

In order to develop this thesis, the chapter is divided into three parts. Part one elaborates the thesis about the primacy of the external factors, discusses existing definitional problems in the use of the concept of the state, and specifies the definition used here. Part two analyses the collision between grass-roots political culture (based on a 'pan' concept, whether Islamic or Arab) and the 'foreign' political culture (based on the territorial concept). It surveys some findings of recent empirical social science research and then addresses itself to the rise and globalisation of the phenomenon of the territorial state and its importation by the Arab world. To develop how the present demarcation of the Arab territorial state is indeed a phenomenon made in Europe (the centre at the time of the emerging international system), three historical phases are traced: (a) the rise and characteristics of the Westphalia system of 1648 which ended Europe's wars of religion and initiated an international system of sovereign states; (b) dismemberment of the Ottoman empire and its integration into the European system; and (c) the rise of the mandate system in its place and the resulting Arab territorial states.

Part three moves from the global to an emphasis on the regional level of analysis: the study of strains in the Arab region resulting from the extension of the territorial inter-state order. Two types of internal strains are studied: section one deals with 'particularistic' tensions associated with early territorial demarcation, with Saudi Arabia in the late 1920s as a sample case: section two deals with strains that arise once the state has been established, i.e. inter-state territorial conflicts. Two sub-regions of the Arab world are surveyed: the Gulf area and North Africa.

The conclusion pulls the threads together to draw lessons from the historical data in order to throw light on the evolving political landscape in the Arab world. For instance, the creation of the state of Israel and the increasing emphasis on resources (oil, water) in regional politics increase the salience of inter-state territorial issues. The chapter ends by raising a nagging question: if the globalisation of the territorial norm explains the origin and the contradictory existence of the Arab territorial state, is the 'outside' enough by itself to explain its present consolidation and continuing 'victory'?

THESIS AND DEFINITIONAL PROBLEMS

In relation to the political organisation of the community, *at-turath* (heritage) emphasises two basic concepts. First, the all-inclusive pan-Islamism with its corollary of *umma*. However, the nineteenth century saw the decline of *Dar al-Islam* and in 1924 the Caliphate was formally abolished as a political institution. Pan-Arabism with its emphasis on 'one Arab nation from the (Atlantic) Ocean to the (Arab) Gulf' was a secular attempt to cope with European patterns of political organisation while salvaging some parts of at-turath. These two concepts of political organisation — as well as the attempts at their 'reconcilability' (*Al-Qawmiyya al-'Arabiyya fi al-Fikr wa al-Mumarasa,* 1980) — still dominate Arab political discourse.

Contemporary inter-Arab relations, however, have been dominated not by the realisation of the Islamic umma or the single Arab state, but rather by polemics over these two issues. In the meantime, (sub-national) territorial Arab states — Algeria, Syria, Libya, Kuwait or Sudan — have acquired international legal personalities and are being consolidated. This is one of the most neglected aspects of the penetration of European political ideas into the Arab value system.

Why does this gap exist between discourse and reality? The thesis of this chapter is that the gap between 'said' and 'done' is a reflection of a contradiction between indigenous grass-roots political culture (which is either 'pan'- or particularistic-ethnic) and the imported elite political culture, which emphasises the nation-state as the frame of reference. This nation-state concept is a relatively modern invention (less than four centuries old) and is a consequence of the rise of a European inter-state system since the Treaty of Westphalia in 1648. Through colonialism, the mandate system in the inter-World War period, and post-World War II political (but not ideational) decolonisation, the European frame of reference became generalised. Consequently, nation-state formation in the Arab world is both hybrid and in transition, two causes of its tension. Intra-state pressures (ethnic, religious or tribal, and Kurdish, Berber or Negroid) and inter-state territorial conflicts are manifestations

49

of this tension. Tense and contradictory, the Arab territorial state is getting increasingly naturalised to become the order of the day.

Penetration of the nation-state concept in the Arab world is not dissimilar from what happened in other parts of the Third World. As Ali Mazrui (1984: 290) remarks:

> The West's cruellest joke at the expense of Africa, is the construction of two contradictory prison-houses — one incorrigibly and rigidly *national* and the other irresistibly *trans-national.* One is the prison-house of the sovereign state, a fortress of political and military sovereignty. The other is the prison-house of capitalism, compulsively trans-national and constantly mocking the very principle of national sovereignty.

In the Arab world, the hiatus between the triumph of imported ideas and the resistance of indigenous reality can be shown in this characterisation of the Jordanian 'state'. Indeed, Jordan (previously known as the British mandated territory of Transjordan):

> ... had the distinction of having the most artificial boundaries, the poorest endowment in natural resources and the least developed feeling of civil loyalty of any country in the Middle East ... Its desert dunes were unsuited for agriculture, and no minerals were discovered. Its coastal city of Aqaba ... was undeveloped as a port and its possession, moreover, disputed by neighbouring Saudi Arabia. All imports, therefore, had to come via the Palestinian ports of Haifa or Tel-Aviv and since 1948, via Beirut and Damascus (Rustow, 1971: 53-4).

This indeed raises the problem of the definition of the state, not only in the Arab world but in general. For even though the state is increasingly at the heart of political analysis, no standard definition has yet been canonised. As early as 1926, MacIver discerned seven uses of the concept of the state. Jessop has found six conceptions in classical Marxist literature alone. This is why Clark and Dear could plausibly assert the existence of eighteen different theories of the state. But Titus is the most discouraging. In 1931, in an article in the *American Political*

Science Review he claims to have identified 145 separate definitions of the state. This is why after reviewing different approaches and definitions, the *International Encyclopedia of the Social Sciences* (143-50) concluded: 'at present ... conflict and parochialism (among approaches) overshadow harmony and the search for common denominators. As a result it is impossible to offer a united definition of the state that would be satisfactory even to a majority of those seriously concerned with the problem.'

Basic differences in the definition of the state do, in fact, reflect the fundamental divide among different schools of thought in political theory. Two such schools are the rights theory of politics versus the power theory of politics. As an example of the first, Hegel defined the state as 'the actuality of the ethical idea'. As an example of the second, Weber defined the state as the organisation which 'monopolises legitimate violence over a given territory' (*A Dictionary of Political Thought*, 1982: 446-7). Though the international dimension is not mentioned, an important definitional component — territory — is emphasised.

Consequently, in this chapter, a state is defined as the establishment of an organised political authority in a recognised territory. Territoriality is thus an integral part of the concept of the state. But an objection might be raised: have not so-called stateless societies enjoyed a territory? Granted. De La Pradelle, writing on international law in 1928, seemed to agree and stated that 'the striking feature of the concept of the boundary is its universal acceptance' (p. 9). The attachment of stateless societies to place or locus, however, could be *ad hoc* and relates much less to bounded areas than to scattered features of the environment: e.g. sources of water, windfall foods or grazing land. We shall see later in this chapter this basic difference between the 'stateless' and 'state-nation' concepts of territory and boundary in the conflict between the *Ikhwan* brotherhood and Al-Saud during contemporary Saudi Arabia's state-formation in the late 1920s. International recognition sanctioned only the latter.

This recognition, i.e. sovereignty (identification of exclusive legal control in a society), is another basic component in the definition of the modern nation-state. The nineteenth-century jurist John Austin, one of the most respected authorities on the concept, linked his definition of the law, and implicitly the concept of the state, to the concept of sovereignty. He held that positive law, on which formal government rested, could only exist in conjunction with a determinate locus of power and ultimate authority. Here then are linked the concepts of territory, sovereignty and state, or formal government, as Austin used to call it (Fried, 1968: 143-50). At this legal level in the definition of the state, we have come to the heart of the importation of European ideas by the countries of the periphery.

THE ENCOUNTER BETWEEN GRASS-ROOTS AND FOREIGN POLITICAL CULTURES

A survey of the constitutions of the Arab countries reveals an explicit insistence on the identification of the state as Islamic and/or Arab, and this does not change whether the state is 'moderate' or 'radical' in political ideology. Thus, Saudi Arabia — which does not yet have a written constitution — has set up an eight-man committee to draw up a 200-article main 'system of rule' based entirely on Islamic principles. In the meantime, the king rules in accordance with the *Shari'ah*. The People's Libyan Arab Jamahiriyya, on the other hand, proclaimed through its General People's Congress in Sebha (2-28 March 1977) its commitment to achieving Arab unity — and that 'the Holy Quran is the social code' of the country. Even Egypt, which pioneered secularisation and Europeanisation in the late eighteenth and early nineteenth centuries and has the dubious distinction of signing the first peace treaty with Israel, has its Constitution declaring that its 'system (is) based on ... the country's historical heritage and the spirit of Islam. The Egyptian people are part of the Arab nation and work toward total Arab unity ... The Islamic code is the principal source of legislation.'

Why this solemn insistence on the 'pan' idea in the face of divergent political behaviour in inter-Arab relations? One answer is to be found in the prevalence of the pan idea at the grass-roots level and hence the attempt by the different regimes to capture this 'aspiration' in their official political texts. Recent empirical surveys of indigenous political culture — especially in its pan-Arab brand — confirm this inference.

The choice of these studies is dictated not by their perfection, but rather by the fact that they are pioneering applications of social science techniques (e.g. content analysis and survey research) to gauge the Arab political culture both in recent history and at present. Thus, despite the usual methodological headaches over the application of such techniques in the 'non-Western world', the results of this research are still useful as indications of the state of indigenous political culture regarding the question of unity (as a counterpart to the territorial state). Two research teams conducted their work in the late 1970s and published their findings in 1980 (Yassin, 1980; Ibrahim, 1980).

Yassin and his team content-analysed some historical Arab writings for the evolution of the concept of unity through four historical periods: (a) pre-World War I; (b) the inter-war period; (c) the two decades 1945-65; and (d) the post-1967 period. Without going into details of the analyses, two findings and their variations across time have to be emphasised for our present concerns.

The first is the relationship between the Arab nation and the umma, or Arabism and Islam. Thus whereas early writings on Arab unity were either ambiguous concerning the relationship or tended to emphasise the religious dimension, later analyses (e.g. al-Husri) tended to be increasingly secular. They thus dealt with Islam not as a theocratic basis of the Arab nation but rather as its principal cultural component. Amin ar-Rihani, for instance, emphasised in 1938 that the Arabs antedated both Christianity and Islam and that Arabism comes first and above everything. A year later, Sami Shawkat — Director of Iraqi Education — went in the same direction to emphasise the pre-Islamic civilisation of the Arabs. 'Ali Nasser was even more explicit; 'religious atheism is relatively unimportant, whereas denial of Arabism is a crime'.

The second variation in findings across time concerns the priorities emphasised in the different writings. Whereas the first two time periods had at the top of the list of priorities the 'rationale for unity' (32 per cent and 27.9 per cent respectively), in the last two time periods this prime place is occupied by 'obstacles on the road to unity' (20 per cent and 49 per cent respectively). Does this increasing concentration on 'obstacles to unity' reflect the writers' consciousness of the growing ascendancy of the concept of the nation-state and *raison d'état* as a frame of reference?

In fact, the second research project (Ibrahim, 1980), surveying Arab political culture on the issue of unity, conducted its work at the ebb of Arab nationalist thinking and increasing crisis in the Arab system associated with Sadat's visit to Jerusalem, the Camp David Agreements and Egypt's conclusion of a separate peace treaty with Israel. For, whereas Yassin traced the evolution of nationalist ideas *across time*, Ibrahim intended to measure their existence at a *specific point in time*, i.e. 1977-9. Consequently, the research technique preferred was not content analysis but survey research. Thus the project regrouped about 200 Arab social scientists who surveyed and analysed a sample of 6,000 persons of different social categories in ten Arab countries. These countries contained two-thirds of the whole population of the Arab world and embraced its different subregions from the Fertile Crescent to North Africa. What could the findings tell us?

Despite the antagonistic mass-media campaigns between Egypt and the rest of the Arab countries and the ideological confusion reigning in the area, 78.5 per cent of those surveyed believed in the existence of an Arab entity, and no less than 77.9 per cent believed that this Arab entity constitutes one nation (with a full 53 per cent of this percentage believing that this nation is divided at present by artificial boundaries). What about doing away with these 'artificial' boundaries and driving for statehood? Only 24.9 per cent believed the disadvantages of such a project predominated over its advantages, whereas 33.4 per cent believed that the advantages/disadvantages balance-sheet was equal and 41.9 per cent believed the advantages predominated. This last finding is amplified and reconfirmed when those sampled were asked about the effects of unity on them as *individuals*. As many as 69.1 per cent thought it would be beneficial (compared to 26.8 per cent who thought it would be harmful), and 81.7 per cent thought it would be even more beneficial for their children (compared to only 14.5 per cent who thought it would be harmful). Arab unity, then, is the wave of the future, not only from an abstract political or symbolic point of view, but from a daily down-to-earth personal one. Why is it then not realised?

There are, of course, many obstacles: 48.5 per cent of those sampled believed that the most important obstacles were those imposed by external forces, 32.5 per cent blamed some Arab leaders, 13.9 per cent attributed the failure to lack of political consciousness among many Arabs, and 4.9 per cent attributed it to the unwillingness of some Arab peoples. This explains, perhaps, why only a little more than a third (or 36.4 per cent) of those asked desired to achieve unity in the short term (i.e. five years), whereas 40.8 per cent aimed at its realisation within 10 years and 22.8 per cent envisaged a longer term: 20 years. More revealingly, only 21.5 per cent thought that the objective should be one state with a central government; whereas the majority (57.3 per cent) preferred a federation based on common foreign and military policies, leaving internal affairs to the jurisdiction of the federated components.

Is this perhaps the golden compromise between the 'return to history' of 'one Arab nation' and the daily reality of the existing *raison d'état*? And does the emphasis on external obstacles to unity reveal consciousness of the historical weight of the outside in shaping the present inter-state Arab system? This brings us to the impact of the global system on the rise of the Arab territorial state.

THE ARAB TERRITORIAL STATE: A PHENOMENON MADE IN EUROPE

In a nutshell, the present inter-state system in the Arab world is part of a global process, of the expansion of international society (Bull and Watson, 1984) or global rift (Stavrianos, 1981). Though increasingly world-wide at present, this global inter-state order only dates back just over three centuries, more precisely to the 1648 Treaty of Westphalia which concluded the Thirty Years War in feudalised Europe and sanctioned the nation-state as the cornerstone of an emerging world order. This post-Westphalia inter-state order followed at least seven pre-modern world orders (Bozeman, 1960; Holsti, 1967; Northedge, 1976) represented by the ancient empires of the Near and Middle East, the Chinese empire, the kingdoms of ancient India, the Greek city-state system, the Roman and Byzantine empires, the political and diplomatic system of Renaissance Italy.

There is a controversy in international historiography about the rise of the modern inter-state system. Some (Bozeman, 1960) put it before the Peace of Westphalia and others (Hinsley, 1963) put it after. Without going into the details of this debate, we can say that, even if the embryo of the inter-state order predated Westphalia, the new international order came of age with that treaty. This view is supported by the shift in focus of the normative apparatus at the basis of a political order: law.

So-called international law (Falk *et al.*, 1985) witnessed a shift after Westphalia: from a naturalistic to a positivistic theory of legal norms. For instance, writing at the beginning of the seventeenth century, Grotius reveals that the rules of international law were identical in any Christian society in which the Bible and 'right reason' (in that order of importance) were the true sources of right and wrong. But writing in the eighteenth century, Vattel had an entirely different conception of international society and international law, one more akin to present-day international norms. Vattel begins not with the single Christian republic of Europe, which is by now a part of history, but with the national state:

> Nations or states are political bodies, societies of men who have united together and combined their forces in order to preserve their mutual welfare and security. Such a society has its own affairs and interests; it deliberates and takes resolutions in common, and thus it becomes a moral person having an understanding and will peculiar to itself and susceptible at once of obligations and rights (Northedge, 1976: 61).

This is the embodiment of the norm of *raison d'état* in its most explicit form at the international level. Consequent international lawyers only elaborated on this idea to emphasise the legal basis of the present inter-state system: state sovereignty, territoriality and equality.

To conclude then: the present inter-state system of Westphalia evolved through a lengthy process from about the seventeenth to the mid-eighteenth century. At the beginning of the seventeenth century

> the modern system began to take shape when the rulers of Europe started to think of their business as essentially material and earthly, rather than religious, or in other words as the conduct of the affairs of the secular state: all of which was not God's but Caesar's domain. By the mid-18th century there was the acceptance of Europe, no longer as a single state, the interests and welfare of which had to be defended against the infidels by sovereign and people alike, but as a

collection of separate entities with interests unique to themselves. These entities were regarded as associated together by principles of law and morality which echoed the older unity of the whole, but which might from time to time have to give way to the even greater necessities of the sovereign state (Northedge, 1976: 64).

This intrinsically European system became universalised to the rest of the world. In the Arab region it did so in successive stages: the co-option of the Ottoman empire into the European balance of power in the nineteenth century, the fragmentation of this same empire and its replacement by the mandate system during and after World War I, and the present interstate Arab order following World War II, shaped by the mandate system.

Integration of the Ottoman empire in the European system

Though from the fourteenth to the nineteenth centuries the Ottoman empire occupied, controlled and administered between a quarter and a third of the European continent, the empire was in but not of Europe. Indeed, the contact between the Ottomans and post-medieval Europe represented a collision between two opposed political cultures. For the

> post-medieval European idea of the state — a territorially defined entity apart from ruler or dynasty organised in accordance with man-made rules — was alien to Muslim political theory. Ottoman theories of state and government derived from the Muslim concept that God is the source of all authority and law, that government exists to enable the community of true believers (Muslims) to fulfil its obligations to God. The community, not the state, constitutes the basic Muslim policy. transcending all boundaries (Naff, 1984: 143).

Thus the Muslim policy represented *Dar-al-Islam*, whereas non-Muslim political entities represented *Dar al-Harb*, abode of war. Between the two there could be no equality of sovereignty as Europe's international law theorised, but a

57

spectrum of relations ranging from *jihad* (Holy War) to provisional truce.

Such a pattern of relations could be practised as long as Istanbul was militarily powerful enough to back up its version of international society. But with the abating of Ottoman military prowess and the challenges it faced on the Asian frontier, in the Balkans and in the north,

> the ruling circle of the Empire turned in on itself, yielding to conservative religious influences often shading into fanaticism. Corruption and self-serving factions destroyed the system that had produced the great leaders of the past, while the Ottoman sense of moral superiority stifled curiosity about Europe, its societies, governments and religions (ibid., 148).

Thus the stream of Ottoman concessions started and multiplied, discreet and unconscious at first but increasingly basic and imposed. Even though Ottoman rulers harboured feelings of Muslim superiority over the 'infidels', they were becoming increasingly integrated into Europe's state-system and hence recognised and accepted the principles of Europe's inter-state order: equality of sovereignty, reciprocity of relations, European diplomatic usages, points of European international law such as extraterritoriality and the 'Law of Nations'. The huge ideological barrier to alliance with European powers and practising the rules of the game was thus demolished. These rules of the game were to turn against the very survival of the empire itself:

> the bonds of tradition were permanently loosened, the old institutions were shaken to their foundations, and the idea of reform itself acquired an inexorable momentum within Ottoman governing circles. One of the most significant changes was a more favourable attitude towards European civilisation by influential Ottomans ... As European travellers in the empire became more common, as the European communities burgeoned, and as, at the same time, the number of special Ottoman missions to the capitals of Europe increased, westward-looking Ottoman officials — small in number but influential — led the empire, often unwittingly, into Europe's international system. Since the Ottoman Empire had no permanent diplomatic representa-

tion in Europe, Europe brought its system to the Sublime Porte. Resident European envoys in Istanbul insisted on instructing the Porte in the niceties of European protocol. The able among them succeeded in making the Ottomans the instrument of their sovereign's foreign policy in eastern Europe (ibid: 155).

The year 1789 saw the seizure of the Crimea by Russia, the first piece of Islamic territory to be taken by a Christian power. Militarily incapable of stopping its dismemberment, the empire under Selim III increasingly sought European allies, starting with Gustav III of Sweden (following his attack on Russia) in July 1789. But the Swedes, contrary to their treaty with the Ottomans and without even referring to it, signed a unilateral peace with Russia one year later (July 1790). Highly disappointed, Selim III stated to his Vizir: 'This is a harmful situation ... Infidels are so unreliable.' The Sultan tried to cope with his ignorance of Europe's *Realpolitik* by more integration in the system, the most significant diplomatic feature being the establishment of Ottoman embassies in Paris, London, Vienna and Berlin.

The following example shows the magnitude of Ottoman assimilation of the basic norms of Europe's inter-state system at the expense of earlier Islamic rationale. When in 1799 the grand Vizir informed Selim III that a squadron of Russian warships had entered the straits unannounced, the Sultan commented:

> My vizier, the *reis effendi* ought to take this opportunity to remind the Russian interpreter in an amicable way of the international rules of conduct and of the reasons for the clauses in the treaty (with Russia) governing this matter. It is contrary to the canons of international law that a war fleet should enter a foreign port without prior notification and without specifying the number of vessels (Nass, 1984: 159-60).

With the French expedition into Egypt and the rise of Napoleon, the Porte effectively joined the continental alliance against France to become the first and only non-Western *de facto* member of Europe's network of alliances.

But as mentioned earlier, assimilation was not limited to the empire's external relations. For throughout the empire's process

of internal reforms to cope with the external challenge, European ideas, institutions and systems served as the model frame
of reference for change. Thus around the mid-nineteenth
century both the empire's upper political and social levels as
well as its bureaucracy and education were Europeanised in
language, ideas and methods. The last barrier to Europe's
swallowing of the empire finally fell.

The rest of the story — from Muhammad Ali's challenge to
the arrival of the mandate system — is well-known. It is this
latter system that needs now to be tackled in order to complete
the story of the globalisation of the European inter-state system
and its implantation in the very heart of Islam: the Arab world.

The mandate system

The story of the triangular relations between the European
powers, the Ottoman empire and the Arabs during and after
World War I need not be detailed here. Suffice it to say that
such historic events as the 1916 Sykes-Picot Agreement, the
1917 Balfour Declaration and the 1920 mandate system had
two common features in relation to our subject: they presided
over the dismemberment of the Ottoman empire and planted
the seeds of fragmentation in the once-deemed-possible Arab
state.

The Sykes-Picot Agreement divided most Ottoman possessions into spheres of influence of Britain and France. The
Balfour Declaration continued the tradition of dismemberment
and also made sure that the emerging territorial state in Palestine would not be Arab. As for the mandate system, it affirmed
that the Arabs were not ready to have even mini-nation-states
and that others (i.e. Britain and France) would decide on the
timing and form of such political organisation. Article 22 of the
Covenant of the League of Nations speaks of 'peoples not yet
able to stand by themselves', whose 'well-being and development ... form a sacred trust of civilisation', consequently, 'tutelage of such peoples should be entrusted to advanced nations ...
as mandatories on behalf of the League'. One small consolation
for the Arabs concerned, they were designated as an 'A'
mandate.

The colonial settlement of 1919, in effect, defined three
classifications of those dominated: the 'A' peoples of the

Middle East (Palestine, Transjordan, Iraq, Syria and Lebanon) who were considered 'civilised' but not yet ready for independence. The mandatories were to give administrative advice and assistance and — in the case of Iraq and Syria — to 'facilitate the progressive development' of these territories 'as independent states'. Constitutions were to be drawn up within three years so that these territories would be able 'to stand alone'. The 'B' category designated the tribal peoples of tropical Africa who could require an indefinite number of years or decades of economic and political advancement under European tutelage. As for the last category, 'C', it designated the 'primitive peoples of the Pacific' and the 'Hottentots' of South West Africa, who probably would remain European subjects at least for a period of centuries, if not forever (Louis, 1984: 201). How different then is the mandate formula from the old-fashioned straight-forward colonial bond?

The question should not be regarded as rhetorical. The traditional idealistic school of history — still influential in many quarters — considered the enactment of the mandate system as the triumph of internationalism over nationalism, the victory of Wilsonian ideas and those of the 1917 Russian Revolution, notably of self-determination. Thus the mandate system was affirmed as a mid-way stop towards a pre-fixed destination and was closely associated with the catchphrase (i.e. self-determination) that the British and French accepted only with great circumspection. The linkage of mandate system and self-determination might indeed have been the intention of some. Was not a Permanent Mandate Commission constituted in February 1921 as an auxiliary political agency of the League? Were not the governments of the mandated territories obliged to present annual reports to the Commission so that the latter could advise the League Council whether or not the conditions of each mandate were being strictly observed? Were not representations from the inhabitants of the various territories heard, and governors and other high officials summoned for questioning? All this is true.

But thus was the formal aspect of the mandate system, its paper-work. Its reality was somewhere else: in the hands of those who held the mandate power. And for them the mandate system was not very different from colonialism. What differed was the humanising veneer or the legal cover. Thus Lord Curzon, in explaining Britain's final decision to endorse the principle of self-determination, put it explicitly in December 1918:

> I am inclined to value the argument of self-determination because I believe that most of the people would determine in our favour ... if we cannot get out of our difficulties in any other way we ought to play self-determination for all it is worth wherever we are involved in difficulties with the French, the Arabs, or anybody else, and leave the case to be settled by that final argument knowing in the bottom of our hearts that we are more likely to benefit from it than anybody else (Louis, 1984: 205).

At the normative level, the inter-state European system did indeed benefit more than anybody else, for whatever interpretation of the mandate system is adopted, the end-result, at least as it concerns our topic, was not different from the colonial relationship. Whether we are talking about colonised Algeria, Mauritania, Tunisia, Aden, or mandated Lebanon or Syria, the result was the same: the institutionalisation and consolidation of territorial states in the image of the European pattern. In a different context, Helms reached the same conclusion:

> The present Middle Eastern borders and thus the whole of the modern Middle Eastern state system are products of this mandate period. From the perspective of the indigenous populations, there was little historical rationale in their formulation except in the most general sense. Many of the borders were linear, as if drawn with a ruler, determined by Europeans to further their own ends, however well-intentioned and idealistic, and to expedite mandate administration (Helms, 1981: 188).

Because of its 'alien' origins, the implanting of the inter-state system was to face two pressures: internal strains within the polity at the time of the system's institutionalisation, and territorial disputes once the inter-state system was established. To examples of each we now turn.

THE TERRITORIAL STATE UNDER PRESSURE

Internal strain

According to some dominant analyses, the Middle East is the home of multiple or mosaic societies where territorial states prove to be failures. Are not cultural or religious diversities the order of the day (e.g. Kurd/Arab, Muslim/Christian), with Lebanon constituting a notorious example? Are not 45 per cent of Morocco's population and 30 per cent of Algeria's Berber communities increasingly self-assertive? There is indeed increasing literature (Chabry, 1984) on this aspect. The ten-year-old civil war in Lebanon has produced literature too voluminous to mention here on 'precarious republics' (Hudson 1968, 1977).

But what about relatively homogeneous societies? Saudi Arabia, for instance, is both 100 per cent Muslim and Arab. Yet the establishment of the territorial state did not prove an unmitigated success and was in fact established with the internal strain symptomatic of 'mosaic societies'. The case of Saudi Arabia could indeed constitute a 'model' or laboratory case, for in both social organisation and political structure (i.e. the predominance of tribal-religious bases) it is nearest to the original Islamic-Arab polity. Moreover, its territorial demarcation in the 1920s reveals the web of relations between al-Saud, the *Ikhwan* brotherhood and — the dominant colonial power in the area — Britain. Britain's dominant role in Saudi territorial demarcation and indeed in the 'internal' al-Saud/Ikhwan conflict shows that internal factors can never be separated from the omnipresent global factors. Briefly, even such a seemingly orthodox leader as 'Abd al-'Aziz ibn Sa'ud was co-opted into Europe's inter-state norms, and this was almost the pre-condition of his survival.

Two elements underline Saudi Arabia's social organisation and political authority: the tribal system based on kinship and *'asabiyya* (sense of tribal solidarity) and Islam (of the strict Hanbali type). Whereas tribal organisation constituted a formidable barrier to the constitution of a centralised state, Islam was the *raison d'être* of the impressive army, al-Ikhwan (literally Muslim Brethren), which fought until central political authority was achieved in the late 1920s.

63

The Ikhwan were Bedouin warriors who left their nomadic life to settle down and lead a life consonant with Islamic teachings and practice. Between the year of their establishment in 1913 and their demise in 1929 after their conflict with 'Abd al-'Aziz ibn Sa'ud, the Ikhwan were able to win for 'Abd al-'Aziz ibn Sa'ud every battle they fought. The Ikhwan replaced tribal segmentation, eternal shifting balances, and *razzias* (tribal raids) with Islam as a unifying element, and thus transformed tribesmen from undisciplined warriors into an army. They achieved this task without losing the fervour and dedication typical of earlier inter-tribal wars. The political control scheme used to weaken the tribal bands was the establishment from 1912 to 1913 of *hijras* — co-operative, agriculturally-oriented colonies that recognised al-Sa'ud as the holder of the lawful Islamic leadership, or imamate. These hijras, which numbered between 200 and 222, gave 'Abd al-Aziz in 1926 a formidable Ikhwan army of 150,000.

In a rare letter dated 17 January 1928, 'Abd al-'Aziz revealed to the British officer Dickson his acute awareness of the problems of political centralisation in a segmented tribal society and the importance of Islam in coping with these problems. 'The Government ... has been established in this wide desert ... by virtue of the social teachings of religion ... (which) has brought all the desert tribes within the lands under our control' (Korany and Dessouki, 1984: 247).

It was on the two issues of territorial control and the role of Islam that al-Sa'ud's leadership faced a serious crisis in the 1920s: a conflict with the Ikhwan. Moreover, confrontation and debate of the two basic issues took place within the imposing context of the presence of the British, *Al-Mushrikun* (the infidels), as the Ikhwan called them.

The Sa'ud/Ikhwan conflict was simmering during the period 1925-9. It involved the incompatible attitudes of both sides toward the responsibilities of an increasingly secular government whose legality and authority were based on a divine right to rule. When the Ikhwan finally rebelled in 1929 and 'Abd al-'Aziz defeated them, he succeeded with the help of the British, a non-Muslim government, and at the price of his 'personal acceptance of Western-style fixed boundaries' (Helms, 1981: 251).

The conflict over secularisation came to the fore in 1925 on the occasion of the successful completion of the Ikhwan campaign to take over Hijaz. The Ikhwan felt that they should be installed as the new governors of the region to apply the strict Wahhabi doctrine. Both because he feared the Ikhwan's rising force and because of the increasing incompatibility between political and purely religious authority, 'Abd al-'Aziz returned the Ikhwan rank and file to their hijras in central Arabia.

This conflict in political culture over the type of authority (religious versus political) was too basic to be settled by a political compromise between the two incompatible philosophies. One of them had to disappear. In this case the rising concept of the Europe-inspired territorial state and its supporters triumphed. The battle of Sibila in March 1929 saw the dispersal of al-Ikhwan as an organised fighting threat. What was left of it were remnants that could not be saved since they could not grasp the formidable foe — the concept of the territorial state and its supporters — against which they were fighting.

Thus the transition in political authority from particularistic political identification to identification with the territorial state was made. Many indigenous elements were confused by this 'new' concept. Witness this poignant answer by the Ikhwan leader, Faisal al-Shiblain, to Dickson, when the latter forbade the Ikhwan from crossing the border on pain of being bombed:

> Where is the boundary? We don't know any boundary, we have never been told anything. If you mean Iraq or Kuwait tribes, we [Ikhwan] understand, and I tell you they are safe (Helms, 1981: 272).

But this assurance could not be integrated into the emerging concept of state based on sovereignty and territoriality. The Ikhwan had to perish in favour of those who could accommodate the concept, and such accommodation was the price of the latter's survival.

But if the different forms and facets of internal pressure were handled and the territorial state was finally institutionalised and legalised according to the norms of Europe's inter-state system, other problems came to the fore. Most important among them are inter-state territorial conflicts.

Territorial conflicts

These have always been a frequent feature of international relations but multiplied with the increasing number of (artificial) states in the post-1945 period:

> The relations between modern states reach their most critical stage in the form of problems relating to territory. Boundary disputes, conflicting claims to newly-discovered lands and invasions by expanding nations into the territory of their weaker neighbours have been conspicuous among the causes of war (Hill, 1976: 3).

Sub-Saharan Africa has been notorious in demonstrating the artificiality of existing state boundaries, and the conflicts that ensue when they are put in question. A recent survey of only *unresolved* border and territorial issues between states around the world counted the existence of more than 70 such cases ranging from the Balkans to the Kenya-Somalia-Ethiopia dispute (Keesing, 1982). The Iran-Iraq war demonstrates that territorial disputes cannot be confined to the level of 'low violence', and the history of the early 1960s shows that territorial issues can go as far as the negation of the state itself (Iraq versus Kuwait, Morocco versus Mauritania). We shall concentrate on the two regions of the Gulf and North Africa as samples of present territorial disputes in the Arab world. (The descriptive data included in this part are taken from Keesing, 1982).

The Arabian peninsula — Gulf area

In this region we find a few difficulties of territorial demarcation combined: basic tribal conglomerations which migrate to water wells or grazing land; desert ecology; the colonial power's imposition of European practices on a different culture (e.g. the 1922 'Uqair Convention). With the coming of political independence and the establishment of many mini- or family-states in the 1960s and 1970s, territorial demarcation has become an increasingly important issue, even if the rise of a militant Islamic Republic in neighbouring Iran has forced the other countries to settle their differences as the deliberations within the 1981 Gulf Co-operation Council show. However, the last two decades have seen the following territorial disputes:

66

The Iraq-Kuwait conflict. Kuwait's political independence was declared on 19 June 1961. But only six days afterwards, General Qasim — Iraq's Prime Minister — denied the existence of Kuwait and argued that it had been an 'integral part' of Basra province under Ottoman rule and that Iraq had succeeded to Turkish territorial sovereignty over Basra with the dissolution of the Ottoman empire after World War I.

British and Saudi forces were immediately brought in to thwart any possible troop movements by Iraq. The issue was debated in the UN Security Council and the Arab League. This latter replaced British and Saudi troops with its own forces, admitted Kuwait as a full member against Iraq's opposition, and decided to regard any aggression against the skeikhdom 'as aggression against the League's members, to be repelled by force if necessary'.

Iraq was thus unsuccessful in gaining international recognition for its claim over Kuwait, and following Qasim's overthrow and 'Aref's accession to power in 1963, Iraq put aside its claim and recognised Kuwait as a sovereign state. However, the status of the two islands of Warba and Bubiyan (under Kuwait's control but claimed by Iraq) is still pending. In 1973, Iraqi troops moved towards this part of the frontier and occupied a border post, from which they were, however, rapidly forced to withdraw in the face of general Arab opposition. Iraq and Kuwait then began a series of negotiations, at times with external mediation, to settle the border issue. The outbreak of the Iran-Iraq war was a big incentive to reach agreement.

The Bahrain-Qatar dispute. At issue are the Hawar Islands situated 2.4 km off the coast of Qatar but under Bahrain's sovereignty. Whereas Bahrain continued to give drilling concessions in the islands to US companies, Qatar's authorities insisted that 'all geographical, historical, legal and logical indications' categorically proved that these 'islands constitute an indivisible part of Qatar since they are situated within its territorial waters'. Saudi Arabia is mediating between the two countries and the Gulf Co-operation Council is actively trying to prevent escalation. Thus at the GCC ministerial council meeting in Riyadh on 7-9 March 1982, both sides agreed to 'freeze the situation and not to cause escalation of the dispute'.

The Iraqi-Saudi Arabia territorial demarcation. The collapse of the Ottoman empire and the emergence of Saudi Arabia and Iraq as the two regional powers in the area was associated with bitter territorial disputes.

Under the aegis of Britain, the 1922 Convention defined the territory and created a neutral zone on the contentious eastern border area between the two countries. But with the 1958 revolution in Iraq, and with the rise of the radicalism/conservatism bipolarity in the Arab system, the border issue reappeared. The 1979 Iranian Revolution and the Iran-Iraq war pushed the two countries to settle the issue once and for all. Prince Nayef, Saudi Minister of the Interior, visited Iraq in December 1981 and signed an agreement defining the border and also dividing the neutral zone between the two countries. According to Nayef, the border has been 'defined and fixed' and the frontier area 'stabilised'.

Kuwait-Saudi Arabia. Initial border demarcation between these two countries was the result of the 1922 'Uqair Convention between the British protectorate of Kuwait and the sultanate of Najd. As usual, Britain established a neutral zone of common sovereignty until settlement could be reached. This zone amounts to 6,500 sq km of desert with about 64 km of coastline in the Arabian Gulf. With the discovery of oil, the zone became increasingly important. The influx of workers and oil company personnel increased the problems involved in jointly administering the area. In 1965, the two countries signed an agreement on the partitioning of the zone and by 1970 they had, as agreed, completed the allocation of properties and facilities in the zone.

However, the status of the two islands of Qaru and Umm el-Maradim, situated some 37 and 26 km respectively off the coast of the northern part of the neutral zone, remained unsettled. At present, the islands remain under Kuwaiti control, but Saudi Arabia has not formally abandoned its claim to sovereignty over them.

Other disputes. Other disputes still exist between the two Yemens, between Saudi Arabia and the Yemens, between Saudi Arabia and the United Arab Emirates, between Oman and the United Arab Emirates, between Oman and South Yemen. None of these disputes constitutes a hot issue at present and several agreements have been concluded to resolve outstanding border questions. Many of the remaining issues, however, are related to bigger contentions in the countries' general political orientation (e.g. Saudi Arabia or Oman versus 'Marxist' South Yemen), and the geo-politics of the region (e.g. Saudi Arabia's hesitation to permit unity between the two Yemens). Though unimportant in themselves, these pending border issues contain potential for future dissension among the states of the area.

North Africa

The Mauritanian issue apart, Morocco has, since its independence in 1956, pressed a claim to sovereignty over the expanse of desert to its south known as the Western Sahara. An area of about 325,000 sq km, its boundaries were specified by the colonial powers. According to the 1974 Spanish census — very much contested by the Polisario — the area's population is 74,000, mainly tribal.

Morocco's ties with the region date back for centuries, but its political control has always been very limited since the area occupied by particular nomadic tribes was constantly changing. For this reason, no reliable maps of the territorial limits of Morocco's old empire can be found. This was one of the main bones of contention when the issue was submitted to the International Court of Justice (ICJ).

Throughout history, however, Moroccan leaders have refused to confirm Spanish rights in the region (e.g. refusal of Spain's Royal Decree of April 1887 attaching Rio de Oro to the General Office of the Captain of the Canary Islands). Moreover, the 1900 Paris Agreement on the delimitation of French and Spanish possessions on the coast of the Sahara and the coast of the Gulf of Guinea established the southern and eastern borders of the 'Spanish Sahara' but not its northern one. With the independence of both Morocco and Algeria, however, border delineation involved the two countries directly. There was already the 1963 *guerre des sables* between the two countries over Wadi Draa and Tindouf, a conflict settled by the Treaty of Ifrane in 1969. Now the Western Sahara war raging between the two countries is a dominant issue in North Africa's political constellation (e.g. the 1984 unity between Morocco and Libya) and is even hampering deliberations of the Organisation for African Unity.

The conflict came to the fore following Spain's announcement on 21 August 1974 to grant independence to the Sahara (in response to the 1972 UN resolution 2938/XXVI). Morocco and Mauritania, which had incompatible claims on the area, settled their differences and agreed in December 1974 to submit the issue to the ICJ. The Court had to answer two questions: (a) whether the Spanish Sahara was a territory belonging to no-one (i.e. *res nullius*) at the time of its colonisation by Spain; and (b) if not, what legal ties existed between the territory and the kingdom of Morocco and the 'Mauritanian entity'. The proposed referendum in the Sahara was postponed while the ICJ considered the issue.

The Court's advisory opinion (published on 16 October 1975) affirmed that, while certain 'legal ties of allegiance' existed between Western Sahara and both Morocco and Mauritania at the time of colonisation by Spain in 1884, these did not support a claim by either Morocco or Mauritania of territorial sovereignty or affect the application of the right of self-determination by the inhabitants of the area. Thus the Spanish Sahara was not *terra nullius*. The Court added that the overlapping of geographical claims by both Morocco and Mauritania indicated the difficulty of disentangling the various relationships existing in Western Sahara at the time of colonisation.

Immediately following the delivery of the Court's advisory opinion to King Hassan II, Morocco's leadership ordered on 6 November 1975 a 'Green (peaceful) March' of 350,000 unarmed Moroccans to symbolise 'recuperation of the land of our forefathers, after 90 years of separation'. Both Spanish and Algerian troops were put on alert, but the king, at UN instigation, ordered the marchers' withdrawal on 9 November. To make their point, however, the marchers had already penetrated 10 km into the north of the Western Sahara, about one km short of Spain's mined 'dissuasion line'. The same month also saw the conclusion of a Spanish-Moroccan-Mauritanian agreement stipulating that Spain hand over its responsibilities to a trio of representatives from Morocco, Mauritania and Jamaa (the Spanish Sahara General Assembly).

Two principal actors condemned this agreement. Algeria insisted on the practice of the right of self-determination for the inhabitants of the area and mounted a world-wide diplomatic campaign to impose its views. The Polisario staged a guerrilla war against both Moroccan and Mauritanian troops in the area in its fight for independence, and moved its headquarters to Algeria.

Both the Algerian and Polisario positions received a big boost from the report of the fact-finding mission of the UN Decolonisation Committee which visited the Sahara in May 1975 and found evidence of widespread support for the Polisario in the region. It stated that the people it had met in the territory were categorically for independence and against the territorial claims of both Morocco and Mauritania. Finally, the Commission's report (published on 14 October 1975) recommended that the people should be enabled to determine their own future 'in complete freedom and in an atmosphere of peace and security'.

The Spanish presence was declared terminated on 26 February 1976 (the troops had already left on 12 January). Opposing claims by the different parties were put into effect. Thus the Jamaa met in al-'Aaiun on the same day (with only two-thirds of its full contingent) and declared its unanimous ratification of the Madrid Agreement. But on 28 February, the Polisario proclaimed the Western Sahara a free, independent and sovereign state known as the Saharan Arab Democratic Republic (SADR), and formed a government recognised immediately by Algeria. Morocco and Mauritania broke off diplomatic relations with Algiers in retaliation.

War on the terrain continued and accelerated, straining the economies of both Morocco and especially Mauritania (in its 1976/7 budget Mauritania was devoting almost 60 per cent to defence). Indeed, when the Mauritanian armed forces overthrew the government in July 1978, they declared that the country was on the verge of bankruptcy. Consequently, the new government entered into negotiations with the Polisario, signed a peace agreement on 5 August 1979 and withdrew its forces from Tiris al-Gharbia during that month. Moroccan troops immediately entered the evacuated area, renamed it Wadi Eddahab (the Arab name for Rio de Oro) and allocated seats in parliament for the new 'province'.

In the meantime, SADR had been increasingly recognised internationally. More than 50 states have given recognition, and the OAU accredited it with membership in 1982 (at the 38th regular session of the Council of Ministers held in Addis Abeba). Thus while the OAU was experiencing its deep rift, little progress was made toward holding a referendum in the Western Sahara.

CONCLUSION

The Arab territorial state is becoming increasingly implanted and naturalised. It is not an indigenous phenomenon and yet it no longer seems a foreign import. It is thus a hybrid product. Though its form represented the primacy and globalisation of the modern European political culture at the basis of the Westphalia inter-state order, its content is increasingly nationalised. Despite this contradiction between form and content, acceptance of it as 'normal' is growing. People have become accustomed to its presence, it is now the order of the day, the standard frame of reference. Did not the 1945 Charter of the Arab League sanction its presence? Moreover, Arab states whose territorial statehood has been questioned or threatened seek political strength by emphasising the sanctity of the principle of territoriality, even in their constitutions. Thus Kuwait's 1962 Constitution stipulates that 'no part of its territory may be relinquished', and Lebanon's constitution affirms as one of its basic principles that 'no part of the territory may be alienated or ceded'.

Moreover, the principal phenomena of the regional landscape reinforce the trend of territorial primacy, e.g. whether we think of the rise of the state of Israel or of petrolism. Thus the plans for the partition of mandated Palestine and the rise of a Jewish state on 'part of Arab territory' heightened consciousness about territorial issues. Similarly, the repeated Arab-Israeli wars, the continuing 'violation of international borders', and even the discussion of possible peace plans increasingly push territorial issues to the fore in regional politics. Even the conclusion of a formal peace treaty did not lessen the ascendancy of these issues, as witnessed by the conflict between Israel and Egypt around the tiny area of Taba.

As for petrolism — as the section on territorial contentions in the Gulf tends to show — it too has been associated with the salience of territorial issues. Oil discoveries or their possibility have given value to erstwhile parts of barren desert and made them overnight an issue of high politics. Consequently, one can forecast that growing attention to other resources — river waters and seabed possibilities — will give importance to inter-state territorial issues. This is where the distinction of high/low politics becomes increasingly dubious.

Thus, a seemingly low-politics issue like water resources

exploitation is no longer separable from a high-politics issue like the establishment of the state of Israel. If the experience of the past is any indicator, the period 1951-67 witnessed — in the area of the Jordan River system alone — eleven cease-fire violations, with the majority involving the UN Security Council (Naff and Matson, 1984: 36-7). And in the 'arid' Middle East with its growing 'strategic' value of water resources, the future does not augur well. Even with present consumption patterns, Jordan and Israel will be short of water long before 1995. Because of its military superiority, Israel has tended to seize by force the water resources of its neighbours and 'it is known that 40 per cent of Israel's current supply originates outside the pre-1967 borders of Israel' (ibid.: 231). Such disputes over vital resources increase obsession with the territorial imperative all over the region.

But the problems of vital water allocation exist also among the Arab territorial states themselves. Thus Iraq and Syria witnessed a minor incident in 1975 because of the water of the Euphrates. The situation could have developed into a major conflict had it not been for the mediation of Saudi Arabia (and the tacit support of the USSR) which made Syria release more water to Iraq 'from Syria's own allocation' as a one-time gesture of good will (ibid.: 232). The problems between Syria and Iraq around the Euphrates, however, are dwarfed by the possible problems around the Nile River basin, given the extent of that territory, its magnitude of annual water flow, and the size of Egypt's and Sudan's populations.

On the other hand, though it heightens obsession with the territorial imperative, regulation of strategic resources attracts attention to the inherent and glaring limitations of the territorial state, as the increasing pace toward integration, even among established European states, shows. Yet Arab territorial states are not only resistant, but seem to be increasing in number. Are not the 'revolutionary' Palestinians and Saharans, who differ in (almost) everything else, united by their taking up arms in the name of achieving territorial statehood? An important question should then be explicitly raised: if the contradictions of the Arab territorial state are closely related to its foreign origin, does this foreign origin provide sufficient and necessary reasons also to explain its continuing consolidation and supremacy?

Though this is a new research problem that goes beyond the scope of this chapter (Ben Dor, 1983), it is a very legitimate problematique. Suffice it to suggest for the moment that consolidation and supremacy of the territorial Arab state could also be a problem of default, a victory facilitated by the absence of an alternative, i.e. the failure up till now to elaborate an operational formula of the 'pan' state, Islamic or Arab nationalist. Indeed, the neglect by Arab nationalist ideology to elaborate on the organisation of the desired Arab state is one of the most important loopholes in the nationalist doctrine. In this sense too, the failure of the short-lived United Arab Republic (1958-61) has, in reality, only boosted the existing territorial Arab state. Would the Islamic fundamentalists fare better and come up with the needed alternative?

3

State-building and Regime Performance in the Greater Maghreb

Elbaki Hermassi

The state in the Maghreb has always tried to establish its legitimacy in the absolute, as when it refers without any further restriction to one nation indivisible: 'a nation whose language is Arabic and whose religion is Islam'. Such a stance does not allow for the fundamental expression of conflicting interests, whether ethnic, religious, or related to class. Instead of putting forward a number of general principles capable of normative and situational adaptation, this prevailing political attitude tends to resist adaptation to differences and disparities and fails to deal with them. It is, however, necessary to consider a thesis (which I believe to be highly unlikely), which dismisses any probability of conferring legitimacy on the state in the Maghreb, due to the existence of an Islamic or an Arab Utopia. These two Utopias are likely to deprive the state of any loyalty whatsoever and may lead to violence, thus turning the state into one of sheer force. Utopia strips individual states of their legitimacy.

There is loyalty, but not related to the state, there is consensus, but not around it. In this case, authority is severed from the law and power from moral authority. The orders of the state are implemented. Projects are achieved. The individual state provides the country with infrastructure, education, employment, organization, etc. All these achievements do not, however, bring loyalty to, or consensus around, the state. This is especially the case if its propaganda is a constant reminder that this is only a stage towards the achievement of the greater Arab State (Laroui, 1981).

In other words, there is a basic contradiction between the

functions undertaken by the state and the nature of the general ideological atmosphere, a contradiction which leads the individual to not take the state and its decisions seriously.

It is clear that propositions of this type fail to distinguish between various levels of political life, reducing them to a single dimension — 'government' being used when 'state' is normally expected — and totally neglecting all others. It is consequently not difficult to demonstrate the invalidity of such propositions in the case of the Maghrebi states.

When we consider the structure of the state in the Maghreb, we are led to distinguish between the states on the one hand, and the regimes on the other, and to feel that people accept the state as a political framework for reference, although they do not necessarily accept the regimes or their policies, especially now that these regimes are being seriously challenged in their legitimacy. Reference is made here to a type of analytical distinction which, if handled properly, could help explain the struggles against, and reactions to, government activities. In addition, it could help evaluate opposition levels and determine whether these are against authority and policies, or against the political class as a whole.

In the last fifty years nationalism has become the prevalent ideology in the Maghreb and it is this ideology which resisted 'the long night of colonialism', as Ferhat Abbas put it. It is also this ideology which, once victorious, took possession of and reinforced the state system and initiated ambitious development projects. Contrary to the Mashreq where the unionist ideology prevailed, the Maghreb saw the rise of the national state and of 'territorial nationalism'. This idea has prevailed since the 1930s when nationalist elites managed to get the better of the traditionalist movement and to reduce liberal and socialist elites to a marginal status.

It is worthy of notice that not a single liberation party in the Maghreb took up the motto of Arab Union. Even the Tangiers Conference, convened under the banner of union for the Maghreb, only managed to extend the demand of a territorial state for Algeria after Tunisia and Morocco had gained their independence.

This does not mean, however, that nationalist elites did not resort to stirring up religious feelings or relying on Arab support; nor did they neglect to mobilise public opinion or to propagate their ideas on how to put an end to social problems.

What needs to be remembered is that all these symbolic and institutional resources were used in favour of Algerian, Moroccan and Tunisian political communities as if these groups represented nations in themselves.

It is therefore clear that attitudes to, and relations with, the state differ somewhat from the Maghreb to the Mashreq. Although double standards in dealing with the authorities are common to both areas, their separate development led to the rise in the Mashreq of an ideology which considers national states as artificial entities created by colonialism to reinforce the political division of the Arab Nation. There is no doubt that the link between imperialism, division and disintegration is a current belief. It is still necessary, however, to state clearly that considering political entities as transient and temporary territorial units is not verified by the objective and personal experience of most Maghrebians. The facts show that the framework of the national state is totally accepted, even if people do not take it in isolation from the Arab world. The framework is, therefore, accepted even if individual regimes have found it difficult to prove their legitimacy.

For our analysis to be comprehensive, it is necessary to list, however briefly, a number of factors: a history characterised by the establishment of relatively powerful political centres, a heritage which the coloniser continued and reinforced; the fact that Islam spread throughout the Maghreb, but that it was not fully Arabised; the geopolitical situation which made the Maghreb a cultural border area.

All these elements tend to give prevalence to the Arab/ Muslim traits without much differentiation between the two. None the less, and in the light of these influences and their various interrelationships, we can understand how permanent and specific political entities emerged on the basis of an acute feeling of collective identity.

Considering the issue in these terms and claiming that the nationalist programme has won the battle at the expense of other alternatives such as a united Maghreb or Arab union, etc., this may mean that building up the territorial unit is the touchstone by which to determine to what extent these experiments succeeded or failed. How, then, are we to evaluate this process over the last twenty five-years?

THE STATE AT THE CENTRE OF THE POLITICAL PROCESS

Previous studies show that almost all aspects of life (the aggregate heritage, the domination effect of foreign models, the erosion of traditional society) have led to a special situation in which people expect the state to be at the centre of integration and development processes and to achieve, for their own benefit, all those things they were denied by colonialism. The various regimes accepted this serious challenge and derived enough ardour from the enthusiasm for independence and the optimism of the economics of development to undertake the building of the state and the initiation of growth in economic, social and cultural terms.

It is extremely important at this stage to consider how the state was institutionally able to undertake this programme. This process could be described as putting the programme under state control (*étatisation*). State control means the administration of reform and rehabilitation programmes by neutralising existing institutions and relying on corporate bodies to channel people in the various sectors.

It is apt to say that the process of *étatisation* is affected by the institutional structure of each society because of the effects of such a structure on the general options and how they are implemented, as well as on the nature of relations in political circles.

In Morocco, the royal family was not only able to contribute to the liberation movement, it also became the cornerstone of society as a whole. There is no doubt that the perpetuation of monarchy is both an indicator and a factor in the perpetuation of traditional values and the inherited social hierarchy. In addition, it hinders radical policies and fosters discretion and conservatism in social and economic reform.

In Tunisia, historical and social factors contributed to the emergence of a regime centred on a single party. This party played a part in leading the liberation movement and building a nationally-oriented state. It also tried to a certain, limited extent, as we shall see, to fight the battle against underdevelopment.

Maghrebians had great expectations regarding the Algerian Revolution. Some even hoped that, led by the National Liberation Front, this revolution would achieve what nationalist movements in Tunisia and Morocco had failed to achieve. But the Algerian Revolution failed to meet these ambitions for, once the peasant rank and file had been discarded and the political party marginalised, the army became the centre of power. Apart from the institutional aspect, there were other crucial factors: class structure, levels of social diversity, capacity for mobilisation. The capitalist class in the agricultural and commercial sectors was far more important in Morocco and Tunisia than in Algeria. On the other hand, mobilisation and determination were at a much higher level in Algeria than anywhere else. It is for all these reasons that the Moroccan regime opted for liberalism and proceeded with it to the limits of acceptability, checked only by a situation of independence. Algeria launched its programme of nationalising industries under a system of state capitalism in which the regime is in theory at the service of workers and small farmers, but is in practice in the hands of the bureaucratic and technocratic elites. As for Tunisia, the regime has always tried to strike a balance between the liberal capitalist model and state capitalism.

With these conditions and the consequent divergence in levels and in style, a general phenomenon is still to be found: the dramatic intervention of the state in problems of reconstruction, integration and development. Any student of Maghrebi affairs can now see the results for himself. Maghrebi societies have undergone considerable change under the effects of centralisation, education, information and the various development plans. These have had their effect on, and reacted with, all sectors and all social groups. It is therefore possible for North African regimes to boast about a relatively important level of economic development. Such development came with a number of structural changes, such as the emergence of a new class of entrepreneurs in both public and private sectors, as well as an increase in the numbers of the work force which gained new awareness of its weight.

DISENCHANTMENT WITH THE STATE

In the 1970s, however, this atmosphere of enthusiasm and optimism started to dissolve. With the new difficulties facing development policies and the ensuing social problems, public opinion began to question the ability of post-independence politicians to formulate new problems and find adequate solutions. In other words, there came the time of disillusionment with regard to the nationalist programme (Béji, 1982).

This is not, in fact, the first time that signs of disagreement and disgruntlement have emerged in the modern Maghreb, but the new situation is different because disagreement is no longer restricted to the elite and has extended to the wider public, and because disenchantment appears more and more like a national crisis. To understand the reasons for this crisis we should keep in mind that most Maghrebians believed in the nationalist project and, as was previously suggested, their reasonable — and less reasonable — ambitions were centred around a national state. In general, the majority trusted the regime and accepted austerity measures in the hope that they or their offspring would benefit from the returns of development policies. That trust was only shaken after more than twenty years of national management and administration, when the profitability of the development programme — in spite of its manifest achievements — proved limited. The programme was also seen as sanctioning existing social disparities as well as creating new types of disparity.

From what we have seen, it appears that the national crisis was caused by social and economic factors and growing intolerance towards inequality. The unusual fierceness of the demands of labour organisations is probably the best indicator of this attitude. The 1970s was a period of numerous strikes, both legal and illegal, even if some had limited goals and were restricted to certain sectors.[1] Others, however, were so aggressive that they represented a challenge to authority and questioned the regime's legitimacy in representing the people (e.g. in Tunisia on 26 January 1978).

It should be observed that social polarisation was exacerbated not only by disparity in income, but also by the behaviour of the *nouveaux riches,* their propensity for ostentatious consumerism and the negative effects of this behaviour: the feeling of deprivation common among the poorer classes and despair amongst the young. Maghrebi youth suffered at the same time from the prospects of a hopeless future and inflated diplomas. Young people lost all hope of social mobility and of even achieving the slightest portion of the privileges of the previous generation.

The crisis also took on a political aspect with the current belief that success (and social mobility) are not related to competence and effort, but to other factors such as nepotism, barratry and regional considerations.

A number of indicators show that public opinion is now changing its attitude towards politicians. The general impression is that politicians, as in Max Weber's famous proposition, live from, rather than for, politics. The difference between the early days of independence and the present is the difference between a period of *étatisation* of society and a period of privatisation of the state.

In addition to social polarisation and the absence of trust in, and enthusiasm for, the regimes, it is now manifest that post-independence regimes have to face new types of rebellion and anger, which show that the nationalist programme has outlived its aims and confirm the pressing need for correction and reform.

THE FUNDAMENTALIST CHALLENGE

It is within this framework that the Islamic fundamentalist opposition can be considered. Although there is an obvious link between changes in class structure and the ensuing isolation and hopelessness of certain social layers, on the one hand, and the emergence of the fundamentalist movement on the other, it would be a gross mistake to reduce the movement to this single dimension. Young fundamentalist militants are more sensitive to cultural and civilisational than to economic options. Given their background, social membership and disenchantment, they tend to consider only the corrupt outward aspect of life and to see in development only those aspects which widen the gap between social classes and exacerbate social injustice.

As a consequence, they reject a model in which they believe there is no place for them. Rather than follow the pattern of opposition parties and labour organisations which direct their criticism to a limited number of policies and try to introduce effectiveness to existing patterns, fundamentalist militants reject wholesale all the regimes' theoretical propositions and ensuing practical measures. The two countries most concerned by the fundamentalist challenge are those which have opted for radical modernising reforms: Algeria and Tunisia. But if we take into account the different evolution of these two countries, we realise that the fundamentalist movement will be violent and utopian in the first case, innovative and interactive with progressive movements in the second.

81

In Morocco, the movement bears the stamp of the prevailing situation; it is characterised by sectarianism and opposition to the left and has little political weight because of the regime's strong religious base.

Whereas the fundamentalists blame the state for obliterating the Arab/Muslim heritage of the country, the Berber rebellion seems to blame it for doing exactly the contrary — exaggerating the Arab/Muslim traits. The Berber movement is not a simple phenomenon since it is possible to distinguish between three different tendencies. The first tendency runs against governmental unity in the name of cultural plurality. The movement does not so much oppose the policy of Arabisation as it demands the formal recognition of the minority's right to keep its specific language and culture.

The second, which opposes the Arabisation policy, is the *Imazighen* Renaissance movement which considers Arabic a foreign language. Such a movement is not difficult to resist because of its ethnic background and its lack of pragmatism.

The third tendency within Berber opposition puts its struggles on a political rather than a cultural level. It works against the monopolisation of political initiative as well as the central government's claim to control and supervise all aspects of national life. Opponents locate their movement within the larger framework of efforts for a democratic political system and consider that linguistic and cultural matters are not state issues, but are related to the interaction between social forces in which the state has no intermediary or supervisory role to play.

Given that Tunisia is fully Arabised and that cultural pluralism is accepted in Morocco, Algeria will be the country most concerned with acute ethnic demands. This was manifest in the bloody events of Tizi Ouzou in April 1980.

As was observed by the militant and historian Muhammad Harbi, there is no place in the political culture of the Algerian Nationalist leadership for respect for differences in opinion, whether among Arabic — or Berber — speakers. The prevalent tendency is 'Jacobinism and despotism and the propensity among every section of society to monopolise the system of government to further its own interests' (Harbi, 1980).

Muhammad Harbi writes further on (p. 36):

The target of the Tizi Ouzou uprising was a despotic state. It drew the attention of Algerian public opinion to the problems of democracy and the right to be different. All those national integration efforts that ignore diversity hinder Algerian unity which not a single Berber questions. It is pure wishful thinking to believe that the army will remain unconcerned by the problems which are tearing Algerian society to pieces. How can the leaders speak about unity when they have been trying ever since Boumédienne died to make use of the regional allegiance of officers to further their own interests? Otherwise, how are we to explain the rash campaign orchestrated by Colonel Belhouichet against the Berber Colonel Mirbah? How to explain the discarding of officers like Tahir ibn Zghoud, Ayet Ouyahya and Larbi al-Hassen, if not by the fear of a potential Berber leadership within the army? Algeria today is in the hands of charlatans who, without principle, play one class against another and do not hesitate to play one region against the other as long as they remain in power.

The absence at the Algerian national level of an organised opposition movement has sometimes led fundamentalist, ethnic and even social movements to be local and spontaneous in nature. Their gravity lies in how sudden and unpredictable they can be. In Morocco and Tunisia, it is the popular uprising of marginal sections of society which represents the most serious challenge to the regime's stability.

This phenomenon became manifest during the January 1984 events. In both countries, after grain prices were raised, the unemployed led the most violent demonstrations ever seen in Moroccan and Tunisian streets. Their anger was fired by social inequality and the narrow base of development, as well as by the ostentation of the affluent and the neglect and inhumanity of the ruling elites.[2] In both cases, the anger was spontaneous in comparison with the labour demonstrations of the late 1970s. The January 1984 riots started in faraway depressed areas and extended to other areas where they were joined by the marginal fringes of society living in the poorer districts, the so-called 'red belts'.

A question which begs an answer is: why did these two regimes resort to raising the prices of basic products in such proportions late in 1983? Admittedly, their economic situation was difficult and called for austerity measures, but did implementation of the International Monetary Fund's guidelines

83

mean the adoption of purely monetary criteria which take no account of social repercussions? It is not surprising that, soon after the riots, the IMF disavowed the Tunisian Government's implementation methods. According to an article in *The Financial Times* in January 1984 'the method adopted by the Tunisian authorities to attenuate the importance of the compensation budget is a clear example of what should not be done even when it is right'. According to the IMF, the mistake does not lie in removing the compensation budget but in the suddenness of the measure and the extent of the increase, and not taking the social and political repercussions of this decision into account.

It should be noted that Tunisia and Morocco opted for the same political style, in the belief that hemming in political opposition and satisfying the demands of the labour organisations would increase the peaceful and smooth acceptance of austerity measures.

It is a well-known fact that political opposition has, for a long time now, been either outlawed or marginalised. Democracy has been sacrificed in the name of national unity, as well as in the name of cultural specificity. On this subject, an important Tunisian official wrote: 'Democracy is a recent concept ... based on practices, experiences and a historical background. Even in the heyday of Islamic civilisation, there were no political parties or councils like those you found in Europe ... Nonetheless, Islamic society had a keen feeling for freedom and justice ...' The same official offers new proof of this:

> At the height of their civilisation, the Arabs translated all Greek philosophical and scientific books. They translated Aristotle and Plato, yet neglected the concept of democracy, that is to say, the concept of democratic organisation. They had no need for it because it is alien to the Arab/Muslim mentality. The citizen himself does not feel the need for choice, whereas he has a keen sense for justice. He needs justice with regard to the police, judges and rulers. These are elements of Arab/Muslim mentality, from God's word to Ibn Khaldun, who never spoke about freedom, but laid the stress on justice which he considered one of the pillars of a thriving society (*Al-I'lan*, November 1982).

These regimes also sacrificed democracy on the altar of

economic development. The general belief among decision-makers was that citizens aspired to meet their material needs (employment, housing etc.) more than they aspired towards political pluralism. As a consequence, they believed that, for developmental purposes, there was a need for a powerful and autocratic state. This belief made political compulsion an institution and sanctioned the idea that freedom is possible under the one-party system (Ibrahimi, 1978: 116-34).

With the years, these arguments lost their edge because Maghrebi societies evolved towards structural disparity and diversity in the levels of their aspirations. It was no longer possible to take for granted spontaneous unity or the existence of specific traits which hindered the possibility of progress. Nor was it possible to sacrifice freedom once the development policies had attained their limits with regard to inequality, deprivation and isolation. Therefore, it was not possible for these regimes to avoid the legitimacy crisis by offering concessions when it was too late. For all these reasons, the January 1984 riots represented a real danger not only for the regimes as such, but for the opposition and labour organisations which proved unable to organise the masses of young people in the streets. Depending on the resources of each country, Maghrebi regimes are, to varying degrees, in the throes of a serious legitimacy crisis characterised by the divorce between the 'legal country' and the 'real country'. What is probably the most dangerous aspect of the crisis is a situation in which the regime is still in place, but without popular support or any real wish for it to stay. It is, however, a situation without any prospect for progress as long as the opposition fails to mobilise the masses and to channel their energy into transcending the situation and achieving their aspirations.

IS UNITY FOR THE MAGHREB POSSIBLE?

In the recent past, a number of indicators have emerged which show that Maghrebi regimes are now aware that they have reached a dead end. They are now looking for new ways of renewal, starting with slogans such as 'open politics', 'decentralisation', 'a united Maghreb'. We have already seen the structural and psychological restraints on the democratic process and the propensity of a given minority around one individual to

85

monopolise the representation of public affairs. We also saw how changes in the structure and prospects of society can lead to a widening of the gap between it and what has become a new *makhzen,* now that the nationalist programme has exhausted its resources. Decentralisation is a difficult option to implement once the state has almost totally done away with medium-level leaders. Until the 1950s they defended the interests of local communities, but as these have no resources and as the election of members is by approval of the central authorities rather than through universal suffrage, they have no credibility. These communities most urgently need 'bridge-men' who, in the past, were able to preserve the cohesion of the community while importing integration. The state has, however, monopolised the innovative process and deprived social communities of their ability to innovate, thus muzzling their existence.

Twenty-five years after the Tangiers Conference, the idea of a united Maghreb has recently made a new start. This can be explained by a number of factors, either specific to individual countries or common to all of them. Despite undeniable achievements and attainments at the individual country level, we could cite recurrent failures and the growing feeling that national structures restrain further progress. In spite of his passion for Tunisian specificity and his wariness of unionist projects, President Bourguiba now believes that 'it is inevitable for us and our brothers to come to an agreement on how to organise our affairs in the manner we see fit. We would not then have to face foreign pressure single-handed, with few resources and little authority' (*as-Sabah,* 8 August 1984). What is even more surprising is that Qadhafi himself at times accepts the stage-by-stage implementation of union:

> If the Tunisian regime, for example, accepts economic complementarity with Libya, we would consider this complementarity a significant step towards union, until the situation in the two countries becomes similar. It will thus be possible to achieve the union with individual countries retaining their political and administrative organisations, as is the case now with Tunisia and Libya (*al-Mustaqbal,* Tunis, 1 March 1982).

Another common factor is the growing awareness among the various leaderships of the gap between them and the younger generation — a generation of young people grown weary of reiterated national legends and monopolised heroism, a generation with no practical means to achieve its identity.[3] The proponents of a united Maghreb obviously wish to open up new prospects for the young.

But there are also specific factors, the most important of which (those which will determine what is feasible and what is not in uniting the Maghreb) are, first, the disagreement of the Maghrebi leadership as to the goals of the union and, second, the competition between Algeria and Morocco as to who will dominate the region.

Everybody knows that Qadhafi does not so much believe in the Maghreb as in a united Arab Nation. This has led a Maghrebi leader to say that

Qadhafi was haunted by a major idea, a united nation. We think it is unrealistic. Qadhafi is now mature, but what he accepts is just closer and smoother relations. This is, in fact, just a 'political epiphany' which brings him closer to his original goal. Because he was not able to find a way into the fortress, he went round the wall looking for a gap through which he could penetrate. The Maghreb is important in his eyes only insofar as it allows him to drag his Moroccan, Algerian and Tunisian partners into the project of Arab union. There are, in fact, two different wagers. We are betting on his adopting the idea of the Maghreb and he is betting on dragging us into his theory of Arab union ... An exquisite argument (*al-Maghreb*, 8 September 1983).

What is more serious, though, is the competition between Algeria and Morocco which goes back nearly twenty-five years. President Boumédienne considered that the Algerian security zone extended all over the Maghreb plus the area between Cairo and Dakar and that no change could take place there without prior agreement with Algeria.

It is not surprising, therefore, that there is a Sahara problem and that hindrances are rife on the road to a united Maghreb. The existence of the 'sacred egoism' of states and the prevalence of domineering tendencies do not lead to union so much as to secondary alliances. Instead of paving the way for union, these have widened the gap and consecrated blocs. When Tunisia and Algeria signed the Friendship and Concord Treaty on 19 March

1983, they called on the rest of the Maghrebi states to join them. Whereas Mauritania complied, Libya and Morocco chose to sign a separate agreement, the Arab-African Union, in August 1984. At the same time, Morocco was indirectly requesting membership of the European Community. The king declared: 'The European Community is a political option and Morocco has made its choice by promoting political pluralism, freedom for labour organisations and free trade. This brought our kingdom closer that any other Arab country to the West' (*Jeune Afrique*, 1 May 1985: 26).

It is clear that all these policies (the open policy, decentralisation, awareness of the necessity for union) call for political determination, a determination willing to put its authority at stake in order to achieve progress and union. Such determination is now lacking. Although they point the way to achieving union, ideas and reforms are presented as ideological arguments to transcend the deadlock of an ideological vacuum, not as practical solutions. In addition, they are not refined enough to constitute a project capable of mobilising the people.

NOTES

1. In Tunisia, the number of strikes rose from 25 in 1970 to 452 in 1977. In Algeria, it rose from 99 to 922 in 1980 and in Morocco, between 1971 and 1981, from 260 to 1062. Taken from data from the Ministry of Social Affairs Publications for Tunisia and from Abdallah Saef, 'Maghrebi Political Society between Continuity and Expression', *Al-Wahda*, March 1985, pp. 67-73 for Morocco.

2. Statistics show that the unemployed represented 20 per cent of the Tunisian and 35 per cent of the Moroccan work force in 1984.

3. An Algerian poem in French describes this situation:
Stop exalting bloodshed,
Stop exalting names,
Stop exalting production,
Stop exalting projects,
The young are not foolish and blind, they know.

Part Two

4

State and Authority in Arabic Political Thought

Charles E. Butterworth

With the possible exception of Lebanon, all contemporary Arab regimes are ruled by one or a few persons. The Gulf Emirates, Jordan, Kuwait, Morocco and Saudi Arabia identify themselves as monarchies. Moreover, despite constitutional provisions for something resembling parliamentary democracy or even direct popular participation in government, there is no doubt that Algeria and the People's Republic of South Yemen are in fact ruled by a small group of military officers, and Iraq, Libya, Syria and North Yemen by a single individual. Though Egypt and Tunisia come very close to the norms for rule by popularly elected representatives, both fall short: in each of these nations, positions of power are distributed among a few individuals from the wealthy privileged class. Precisely because the phenomenon is so all-encompassing, it cannot be explained solely in terms of chance. Nor will speculations about the way religion or a particular mind-set influence politics go very far, given the diverse attitudes towards religion among these various regimes and the totally different kinds of people they embrace. Yet in so far as all of these regimes are Arab and thus share a common cultural heritage, one might ask whether there is anything in the history of Arabic thought — especially Arabic political thought — which favours the emergence and continuation of such regimes or which disposes the descendants of the tradition to acquiesce in such rule.

In what follows, I shall argue that it is not any particular set of ideas in Arabic political thought, but rather its absence, which facilitates the acceptance of regimes based on rule by one or a few. Simply stated, there is nothing within the history of Arabic political thought comparable to the radical break with the past effected by Machiavelli and Hobbes in the sixteenth and seventeenth centuries and then refined into a doctrine of liberal democracy in succeeding generations by Locke and Rousseau so that the notion of popular sovereignty became an unquestioned, perhaps even an unquestionable, principle. When these or similar ideas did start to gain sway in the Arab world in the latter part of the nineteenth and early part of the twentieth centuries, more attention was paid to how such reasoning might justify self-determination than to how individual self-rule might be promoted.

To begin with, I shall distinguish between the different kinds of political thought in the history of Arabic political thought from high medieval times to the present and identify the subjects investigated in each one. By 'high medieval times,' I mean that period of time beginning in about the middle of the ninth century and lasting for slightly more than three hundred years, during which philosophy, theology, jurisprudence, history and science flourished, and of whose first hundred or so years one usually thinks when speaking of the summit, the golden age, or even the classical period in Arabic culture. There is, to be sure, no discussion of 'state' and 'authority' *per se* in Arabic writings until very recent times. What we find instead are discussions about political regimes, the administration of politics, transfer of rule or succession, qualifications for rule, justice and the limits to obedience. Though similar in some respects to what the terms 'state' and 'authority' comprise, these topics are none the less different. To understand what characterises modern and contemporary thought, to shed light on it by recourse to ancient and medieval thought, it is necessary to respect these differences. Professor Ann K. Lambton's book, *State and Government in Medieval Islam*, provides a good example for this contention. Useful as her study is as an introduction to what various medieval jurists and men of letters had to say about recognising the rightful successor to the Prophet, confirming such an individual in power, or applying the revealed law, it tells us nothing about what constitutes a state or how it differs, if at all, from an empire. Moreover, it is utterly silent about the way politics were actually carried out during this period, that is, about government.

Subsequently, I shall indicate the parallels between Arabic political thought viewed in this light and pre-modern Western political thought, my point being that the differences between the two traditions come to the fore only with the advent of Machiavelli and that those differences become decisive because of what he sets in motion. Finally, I shall address myself to the question of why political regimes in the contemporary Arab world tend to be so different from political regimes in the contemporary Western world.

AL-FUQAHA, AL-FALASIFA AND POLITICS

The history of Arabic culture will be discussed in this exposition as though it were the same as that of Islamic culture. Although it might be useful to reflect upon the way Islamic culture embraces non-Arabic traditions such as those of the Berbers, Turks, Persians, Indians, and Indonesians or upon the way Arabic culture and history affect, and are affected by, Christian and Jewish Arabic-speaking peoples, it would serve no useful purpose here. Arabic political thought may be divided into at least four categories: political philosophy, jurisprudence, applied theology, and *belles lettres*.

Those who engage in the first base themselves on unassisted human reason and seek through it to determine the characteristics of the best regime and the attributes of the best ruler. The political philosophers — individuals like al-Farabi, Avicenna (Ibn Sina), Ibn Tufayl, Ibn Bajah, Averroes (Ibn Rushd), and to a certain extent Ibn Khaldun — consciously take their bearings from Plato and Aristotle, not from revelation nor from the traditional accounts of the Prophet's sayings and actions. Though fully aware of the importance of revelation and of its effects upon the community of believers, they perceive it as a phenomenon to be rationally understood rather than unquestioningly accepted and thus attempt to explore the meaning of prophecy as well as the merits of the beliefs and actions enjoined by Islam. They turn to Plato and Aristotle to pursue yet unresolved questions or to continue a dialogue and thus frequently disagree with the teaching of these two ancients as well as with that of their fellow philosophers.

Common to all the political philosophers is the primacy of the inquiry into why political association needs to exist; only after that has been established and the goals of political association clearly delineated, do they turn to a consideration of how to guarantee its soundness. They disagree, to be sure, about why

93

human beings live in potential communities. Some, al-Farabi and Averroes for example, insist that the political community exists primarily to provide for the development of the human virtues and deem of lesser importance that it also permits basic human needs to be met, while someone like Avicenna reverses the order. With the exception of Avicenna and Ibn Khaldun, the political philosophers speak about the political community as a city or an association of cities. Vague as Avicenna is about the proper size of the best political community, his remarks unmistakably conjure up a regime founded by a prophet-legislator and thus allow one to speculate about how a well-governed Islamic dynasty or empire might function. Ibn Khaldun is more precise. He speaks about cities (*mudun*, sing. *madinah*), countries (*buldan*, sing. *balad*), nations (*umam*, sing. *umma*) and dynasties or empires (*duwal*, sing *dawlah*), arguing that a well-governed dynasty or empire of modest proportions best provides for the kind of luxurious sedentary life in which human excellence can flourish.

Of paramount importance for the philosophers, whether they rank it as the primary goal of political association or as something to be pursued once existence is assured, is the development of the human faculties, that is, the powers of the soul, and especially those having to do with reason. Man, for them, is the rational animal. Just as man's ability to reason distinguishes him from the other animals and constitutes his superiority over them, even justifying his exploitation of them to serve his own needs, so does one man's intellectual merit set him above his fellows. On the grounds that a man possessed of intellectual virtue can desire nothing but the good of his fellow men, it also justifies his exploiting them or obliging them to perform tasks whose merit they may not otherwise discern or which they find simply repugnant. This latter point is argued in various ways. Generally speaking, however, the political philosophers agree that one cannot have true intellectual virtue without being practically wise and one cannot be practically wise without being morally virtuous and knowledgeable about the practical arts, in short, without having all of the qualities and inclinations of an excellent ruler. Consequently, they concur in urging that such an individual should rule his fellow human beings in order to help them — by persuasion if at all possible and by compulsion if not — develop the human virtues to the extent they are able.

Like Plato and Aristotle, the Arab political philosophers define happiness as the development of human virtue, especially intellectual virtue. In so far as intellectual virtue permits one to know God, to see His face as it were, they also can and do argue that such a pursuit allows one to obtain ultimate happiness in this world and in the next. Persuaded by study and observation that the human virtues are acquired only with much effort, that it is difficult if not impossible for one person to acquire them all, and that they are naturally in short supply, the Arab political philosophers set down as the criterion by which to judge the worth of different political communities the importance these communities attach to the pursuit of the human virtues and their effectiveness in helping their citizens achieve them. Freedom is not desired as an end in itself any more than is the pursuit of victory as an end or wealth for its own sake, all of these being at best only tools for the acquisition of the virtues. To the extent that they do speak about forms of political rule, then, they endorse rule by those who have in fact acquired virtue — however few they may be — over those who have not yet done so.

Clarity about the purpose of political association stated in terms of the acquisition of human virtue, hierarchical stratification, the endorsement of compulsion as well as gentle persuasion, and a willingness to speak in terms and images highly reminiscent of the language of revelation thus characterise Arabic political philosophy. More importantly, it represents an inquiry into human existence that takes nothing for granted and deems no assumption impervious to challenge, although never couched in the strident tones or clarion-like declarations made popular by early modern and contemporary Western philosophers. Scholars eager to portray these philosophers as mindless spokesmen for religion, E.I.J. Rosenthal and Richard Walzer being excellent cases in point, have failed to pay sufficient attention to literary style and, above all, to consider whether there might not be sound grounds for arguing, precisely as these philosophers do argue, that there is a commonality of purpose between philosophy and revelation properly understood. The real spokesmen for religion in the history of Arabic thought, those who do not question its assumptions, are not the political philosophers but the jurists and theologians.

Ever eager to distinguish themselves from both of these groups, the philosophers point out that the jurists accept the revealed law (*Shari'ah*) as given and seek to explain how it is to be applied, while the theologians, also accepting the revealed law as given, devote themselves to arguing for its soundness and defending it against putative critics. For the jurists as for the theologians, then, reason follows upon, and is in the service of, faith. One does not use reason to inquire into what is the best political regime or even to consider why human beings must live together in political association. It can be inferred, however, that Muslims should live together in political association in order to observe more readily their duties of worship and to encourage one another to abide by the beliefs and actions which constitute the faith. Consequently, the best political regime is the one regulated according to the prescriptions of the revealed law and most in keeping with the community first organised by the Prophet in Medina and then continued after his return to Mecca. Guidance about what to do with respect to matters not explicitly covered by the revealed law may be acquired by reflecting on the intention of those explicit prescriptions, by reference to the deeds as well as to the sayings of the Prophet, and occasionally by recourse to analogical reasoning.

Whereas the philosophers arrive at their understanding of the political and human good by reflecting on the nature of man and on his end as a rational being, the jurists and theologians reflect only on the message of the revelation. According to it, man's good is to lead the kind of life here below that will qualify him for admission to paradise in the life to come. Consequently, the well-ordered political community must encourage its citizens to perform the actions and hold the beliefs which permit them to aspire to such a reward and must discourage or even restrain them from those actions and beliefs which would make them risk perdition. The philosophers are not, to be sure, terribly sanguine about the likelihood of most human beings attaining ultimate happiness. Nor, on the other hand, are they terribly pessimistic about them. They seem to think the majority will simply muddle along, rising neither to a very great height of human excellence nor descending to a profound depth. Their critique of the majority is thus cast primarily in terms of how their pursuit of erroneous goals prevents the excellent few from attaining the happiness that might otherwise be theirs. It is for this reason that there occurs so frequently in their writings the theme of how the solitary excellent man might guide himself in the midst of so many who are foolish and how he might benefit from association with those few who resemble him. Nothing of the sort is to be found in the writings of the jurists or theologians. For them, the law exists and must be applied to all believers without exception as well as to all non-believers in so far as that is prescribed. Human beings are to be restrained and limited; they are to follow the precepts of the law, not the promptings of reason. Precisely because human beings once did follow the promptings of reason and turned away from the earlier revelations of the Torah and the Gospel the revelation of the Quran was accorded to Muhammad (see Quran, 5: 59-77).

This is why the best regime is that of the community of believers guided by someone who qualifies as a true successor (*khalifah*, i.e. Caliph) of the Prophet or at least by someone who is qualified to lead the community in prayer, that is, one who is an *imam*. Now whereas al-Farabi equates the imam with the philosopher, the law-giver, and the first ruler, the jurists and theologians think of him as what al-Farabi would call the second ruler, that is, the ruler whose task is to preserve the laws set down by the first ruler and to guide the community along the path traced out by him. The law-giver has already set down the law for the community; there is no reason to ask about the qualities which distinguish the law-giver, for no subsequent law-giver is expected. Thus, in keeping with his more limited tasks, the qualities demanded of the Caliph or imam are less than would be expected of a prophet. Though there is some variation in what the jurists and theologians deem to be these necessary qualifications, they generally agree in stipulating that he be morally honest or just, knowledgeable with respect to the revealed law, possessed of sound judgement, and courageous enough to defend the interests of the community by waging war.

No definite size is set down for the community of believers. Unlike the revealed law, it may vary. Constituted by all those who accept to be guided by the Prophet's revelation and to be ruled as he ruled the original community, it must stretch to as many lands and climes as they occupy. Consequently, rather than speculate about the optimal size for a well-governed regime, the jurists and theologians concern themselves with the regime as it is and recommend how it may be better governed. It is for this reason that someone like al-Mawardi carefully explains in the *Kitab al-Ahkam as-Sultaniyyah* how the imam may delegate power to different ministers and they in turn to subordinate rulers, while someone like al-Ghazali proposes in his *Iqtisad al-I'tiqad* enlisting those learned in religion (the *ulama*) to carry out the various religious duties of the imam.

The philosophers favour rule by one or a few because they deem it necessary for the ruler or rulers to be of pre-eminent virtue, something to which few can aspire and which even fewer will actually achieve. It is expected that the one or few will have a better understanding of what is in the best interest of the majority than they themselves. When the jurists and theologians do speculate about such questions, it is clear that they are guided by somewhat the same notion. Thus they portray the Caliph and imam as the shepherd of the people, the representative of God on earth, the trustee for the revealed law and the one charged to carry out God's commands. Yet what is implied by these many titles suggests wherein the jurists and theologians differ from the philsophers about the functions of the ruler. For the former, it is the ruler who acts for the people, who protects them from their own destructive tendencies, as it were. Their function is one of passive restraint at best and of repression at worst; they must forestall the evil tendencies of human beings. As has already been noted, the philosophers are less pessimistic about human urgings and thus portray the ruler as more of a guide or teacher.

Because of their pessimistic view of what humans might do if left to their own devices, the jurists and theologians are little concerned with safeguarding human freedom. In his *As-Siyasah Ash-Shar'iyyah*, Ibn Taymiyyah poignantly captures this idea by claiming that experience proves only too well the accuracy of the saying 'sixty years under an unjust imam are better than a single night without a ruler' (Ibn Taymiyyah, 1951: 173). Similarly, urging that people must be forced by political rule to fulfil the prescriptions of the revealed law — that is, to struggle on behalf of God or engage in *jihad,* deal justly with one another, perform the pilgrimage, respect the Friday prayers and holy days, combat evil, and refrain from theft, murder and adultery — he cites the saying 'the ruler is God's shadow on earth' to buttress his point. Discussion about the conditions necessary for confirming the Caliph or imam in power, the qualities requisite for those who are to pronounce on his fitness for office, the duties of his office, in short, discussion about basic administrative questions, is far more dominant than inquiries into the extent of the ruler's power or what excuses a citizen from the obligation to obey his every order.

In sum, the political horizon is considerably narrower for the jurists and theologians than for the philosophers. For the former, it is far more important that the political community continue to exist than that it be governed well. Thus one never encounters in their writings the kind of criticisms against the existing rulers made by Averroes in his *Commentary on Plato's Republic*. Presumably, no jurist or theologian would permit himself to consider the merits of Socrates' argument in favour of making women and children common to all citizens or arranging marriages of limited duration (that is, until pregnancy results) between the most physically attractive and intelligent citizens — as Averroes does, for example, in this same commentary. Nor would any jurist or theologian be willing to align himself with Averroes' endorsements of these novel prescriptions and his castigations of the traditional, religiously based, arrangements. It is not that the jurists and theologians are pious whereas the philosophers are impious, but that philosophers seek by playfulness, imagination and daring to probe the reasons for the prescriptions and proscriptions on which excellent political rule is based. The jurists and theologians, on the other hand, are concerned less with understanding why these regulations exist and how they contribute to political well-being than with ensuring that they are put into practice.

The fourth category of Arabic political thought, *belles lettres* or literature, is also characterised by imagination and playfulness, but lacks the daring and inquisitiveness common to philosophical writing. Nizam al-Mulk's *Siyasat-nama* (or Book of Government) comes readily to mind as a case in point, as does the *Risalah fi as-Sahabah* of Ibn al-Muqaffa', the *Qabus-nama* of Kai Kaus, and the duly famous stories of the *Thousand and One Nights*. The frame story of the latter depicts how Sheherazade manages, by means of clever tale-telling (the stories are never completed at the break of day), to so enchant her sovereign-husband during the night that he delays killing her in the morning as he had resolved upon doing and had actually done with numerous wives before her in order to protect himself from the pervasive infidelity of women. As the tales unfold, one begins to discern a pattern which, in the end, embodies a general lesson of political prudence. Sheherazade eventually teaches her husband how to rule in a world confronted by unprecedented problems, one in which the claims of new religions have to be faced and threats from hitherto benevolent foreign powers parried. Nizam al-Mulk's book is not quite so fanciful and certainly nowhere near so fascinating. He seeks to explain in a series of stories and stories within stories, as well as in more direct prose, those matters a ruler must consider in order to rule well and the personal qualities required of a good ruler.

Those who write in this form, generally described as the 'mirrors for princes' genre, accept the *status quo* as given and as unlikely to undergo radical transformation. Consequently, no discussion of alternative regimes is to be found in these writings nor any inquiry into the best form of political association. These authors focus their attention on pointing out how the present regime might be made more effective — that is, more responsive to its own declared goals — rather than on identifying new goals to which it might aspire. Similarly, they consider how the ruler's conduct can contribute to the ends of political association as they are generally understood, and show no inclination to inquire into other ends. As the title of the genre indicates, these authors are writing for those who rule monarchically. Whether the ruler in question is a provincial warlord or a Caliph who is counselled by a just and pious tailor, the rule is the rule of one. No attempt is made to argue that other forms of government might be more equitable or otherwise preferable. Like Ibn al-Muqaffaʻ, the authors writing in this genre may restrict themselves to a discussion of one aspect of the existing regime in order to make precise recommendations for its improvement or, like Nizam al-Mulk, explore the various central and provincial ministries as well as the key offices of the regime in order to suggest additional benefits accruing to the ruler — primarily ensuring the continuation of his rule — by administering them more effectively.

In keeping with their explicit acceptance of the *status quo* and reluctance to alter it radically, the authors writing in this genre act as though they accept the basic soundness of the revealed law without question. They frequently resolve questions by pronouncing in favour of what revelation says rather than by conducting an independent investigation as the philosophers might do. Nor do they pause to inquire into the reasons for human beings living together in political association. Though they do occasionally reflect on the optimal size of a political community, they usually present these observations as administrative concerns and thereby avoid discourse about the ends which a regime ought to pursue. However, paradoxical as it seems, one might argue that there are allusive discussions of all of these questions in this genre. Precisely because of their recourse to stories and anecdotes to illustrate their basic points, it is sometimes possible to discern in the authors writing in this genre observations which approach the concerns of the philosophers. Yet the crucial difference is that these issues are never fully pursued here; they are only intimated. In Nizam al-Mulk, for example, numerous allusions to the greed which motivates human beings and stories about how wise rulers hold it in check among their subordinates or punish its manifestations lead the reader to wonder whether what impedes just rule is a single moral vice or whether there are several such impediments. Similarly, in both Nizam al-Mulk and in the *Thousand and One Nights* instances of how women do, in fact, influence male rulers give rise to the question of whether they might not be as competent to rule as men, perhaps even more qualified. Unfortunately, tantalising as are these hints, they are pursued no more assiduously in these works than in the works which take their place today. For example, the thorny question of God's equity raised in Neguib Mahfouz's *Children of Gebelawi* is never fully pursued there, the criticism of corruption and of government censorship of the press to protect powerful criminals is no more than suggested in the famous film *al-Ghul*, nor is the condemnation of the way the false values of the mass of citizens wreak havoc upon the lives of others sufficiently developed in the otherwise entertaining *Banat Iblis*.

From this discussion it is evident that the focus in medieval Arabic political thought was either on the best or on the actual political regime. Those interested in exploring the first considered the size of the regime of prime importance and urged that it be a city or at best a group of cities, whereas those interested in the second did not. They accepted the Islamic umma as it existed, originally a small community the size of a city but later an entity whose hegemony stretched across numerous lands and which had all the traits of a dynasty or empire. This umma was no more a nation properly speaking than, as a dynasty or empire, it was a state. At times it was a group of nations or, better yet, of principalities; at other times it was merely a chaotic assemblage of diverse political entities whose rulers found it convenient to maintain the fiction that they governed by reference to the revealed law of Islam and deemed themselves the servants of Mohammad's successor, that is, the Caliph. The occasional quandary into which such pretensions put those who tried to explain current politics as the administration of the revealed law can be recognised in al-Mawardi's and other jurists' discussion of whether there can be more than one Caliph to whom allegiance is owed at any one time and what to do when such a situation occurs. Yet, however they approached the question of the regime's size and functions, all medieval Arabic political thinkers agreed on the principle that rule should be in the hands of one or a few. They differed about the qualities which should give title to rule, with the philosophers and those within the *belles lettres* tradition placing primary emphasis on intellectual excellence while the jurists and theologians prized family lineage as well as the moral virtues and practical wisdom. Similarly, though of the same mind about the need for the regime to be grounded in justice, the philosophers deemed it necessary to define justice by investigating the natural order and man's place in it, whereas the other thinkers were content to look to the revealed law for guidance. Finally, no one within this group of medieval Arabic political thinkers was willing to argue that non-political communal life was desirable.

POPULAR SOVEREIGNTY AND DEMOCRACY: TWO WESTERN CONCEPTS

As has already been noted, the Arab political philosophers took their bearings from Plato and Aristotle. So, too, did most of the political philosophers in the West during late classical and medieval times. Consequently, until Machiavelli, these political philosophers directed their attention to identifying the characteristics of the best political regime and paid little heed to how they might improve the actual regimes surrounding them. They agreed upon the principle of rule by one or a few, basing this judgement on the argument that excellence alone qualified a person for rulership and that it was rarely to be found in more than a few individuals. They also defended the idea of educating the citizens according to their varying abilities and, concomitantly, of structuring the regime in such a manner that different kinds of duties and privileges, that is, different social roles followed from these different abilities and different kinds of education. Stated in such terms, justice for them encompassed more than immediate material concerns — for example, the equitable distribution of goods — though it did take such concerns into account; it went further in so far as it aimed both at ensuring the spiritual well-being of the citizen body and at developing the physical and mental faculties of the citizens so that they might lead a completely human life.

Only with respect to the size of the political community did serious disagreement with Plato and Aristotle arise. Dante, for example, saw no reason to restrict the political horizon to a city, whatever its size, or even to a confederacy of cities. He called instead for an imperial government which would embrace the whole world and be under the tutelage of a secular monarch. None the less, his argument was cast in rigid Aristotelian terms, his disagreement with Aristotle about the proper size of the political community stemming from his desire to apply Aristotle's principles universally, that is, to all of mankind and not just to a limited group of people. For Dante, it was imperative to bring the whole human race under political control so that together all human beings could work for the attainment of virtue and thereby ensure its acquisition. Thus, accepting Aristotle's premises about the scarcity of virtue and about the difficulty of human beings achieving it in isolation, premises fundamental to Aristotle's insistence on the natural character of political life, Dante parted company with the Stagirite only in so far as he took that teaching a step further.

The similarities between medieval Western and medieval Arab political thought become fewer the further one moves away from political philosophy. Though there are, indeed, juristic and theological writers as well as authors who fit into the *belles lettres* tradition, their concerns are other than those of their medieval Arab counterparts. Partly because of the different character of Christianity, partly because of the greater receptivity to philosophy, both pagan and Christian, among the jurists and theologians within the Western tradition, the questions raised by such writers in the medieval West differ from those raised by jurists and theologians in the medieval Arab world. Little attention is paid to justifying the *status quo*, few attempts are made to show that the current form of rulership is alone viable, and far more emphasis is laid on the fundamental differences between the demands of secular rule and those of divine rule. The voices which stand out most massively within this category of medieval Western political thought are those calling not for the application of the divine law in the political forum nor for rule to be placed in the hands of those skilled in divine matters, but for a separation of political and ecclesiastical functions. Whether one turns to St Augustine, St Thomas Aquinas, or Marsilius, one learns that the end of political life is not the same as that of life informed by revelation, that the two must not be confused and that success in one does not lead to success in the other. Because Jesus was understood to be the Messiah or Saviour and thus to be unique, accomplishing a mission that could never be replicated, there was no reason for jurists and theologians to inquire into the characteristics which would qualify anyone as a successor. Nor, given the eschatological character of the Christian revelation, was it appropriate to attempt to deduce from it a set of rules which would explain how the community of believers ought to organise themselves politically. For such questions, recourse was had instead to the teachings of the philosophers and to reflection on natural law.

These differences notwithstanding, there are important points of convergence between the jurists and theologians in both traditions. Intent as the jurists and theologians of the medieval West are to urge the separation of political and ecclesiastical functions, they none the less tend to assume that authority, whether political or ecclesiastical, will be in the hands of a single individual. Moreover, like their counterparts in the medieval Arab world, they are more pessimistic about the human condition than are the philosophers. In fact, making frequent reference to the soteriological mission of Jesus, they dwell at even greater length on human frailty than do the Arab jurists and theologians.

In the category of *belles lettres*, yet other differences between Western authors of the classical and medieval ages and medieval Arab authors are to be encountered. In the West, epic and tragic poetry is most frequently used to express political ideas along with occasional recourse to dialogue, moralistic novels, and extensive historical essays. Homer's *Iliad* and *Odyssey*, Virgil's *Aeneid*, Tasso's *Jerusalem Delivered* and Anosto's *Orlando Furioso* provide marvellous analyses of the human soul under the most trying conditions, present political dilemmas that must be reflected upon if one is to understand how justice can be served or thwarted, and return again and again to the fundamental problem of the relative merit among the various goals to be pursued for a full human life: honour, wealth, or wisdom. Similarly, in the *Cyropaedia*, a somewhat fanciful account of the life of Cyrus, Xenophon recounts several anecdotes which raise the question of whether justice is ultimately grounded in respect for private property or in striving to bring about a seemly distribution of goods, what goal a ruler should have in mind when meting out punishment, and the purpose of political rule. Whether one turns to Thucydides and his explicit announcement at the beginning of the *Peloponnesian Wars* that he will invent speeches as he deems appropriate or to Herodotus and his accounts of events and human beings long forgotten, similar questions and problems are posed. We see in these works, as in the *Antigone* and *Oedipus Tyranus* of Sophocles, not to mention the tragedies of Euripedes and Aeschylus, human beings brought to ruin because of a fatal flaw in their character or an unwillingness to explore their differences and seek compromise.[1]

Plutarch's semi-historical *Lives of Illustrious Men* and his moral essays also fit into this genre. In the former, he provides numerous instances of how exceptional human beings have achieved greatness and does so in a manner which prompts the reader to emulate these individuals or at least to consider what precise character traits contributed to their exemplary accomplishments. In the latter, he dwells at length on many of the subtle questions which arise when one tries to apply moral principles to practical situations.

Though not addressed to a particular ruler nor written to teach any single individual how to safeguard his regime, the theme that the best rule is that of one or a few pervades these works. It is the excellent few who are praised and whose actions we are urged to emulate, not the otherwise nondescript many. As with Arabic works in the same *belles lettres* category, questions are raised indirectly in these writings. That is, the reader must pay careful attention to allusions and ask about the implications of the anecdotes or incidents related in order to make sense of a particular work. And as with the *belles lettres* writings in the medieval Arab world, the emphasis in these works is clearly on moral virtue, on how human beings should live.

In sum, then, despite differences in approach and even differences in opinion about the role of divine providence in

105

human affairs, there is much in common between classical and medieval Western political thought on the one hand and medieval Arabic political thought on the other. They certainly share far more than modern Western political thought shares with classical and medieval Western political thought. For whether modern Western political thought is deemed to take its direction from Machiavelli's disparaging of all previous thinkers in Chapter XV of the *Prince* for the innocent and ineffective insistence on speaking about how regimes might be ruled rather than about how they are indeed ruled, from Bacon's rejection of Aristotelian reasoning and its consequences in the opening of the *New Organon*, or from Hobbes' materialistic account of the human soul in the first twelve chapters of the *Leviathan*, it sets itself radically apart from its classical and medieval antecedents.

In the *Discourses* as well as in the *Prince*, Machiavelli firmly stresses the novel realism in his teaching. He is a political Columbus as it were, a thinker who will reveal new horizons and discover new routes for the ship of state to ply, horizons and routes that are distinctly within the reach of human beings rather than hovering always beyond their grasp. The problem with the ancients and their medieval successors was that they dwelt too much on what men ought to do and devoted too much attention to what political regimes ought to be like, thereby neglecting what men actually do, the goals they actually pursue, and failing to note how regimes in fact function. They harmed themselves and those who heeded them by pursuing such a course. Not only did they fail to achieve their goals, they became the unwitting victims of those who assiduously stalked a more limited end. Because those old standards are useless, even harmful, Machiavelli will have nothing to do with them.

> There is so much distance between the way people live and the way they ought to live that he who rejects what people do in favour of what they ought to do brings about his ruin rather than his preservation; for a man who wants to do good in every matter comes to ruin among so many who are not good. Thus it is necessary that a prince who wants to maintain himself learn to be able not to be good and to use goodness or not use it as necessity demands (Machiavelli, chapter XV).

He denies that nature or revelation can provide any kind of guidance for private or public conduct and insists that what really prompts human greatness is a desire for glory. Then, having identified what humans in fact strive for, he explains how it can be attained either in a city ruled by a few dedicated individuals or in a principality ruled by a single person. There is no need to deliberate here about whether Machiavelli is ultimately a teacher of oppressive princes or a devoted friend of republican liberty, it being enough for the present to note simply how effectively he redirected political thought and political discourse. After Machiavelli it is no longer possible to speculate about the best regime or the best human life as defined by some vision never known to have existed; now we must reflect upon what really happens in the political arena, observe the way human beings truly act and direct our own actions accordingly.

If anything, Hobbes lowers the standards for political thought and discourse even more than Machiavelli. Not glory, but mere self-preservation is what he takes to be the end of political association. He deems human beings to be so concupiscent that they will seize the goods and threaten the well-being of others unless restrained by force, hence the need for political association. Accordingly, Hobbes blames his classical and medieval predecessors less for speaking about regimes that have not been realised or goals for human conduct that are beyond the reach of most human beings than for weakening the force of existent regimes by their reflections upon what might be. The alternative to political order — namely, a state which must result in continuous war of all against all, one in which as Hobbes puts it, life is 'solitary, poor, nasty, brutish, and short' — is so frightening that he considers any regime preferable to anarchy. None the less, on the grounds of efficiency and stability, he ultimately opts for the rule of one.

It is not until Locke that the principles set down by Machiavelli and Hobbes are formulated in such a manner as to promote popular rule. Though he denies that human beings must necessarily be at war with one another when living outside of political society, that is, when living in what Hobbes termed a state of nature, Locke recognises that there is always the danger of one person trying to seize the goods of another or threatening his person. Moreover, because he holds that all human beings are by nature free, endowed with a natural right to those things which conduce to their self-preservation and to those they have acquired by their own efforts, he urges that political society be organised so as to allow all the appeal to a common judge whenever they find their interests threatened. The judge has the authority to decide differences but is none the less subservient to the laws of association which govern the community, the purpose of association being thwarted whenever he comes to have absolute power.

Rousseau radicalises Locke's insight, insisting that nothing justifies one individual being subservient to another and that all political power must therefore be traced to a conventional arrangement among naturally free and independent human beings. Because no one can reasonably surrender life or liberty, the political community is grounded on the principle of self-rule. The will of each citizen is always consulted before a decision binding the community is taken, the terms of their original association being such that by responding to these kinds of queries solely in terms of what each considers good for himself the common good inevitably results. Though restrictions must be placed on the citizens, Rousseau carefully explains how these restrictions and the penalties — even capital punishment — resulting from the infringement of laws in principle made or approved by the citizens necessarily safeguard the freedom of all; they are intended as ultimate restraints, nothing more (Rousseau: Bk II, Chap. 5 and Bk IV, Chap. 2).

The principles set down by Locke and Rousseau bear their first fruit with the American Declaration of Independence and the Abbé de Siéyès' Déclaration des Droits de l'Homme. Their influence can also be recognised in the fiery rhetoric of libertarians like Thomas Paine and their practical consequences in the American as well as the French Revolution. As early as the first third of the nineteenth century, it was clear to an observer like De Tocqueville that a new political order based on these same principles was coming into being. The new order has indeed now become firmly established. Today no one would dream of denying that human beings are by nature free. Nor would anyone dare contest the theoretical and practical consequences of such an assertion, namely, that each individual alone has authority over himself and that no-one has the right to rule another without his consent.

Though now an integral part of political rhetoric within the Arab world, these principles have by no means been applied in

Arab nations to the same extent that they have in Western nations. They do not influence practice in the Arab world as they do in the West because they are still relatively new to Arabic political thought. With the death of Ibn Khaldun in 1406, Arabic political philosophy came to an end. For almost five hundred years thereafer, the jurists and theologians were the sole exponents of political thought within the Arab world. Never forced to face anything resembling the challenge posed by Machiavelli and Hobbes, then Locke and Rousseau, they persisted in their traditional defence of the regime of the day, arguing again and again about what qualified an individual for the title of Caliph or pleading for a return to earlier ways of conduct. The same sort of complacency characterises the genre of *belles lettres* during this period of time, no-one apparently feeling compelled to question the old opinions and procedures.

It was not until the latter part of the nineteenth century with the advent of Jamal ad-Din al-Afghani that this quiescent mood was shattered. Shocked that the very people who once held sway over culture and learning should have come to be under the political domination of their former pupils, he argued passionately for religion to ally itself with philosophy and science. At the same time he acknowledged the merit of Rousseau's arguments in favour of popular sovereignty, understanding them as pointing above all to the goal of national self-determination. Though he and Muhammad 'Abduh denied that the British or any other colonial power had any legitimate right to rule Indians, Persians, Sudanese, or Egyptians, both none the less insisted on the necessity for these same peoples to be ruled by a benevolent despot who would slowly prepare them to govern themselves.

Subsequently, other voices were raised to defend the principle of self-government. For at least two reasons they have not succeeded in redirecting thought and practice. One is that the plea for self-government was frequently ancillary to another goal. Al-Mawdudi, for example, was above all intent upon showing that popular rule had always been central to Islamic statecraft, hoping thereby to prove the perfect harmony between Islam and contemporary Western aspirations. The second is that those urging popular rule have simply failed to consider how it may be brought about. Shari'ati provides a good case in point. Despite all his praise for democratic principles and his insistence

109

on their congruity with the revealed law of Islam, he could say nothing about how they might actually be applied. In sum, then, the absence of an unquestioned, perhaps unquestionable, belief in the fundamental need for popular sovereignty is what primarily explains why political life in the Arab world differs so markedly from political life in the West.

This said, it must none the less be noted that citizens in Arab countries do not protest very much against the non-popular regimes under which they live. Whether it be that economic development is tacitly agreed to be so important a goal as to justify the continuation of rule by a few or that most politically aware citizens recognise how little has yet been accomplished in preparing the multitude of poorly educated, even illiterate, workers and peasants for the responsibilities of self-government, opposition to the current forms of leadership is almost non-existent. Yet another reason for this quietistic acceptance of non-democratic government is that private life, which is after all of primary importance for most individuals, is as independent today as it was in medieval times. Individuals are far more constrained in their daily life by social conventions and time-honoured traditions than by political laws or regulations. For the most part laws and regulations are simply ignored, government officials being notoriously unwilling or unable to ensure their application. Consequently, until the domestic economy is greatly improved, the bulk of citizens provided with basic educational skills, and government itself made more efficient, as well as more responsive to the daily needs of the citizens — all factors which accomplished the spread of popular government in the West during the late eighteenth and early nineteenth centuries — there is no reason to expect any far-reaching changes in the modes of rulership within the Arab world.

NOTES

1. For example, though Creon blamed Oedipus at one point for confusing his own good with that of the city, he is eventually brought to ruin because he himself is unable to distinguish between what is his own and what belongs to the city. He punishes Antigone not because her action of burying her brother will harm the city but because it represents a refusal to heed a command he has given — one which has no historical precedent or reasonable grounding and one which only expresses *his*

will about what shall be done in *his* city. Antigone, on the other hand, refuses to consider why Creon might reasonably want to distinguish between the way the bodies of her brothers are treated; she also forecloses any possibility of exploring with him how the putative honour of the city might be safeguarded without in any way neglecting what the gods seem to order about the burial of the dead: apparently more intent upon bringing about her own death as a sign of devotion to the gods than actually burying her brother, Antigone achieves death but not his burial.

5

Notions of the State in Contemporary Arab-Islamic Writings

Fahmi Jadaane

In 1922, following the revolution of Mustapha Kamal, the National Turkish Assembly issued an edict requiring the separation of the sultanate from the Caliphate. This edict was accompanied by a manifesto entitled 'The Caliphate and the People's Power', published in both Arabic and Turkish. The manifesto acknowledged the legal basis for the principle of succession in Islam, but insisted that its actual conditions were not met except in the orthodox Caliphs. The other Caliphs who emerged later were nothing but 'heads of the Muslim community', with their rule having administrative but not spiritual significance.

The manifesto distinguished between a genuine and non-genuine Caliphate on the ground that the former satisfies all the conditions that are necessary for the official instatement of the Caliph, and specifically that the Caliph is voted into office by the nation; whereas the latter lacks these conditions, as the Caliph is brought to office by conquest and use of power. The rule of the latter is a reign but not a Caliphate. This conclusion applied to Umayyad rule — except for 'Umar ibn 'Abd al-'Aziz, and to Abbasid rule in general.

The authors of the manifesto used a quotation from the Azharite al-Iji, author of *al-Mawaqif*, in which he states 'the necessity of installing an *imam* over the Muslims when a person is found to qualify for the conditions of an imam and not otherwise'. They took this to mean 'that a government could be established and a person inaugurated without the former being called a Caliphate, nor its head a Caliph, and without any harm coming to the Islamic nation from that' ('Abd al-Ghani Sani Bey, 1924: 22). The manifesto concluded that a genuine Caliphate cannot be restricted, because it is one of prophecy, but a nominal Caliphate may be. Since the Caliphate has become synonymous with authority and reign, i.e. it has become a purely political matter conducted in an arbitrary manner, it is imperative, in these 'later times', to restrict it so that power will be placed in the hands of the nation, its true owner (ibid.: 66).

This formulation, in fact, was a preparation for the radical edict that was issued in March 1924 officially abolishing the Caliphate and instituting a 'civilian' rule and a secular state. In Islamic circles throughout the Muslim world, and particularly in Egypt, strong protests and violent reactions were generated by that edict. Some thinkers, however, received it positively and publicly supported it, setting off a controversy that pushed the issue of 'state religion' to the forefront in the writing of the constitutions of modern Islamic states that were achieving independence or forming between the two world wars and thereafter. The issue that was raised is: what is the place that religion ought to occupy within the general political structure of the state? Naturally this issue is not considered problematic by contemporary Arab thinkers who follow a liberal, secular or positivistic line. It is resolved by them *a priori* in the process of a decisive separation between the religious and the political or the worldly spheres. The former encompasses the personal spiritual life of the individual and the latter is the basis for the modern state and the means by which it organises its affairs and the societies that depend upon it.

Matters are not so simple for Muslim Arab thinkers who believe that Islam loses its basic significance if it is deprived of its social dimension or political connotations. The great pheno-menon of modern 'civilisation' and the backwardness of the Islamic world, the receding of its culture and the weakness of its states, are evident. Today's Muslim is thus unlikely to be trustful of the dogmatism of traditionalist writers who reject political and social changes. And yet, eliminating the problem simply by abolishing the political and social role of Islam is not the solution. Muslim Arab thinkers have debated this matter since 1924. Their experiences diverge sometimes and converge at other times to the extent that it can be said that, in spite of their undoubted common adherence to Islam, these thinkers repre-sent a vast range of ideas, with some at the limits of 'radical temporal thought' and others at the limits of 'radical religious',

113

or, one might say, 'theocratic thought' and numerous currents in between.

'ALI 'ABD AL-RAZIQ: THE BOOK AND THE WAVES

The first radical expression in the Arab countries following Kamal's overthrow of the Ottoman Government was shaykh 'Ali 'Abd al-Raziq's book on the Caliphate. In 1925, this Egyptian Azhari judge published a book entitled *al-Islam wa 'Usul al-Hukm* (Islam and the Principles of Government) in which he developed a new doctrine of Islam. Is the Caliphate necessary, he asked, or required by Islamic law? Is there a specific Islamic system of rule? His answer is that the Caliphate is not an integral part of Islam, for neither the Quran nor the *Hadith* refer to it, nor is there consensus on it. Its historical existence does not imply the necessity of its continuation. Moreover, the presence of a Caliph is not necessary for worship nor the realisation of the common good. He sums up by saying:

Islam has nothing to do with the kind of Caliphate known to Muslims, with the desire, awe, glory and power with which they surround it, with any legal system or any other function of government, or state positions. All of these are purely political schemes which have nothing to do with religion. Religion neither acknowledges nor denies them, neither stipulates nor prohibits them. It left them for us to tackle by resorting to rational principles, the experiences of nations and the rules of politics. The falsehood that has been spreading among people, concerning the Caliphate being a part of religion and of 'monotheistic beliefs', is the fabrication of kings and sultans who used it to defend their interests and thrones. There have been dire consequences of this for the Muslims. Thus, there is nothing in religion to prevent Muslims from competing with other nations in all social and political spheres, and from destroying the old system to which they submitted and through which they became degraded, establishing the rules of their reign and the system of their government on the basis of modern reasoning and the most solid aspects of what the experience of nations have shown to be the best rules of government.

This view was so daring that it led the council of learned elders of al-Azhar to attack the book and bring its author to trial. This ultimately led to his name being struck from the register of learned men of al-Azhar and to his being deprived of all legal and administrative positions.

A wider circle of critics, both in and outside Egypt, responded to and attacked 'Abd al-Raziq's thesis, because it justifies the idea of a secular state à la Ataturk.

For a long time, 'Abd al-Raziq did not respond at all, although he remained convinced that his stand did Islam a great service, opening its eyes to the evil of the exploitation of dictators and the folly of those to whom affairs were entrusted, but who were concerned only with their own interests. It is probable that he knew that a thesis like his could never be well-received in a traditionalist Islamic environment, and, indeed, it did not evoke any positive response among the learned men of religion and religious law.

The other case that deserves mention is very similar to 'Abd al-Raziq's, and is that of another Azhari, Khalid Muhammad Khalid who, a quarter of a century later, published a book entitled *Min Huna Nabda'* (From Here we Start) in which he showed complete agreement with the political opinions of 'Abd al-Raziq and attacked those he called the 'men of the priesthood', calling on governments and societies with respect and concern for their religion to take all possible initiatives to 'isolate the wicked priesthood and purify religion of its defects' (Khalid, 1950: 47). In his opinion, religious government is nothing but an instrument of dictatorship creating only disasters and suffering for humanity. The renaissance of society as well as the survival of religion itself are not possible without limiting the power of the priesthood and separating civilian from religious power. In this way, religion can achieve the ends for which it was revealed: love, the glorification of God, and the unification of people.

Khalid acknowledged that the Prophet engaged in negotiations, contracted treaties and was involved in many aspects of political power, but he only did this for necessary social reasons beyond his control. Had it not been for these reasons, he would have preferred to devote himself to spiritual affairs alone. It was he who said to 'Umar: 'Easy, 'Umar! Do you think it is Xerxesian? It is a prophecy and not a rule.' He said to his companions: 'You know more about your earthly affairs',

115

indicating by this that it is for the people to manage their worldly affairs.

Furthermore, in Khalid's opinion, combining religious with worldly power endangers the existence of religion itself, for religion represents eternal spiritual truths not subject to variation, whereas the opposite holds true of political aims and means. Thus, if no separation is effected between religion and the state, then religious truths become subject to change and their destiny becomes intertwined with that of the state and its constantly varying political means (ibid.: 47). This damages religion, although it is meant to benefit it.

We could place shaykh 'Abd al-Hamid ibn Badis' position in line with that of 'Ali 'Abd al-Raziq concerning the Caliphate. His untimely death in 1940, while his country suffered under French colonialism, made it impossible for him — the founder of the Association of Algerian Learned Muslims — to follow 'Abd al-Raziq more than halfway (Jadaane, 1981: 334-48).

Ibn Badis openly decried the state in which the Ottoman Caliphate ended and the call of some Azharis for the Caliphate to be turned over to the king of Egypt. In this he showed agreement with 'Abd al-Raziq, for whom this issue constituted one of the driving forces behind his writing *al-Islam wa 'Usul al-Hukm*. Ibn Badis, in tracing the development of the Caliphate system, said:

> The Caliphate is the highest Islamic position designed for the execution of Islamic law and its protection through knowledgeable, experienced and insightful councillors who have wide powers, and through the force of soldiers, commanders and other means of defence. One person occupied this position at the start of Islam and, despite some disagreement, for some time thereafter. But then it became necessary to have more than one position in the East and West and ultimately it was stripped of its original meaning and reduced to a superficial, sanctifying symbol that had nothing to do with the realities of Islam. The day the Turks abolished the Caliphate — and we are not justifying all of their actions — they did not abolish the Islamic Caliphate in its Islamic meaning, but abolished a system of government peculiar to them and removed a fictitious symbol that needlessly captivated the Muslims and turned against them fanatical

Western states frightened by the spectre of Islam (Ibn Badis, 1968: Vol.2, 410-12).

Ibn Badis observed that some colonial powers, especially Britain, — knowing the Muslim fascination with the name Caliph — wanted instrumentally to restore the idea. He strongly warned against this and cried: 'Islamic nation today, stop being vain and deceived and enslaved by these scare-tactics, even if they do emanate from under cloaks and turbans!' The reference here is to the claim of the Azharis with regard to the Caliphate of the king of Egypt.

Ibn Badis did not hesitate to say 'that the Caliphate is a dream that won't come true. Muslims — God willing — will some day come to this opinion.' This might suggest to some that Ibn Badis totally adopted 'Abd al-Raziq's doctrine in depriving Islam of its political aspect. But what he, in fact, intended was to insinuate that the Association of Learned Muslims, because it operated under the shadow of French colonialism, should not interfere in political affairs to avoid any harm being done to its members at colonial hands. And when, given the transitional conditions of the times, he called for replacing the power of the Caliphate with a Muslim group — a group composed of knowledgeable and experienced persons — he was primarily interested in keeping the hands of the occupiers away from the religious and educational administrative bodies of Algeria, so that the latter could preserve its Algerian-Arab-Islamic character. Thus, the Algerians, and not the French, would maintain control over their own affairs.

Otherwise, Ibn Badis maintained openly that 'there are two aspects to the Muslims, as there are to other peoples belonging to different nations: a political aspect connected with state affairs, and a social-educational aspect'. If they have no say on the political aspect, it is because political guidance is a matter for independent Muslim nations, whereas religious and educational guidance is a matter for both independent and dependent nations.

Nevertheless, careful examination of the thirteen rules he set for a political system in Islam, taking as his point of departure Abu Bakr as-Siddiq's famous scheme when he was inaugurated Caliph, clearly denotes that Ibn Badis saw the nation as the source of all power. For him, no nation should be ruled except in accordance with the law that it chooses for itself, and to the execution of which it commits its rulers. That responsibility should be shared by the state and the citizens, within the limits of the law (*ash-Shihab*, January 1938: 468-71). More importantly, he believed that the conditions for an advanced and progressive life are equally available to the entire human race and that whoever avails himself of such conditions achieves the desired results, whether pious or not, believer or otherwise. When the Muslims took to urbanisation in accordance with the dictates of their religion, they prevailed in the world and raised the banner of genuine civilisation with their science and industry. When they neglected the conditions of urbanisation, they fell behind:

> to the extent of almost coming behind all other nations ... They, as a result, lost their worldly goods, having gone against God's will, and were condemned to the low and degraded state they are in. The best medicine for the backward Muslim's fascination with the advanced non-Muslim is to realise that his being a Muslim is not the cause of his backwardness. The non-Muslim does not progress because of not being a Muslim. The cause for progress or backwardness lies in whether or not one satisfies the proper conditions (Ibn Badis, 1964: 78).

One can therefore say that Ibn Badis, in agreement with 'Ali 'Abd al-Raziq in rejecting the altered or distorted Caliphate system, did not go along with him in ascribing religion to the purely spiritual. What appears to be the case is that, for practical reasons, he set aside the political role of religion, pending the stage of independence. But the fact that he tied the political system to the power of the nation and the rule of law, and his belief that progress and backwardness are a matter of adhering to or neglecting worldly conditions, bring him decisively closer to the main issue that 'Abd al-Raziq defended and made dominant in his book.

THE 'RADICAL RELIGIOUS' CURRENT

The effect left by 'Abd al-Raziq's argument was felt in the crystallisation of new Islamic political ideas around questions of rule, power, state and nation. Yet, it would indeed be a gross exaggeration to believe that these new ideas were a response to one single stimulus, namely the provocative work of 'Abd al-Raziq. In addition to it, various Muslim countries were being Westernised, owing to the control by colonial powers over them. There were also modern political institutions based on Western rationalism, which the Muslim learned and intellectuals could no longer completely and unconditionally reject without falling into curious paradoxes.

Thus we find that the strongest voice opposed to 'Abd al-Raziq's theses, namely that of shaykh Muhammad Bakhit al-Muti'i, ultimately set aside the idea that the power of the Caliph is directly derived from God, arguing that the nation is the source of the Caliph's power and that Islamic rule is democratic, free, and consultative, with the Quran and tradition acting as its constitution. This stance made it appear possible to reconcile Islamic with modern concepts.

Viewed from a different perspective, however, it did not represent a retreat with regard to the question of the separation of religion and the state. A strong current against this separation began to make headway and gain support, calling for the re-establishment of the Islamic state and Islamic society under the umbrella of Islamic law. One consequence of the influence of this current was the fact that modern Islamic states introduced into their constitutions a provision to the effect that Islam is the religion of the state or that Islamic law is one basic source of legislation in the state, if not the main source. But these constitutional details are, on the whole, formal and did not suffice in the eyes of some religious movements to force them to swerve from their solitary and radical demands and struggle for the establishment of an Islamic political system and state, as well as for the re-establishment of a Caliphate.

HASAN AL-BANNA AND THE MUSLIM BROTHERS

The new movement born in response to 'Ali 'Abd al-Raziq's provocative claims, goes back to shaykh Muhammad Rashid Rida (d. 1935), who was among the great advocates of traditionalism (as-salafiyyah). He himself described al-Raziq's book as one that constitutes 'a last attempt on the part of the enemies of Islam to weaken this religion and divide it from within'. He affirmed, with shaykh Bakhit al-Muti'i, (al-Muti'i, 1344; Ibn

119

'Ashur, 1344) that Islamic law requires power to maintain and apply it and that it is not possible to reform Islamic law without re-establishing that Islamic state and instating a Caliph endowed with the power to interpret the law (through *ijtihad*). 'The Caliph should see to it that the law is observed and that the government is based on *shura* and should seek to revive Islamic civilisation and strengthen it with the knowledge and technological skill necessary for a strong structure and impregnable progress.'

It was Hasan al-Banna who headed this new movement, inspired by the traditionalism of Rashid Rida and contemporary events. The Muslim Brotherhood, which he began to form in Isma'iliya in 1928, was the most outstanding contemporary Arab-Islamic movement among those who sought to manifest Islam in a society ruled by an openly Islamic authority. But it must be emphasised here that no final crystallisation of the elements of the Brotherhood's understanding of Islam as a political system can be seen. The ideas of Hasan al-Banna and 'Abd al-Qadir 'Awdah represent the primary sources for this understanding; very little has been contributed by writers in the following twenty years. The novelty that might be encountered in an intellectual belonging to the Brotherhood, like Sayyid Qutb or Yusuf al-Qardawi, reflects a practical radicalism related to the application of principles more than to innovation in theoretical concepts.

As for Hasan al-Banna, his thought must be related to the prevailing climate in Egypt in the 1930s and 1940s, charged with political enmities, warring parties, British occupation and the strong current of Westernisation. In the speech which he addressed to the king of Egypt and the rulers of other Muslim countries in 1366 AH, the General Guide of the Muslim Brothers spoke of a dual task:

> The first is that of freeing the nation from its political shackles in order to attain its freedom and regain its lost independence and sovereignty, and the second is that of rebuilding it so that it can advance alongside other nations and rival them in the field of social perfections.

When he called on his audience to determine the path which they must take, he could envisage for them only two alternatives: 'The first is that of Islam, its principles, rules, culture and civilisation; the second is that of the West, its modes of life, its systems and styles.' Naturally, for him, 'the way of Islam and its rules and principles, is the only way we must take and to which we must guide the whole nation, now and in the future' (al-Banna, 1981: 274). He saw Islam as

> a comprehensive system embracing all aspects of life: it is a state and a country, a government and a nation: it is morality, power, mercy and justice; it is culture, law, knowledge and legislation; it is material good, wealth, profit and richness; it is a struggle, a message for an army and an idea; in as much as it is a true doctrine and religion (ibid.: 256).

Islam alone is capable of rebuilding the unity of a nation shaken by a system of political party pluralism and infighting. In spite of the fact that al-Banna called for strengthening the relations between all Islamic countries, especially Arab ones, in preparation for serious and practical thinking about the issue of the lost Caliphate (ibid.: 290), he did not argue for the latter system. What really preoccupied him was the establishment of a genuine Islamic government. Islam does not accept chaos and does not permit the Islamic group to remain without a leader (imam). Anybody 'who thinks that religion, or more accurately, Islam, does not deal with politics or that politics is not of its concerns does injustice to himself and to his knowledge of Islam'. The Islamic state has a message that does not depend on the establishment of a static, dispirited administration or government, but on a state apparatus that 'protects, spreads, conveys and strengthens it'. The greatest mistake Muslims committed, lies in the fact that they forgot this foundation and separated religion from politics, although admitting the close connection between the two.

Al-Banna then turns to Egypt where the Constitution explicitly states that Islam is the state religion. But in his eyes this did not prevent politicians and leaders of political bodies from corrupting Muslim ideas, sensibilities, and tastes, by trying to drive a wedge between the instruction of religion and the requirements of politics. And this was the beginning of weakness and the source of corruption.

The solution lies in the establishment of an Islamic government based on the following foundations: responsibility of the ruler, social and spiritual unity of the nation within a fraternal framework, and respect for the nation's will and commitment to its opinion. A sound application of these rules creates a balanced society, and the function of the representative body of the nation is the observation and maintenance of these rules. This does not necessarily mean resorting to parties to operate this representation. For although parties are one of the bases of the parliamentary system, it is possible to bring about such a system without parties, that is, through a limited representative electoral system where those who are elected and become the holders of real power are qualified persons, free from any pressure or control dictated by an external force, whose campaign claims are subject to moral criteria and restrictions, and where violators do not go unpunished (ibid.: 317-33).

Thus, Hasan al-Banna comes conspicuously closer to the Western concept of democracy, so much so that he himself declares that there is nothing in the parliamentary system that contradicts the rules of the Islamic system of government. In that respect 'it is neither far from the Islamic system nor extraneous to it' (ibid.: 322). Even with regard to the question of the responsibility of the ruler, in al-Banna's opinion the element of Islam's doctrine that states that the head of state is responsible and, as al-Mawardi showed in *al-Ahkam as-Sultaniyyah*, can delegate power to others, has a counterpart in modern constitutions, especially in that of the United States.

Al-Banna, however, contented himself with these few principles which later became the guide for the Muslim Brotherhood's political writers, at the forefront of which is 'Abd al-Qadir 'Awdah. Considered the greatest political theoretician of the Brotherhood, he was the first to dedicate a whole book to the political question, dealing with the matter of an Islamic government, its functions and characteristics; the Caliphate and its conditions; the consultative bodies (al-shura) and powers in the Islamic state (Jadaane, 1981: 363-72).

Who rules? This is the central question for 'Abd al-Qadir 'Awdah. The answer to it is not difficult: 'God rules and commands' and human beings, whom God has delegated, have no choice but to obey His command, refrain from what He prohibits, and resolve differences by reference to what He revealed, for their being delegated is subject to their abiding by the law of God. The Quran, which was revealed to His Prophet, was revealed to become the ultimate law of mankind, and whoever refrains from judging by what God revealed is an 'infidel', is 'unjust' or is disobedient to God ('Awdah, 1951: 55-9).

> Rule is the unifying origin and it is supported in Islam, for Islam is not merely a doctrine but also a system, and it is not merely a religion but also a state. Every order in the Quran and the *Sunnah* requires, for its execution, the establishment of Islamic rule and an Islamic state. For Islam to become established within the limits set by God and shown by the Messenger, it is required that an Islamic state be established that founds Islam within its set limits.

The application of most of the practical principles of Islam is not a matter for individuals but for governments, and this alone decisively shows that to rule is in the nature of Islam and its requirements and that Islam is a religion and a state. The ideal state in Islam is the state which subjects the worldly to the religious, 'where religion cannot exist without the state, nor can the state be sound without religion' (ibid.: 68).

If governments originally arise for necessary social reasons, then it is imperative that they be Islamic. This does not mean that the rulers must be Muslims but they should refer to Islam and take the Quran as the 'constitution for rulers and ruled'. For the function of a government is 'to do what God commands' and to judge by what He revealed. It is obligatory for the ruled to obey their governments and those in charge as long as the latter obey God. If that is not the case, the ruled may renounce obedience to the government.

An Islamic government is unique and distinct with respect to three characteristics. The first is that it is a Quranic government, i.e. the Quran — the revealed Word of God — is its ultimate law. The second is that it is a government of shura limited by Islamic law. The third is that it is a Caliphate or imam government, in a sense which 'indicates a specific type of government', since the Caliphate, imamate and great imamate are synonyms denoting one thing, namely the higher presidency of the state and nothing more (ibid.: 72-7).

The government 'represents the community to bring it under God's law and to supervise its interests'. The Caliph or imam is 'the representative of the first government', thus, he represents the entire community in his capacity as Caliph and is instated by the community in order to represent it. 'His power is and always will be derived exclusively from his position as a representative of the community which instated him and has the right to check him and prevent him from stepping outside the limits of his representative position' (ibid.: 81).

The government of a Caliph is not complete unless chosen by the community, not only because choice is a logical or social necessity but also because the Quran imposed on Muslims to manage their affairs by consultation (shura).

> Choosing a Caliph in this manner confirms that the Caliphate is no more than a representative contract (*'aqd niabah*) between the community and the Caliph, whereby the community entrusts the Caliph with transacting what God commands and managing its affairs within the limits of what God revealed. The Caliph, in turn, accepts to carry out such an assignment in accordance with God's commandments. So long as the Caliph does what God commands, he may remain in office indefinitely. If, however, he deviates from what God commands or develops some trait that requires deposition, then the community should be able to depose him from office and instate another in his place. When he dies, his reign ends with his death (ibid.: 81-2).

An Islamic government is therefore not an 'absolute dictatorship', because it is limited by the Quran as a constitution. Nor is it a 'legally-based government', that is, subject to human laws, for its edicts originate from God, are fixed and permanent and cater neither to the whims of the rulers nor to those of the ruled.

> Although parliamentary governments in the world are based on some form of shura, it remains the case that shura in Islamic government is not similar to the one on which parliamentary governments are based (ibid.: 83).

And in spite of the fact that one of the functions of an Islamic government is to uphold religion,

> it is not to be considered the kind of religious government that constitutional law calls theocratic. For an Islamic government does not derive its power from God but from the community. It does not achieve power or resign it without the

community's decision. It is limited in all its actions by public opinion. This is so since Islam does not deprive people of their freedom of action nor does it reign over all their affairs. It leaves it to them to organize themselves and look after their private and general interests. The Quranic texts yield comprehensive judgements and general outlines for the way to govern and administer and leave what ranks below this to the men of power to organize in accordance with the laws they set (ibid.: 82-3).

Furthermore, the Islamic system of government differs from democracy in that 'it does not leave it to human beings to set the criteria determining the limits to justice, equality and the rest of human virtues', for Islam itself sets these higher criteria for human life. Even though the Islamic system is similar to the republican one with regard to the way the president of the republic is chosen, it differs from the latter in allowing a mandate for life. But it also differs from a monarchy in leaving it to the community to choose as ruler whoever they deem best and most able.

The Islamic system is therefore unique. Muslims did not put the Islamic system into effect after the death of the Prophet except during the era of the orthodox Caliphs, after which the system was transformed by individual whim into a formidable reign that did not hesitate to obstruct the application of Islamic rules. The state was, however, built on a sound basis during the era of the Prophet himself. Material power was built on spiritual power and the state was founded on the four basic pillars: people, political independence, land and sovereignty. Thus the existence of a state is not to be doubted even if we grant, for argument's sake, the absence in that state of internal procedures such as the appointment of judges and rulers, the existence of accounting offices and a proper budget, as well as the absence of any talk about the system of rule and the grounds for shura — to which some (and the reference is to 'Ali 'Abd al-Raziq) appealed to raise doubts about the existence of an Islamic state during the Messenger's time (ibid.: 97).

Following this, 'Abd al-Qadir 'Awdah gives a detailed and complete picture of the Islamic state through a discussion of the following three issues: the Caliphate or great imamhood, shura and the people's power, and the distribution of powers in the Islamic state.

On the Caliphate, his opinions do not, on the whole, deviate from what was determined by legal experts, Ibn Khaldun and the author of *al-Ahkam as-Sultaniyyah*. The function of the Caliphate is 'to uphold Islam', i.e. to uphold religious and state matters within the limits drawn by Islam, for the Caliphate 'as a presidential office, has wide powers ranging from the management of religious to worldly matters in the name of the Prophet'. Upholding it is a duty, neglecting it is a sin. It is 'rationally obligatory', as al-Iji claimed in *al-Mawaqif*. The conditions that must be met by a Caliph or an imam are: being a Muslim, male, responsible, knowledgeable, just, competent, sound and a descendant of Quraysh. The last condition is controversial. 'Nothing, of course, can prevent the setting of other conditions if required by the general good', or 'the circumstances of life which vary with time'.

For the instatement of an imam in office, the only legitimate way is through choice by key powerful figures and the candidate's acceptance of the office. This amounts to a contract that takes the form of readiness and acceptance: readiness of the men of shura to choose a Caliph, and acceptance by the latter to serve in the office for which he has been chosen. 'Imama based on conquest, though approved by some Muslim legal theoreticians, has led to the worst kind of wrongs and to the division of the Muslims, weakening them and destroying the bases of Islam. Had those legal theoreticians foreseen these consequences, they would not have licensed it for a single moment'.

The same applies to acquiescence in the idea of regency as formulated by Mu'awiyah after the fashion of *istikhlaf* utilised by Abu Bakr to prepare the way for 'Umar to succeed him. Istikhlaf is nothing but an 'act of nomination' performed by the key powerful figures. The idea of regency, however, betrays the interests of the Islamic nation and deprives it of its right to choose rulers or remove them from office. To acquiesce in it is to acquiesce in a falsehood and to disobey God ('Awdah, 1951: 138).

The Caliph is an individual representing the nation. His power is derived from the fact that he represents the Islamic nation. His government is considered representative of the community and it is up to the people to widen or narrow the scope of the Caliph's power. If he deviates from majority opinion, then they no longer owe him obedience. It is in the

126

Caliph's or great imam's power to ask the help of others to deal with the affairs of state in their capacity as ministers, directors, judges and officials of all kinds. Legally, they are considered empowered to speak for the nation and are not to be removed if the Caliph is removed from office or if he dies, as long as they do their job properly. The Caliph should not be treated as sacred, nor should he receive any special treatment. If he makes an error, there is nothing to absolve him from responsibility and thus he is subject to punishment like everybody else. His representation of the people in upholding Islamic law is not limited in time, and may last as long as he lives and is able to do his work and does nothing that requires his removal from office. That is, as long as he does nothing that could 'change his condition' in a way that reflects a loss of some of the traits which constituted the basis for his being chosen for the Caliphate. For example, if 'his justice is tarnished' or his 'body maimed' through the loss of senses or limbs, or if his behaviour is so affected that he loses control over things and becomes subject to others or subdued by an enemy with no chance of escape, his replacement could be considered.

Shura is a central pillar, not only of faith, but of Islamic rule in particular, and it is obligatory for the rulers and ruled. Legal experts have determined that it is one of the principles of Islamic law, and any ruler who rejects it ought to be removed from office. Shura, however, is not absolute, but limited by the provisions and spirit of Islamic legislation. It is to be applied only in cases where provisions are lacking and should not go beyond the limits of Islam. It is subject to certain rules: it is a determined right for the rulers and the ruled; it is one of the duties of the rulers but not one of their rights; it should be based on sincerity to God and a desire to elevate Islam; the opinion of the majority of consultants only and not a unanimity is required; the minority should follow the opinion of the majority. Thus, if shura were applied soundly, it would lead to the good of the world, and would help to avoid the failure that has afflicted democracies and dictatorships alike.

But, who, in fact, are the men of shura? They are figures of power and councillors of the Islamic nation, chosen from among those who are 'familiar with Islamic law, with the branches of knowledge, arts, crafts and other affairs pertaining to the interests of the nation'. The determination of their number and way of choosing them depends on circumstances, but they must satisfy requirements such as justice, knowledge in its widest sense, ability and wisdom. Their power is the power of the people themselves, because they in fact speak for the people and are the men of opinion and influence in the nation and the representatives of the nation's will. Rulers 'are committed to executing what is yielded by shura and to upholding it in the manner approved by the representatives of the nation. The nation in this case is the source of their power' ('Awdah, 1951: 17).

There are five powers in the Islamic state (i) the executive power, at the top of which comes the head of state, i.e. the imam who holds it alone with those who assist him such as ministers and rulers, etc.; (ii) the legislative power which is held by those who have the ultimate say among the people, i.e. the imam and the councillors; (iii) the judiciary power which is represented by judges who are appointed by the imam in his capacity as a representative of the people; (iv) the financial power whose administrators are appointed, removed from office and supervised by the imam; (v) the power of observation and evaluation which is held by the people as a whole and involves observing and evaluating the rulers. Councillors, learned men and jurists represent the nation in this task.

FROM AL-BANNA TO AN-NABHANI

Several writers followed the line originally stated by Hasan al-Banna: writers like 'Abd al-Karim al-Khatib, Taha 'Abd al-Baqi Surur, Muhammad Yusuf Musa, Muhammad al-Mubarak and Yusuf al-Qardawi. These writers openly state that Islam is a religion and a state, that it is obligatory for a Caliph or imam to execute Islamic law, that the nation is the source of state power and sovereignty, that the function of an Islamic state is to act as the guardian of the faith and administrator of worldly policy, and that the Islamic system is unique: it is neither theocratic nor monarchic, it is merely Islamic (al-Khatib, 1963; Musa, 1964). Though these writers often come close to the democratic concept of the state, they are careful to renounce it in favour of the concept of a distinct system which constitutes a unique synthesis between the religious and the worldly. For this reason they do not hide their preference for the term Caliphate or imama in spite of their emphasis that what is intended is merely the presidency and politics conducted in accordance with the rules of Islamic law.

Muhammad al-Mubarak presents us with the final aspect of the Islamic system of government as seen by this group of theoreticians, an understanding that reaches its zenith in the writings of Abu al-A'la al-Mawdudi (al-Mawdudi, 1967). Muhammad al-Mubarak's central question is: does Islam itself, in what it basically teaches and requires, impose on its believers the task of establishing a state based on it? The answer is undoubtedly in the affirmative. All contexts indicate the necessity of such a state: the Quran contains rulings whose applications cannot be conceived without a state or political power adopting them — rulings covering matters such as restrictions, inheritance, *zakat*, the call to *jihad*, as well as rulings pertaining to the ruler himself and his subjects. Secondly, the general conception of existence in the Quran must find expression in a social and vital frame of reference that can safeguard and nourish it. This can only be achieved within the context of an Islamic state. Thirdly, there are many instances in *Hadith* that commit us to establishing rule; and, finally, the Prophet himself established a state, the preservation and continuity of which the Muslims have ensured, generation after generation (al-Mubarak, 1981: 12-18).

The purpose of establishing an Islamic state is 'the safeguarding of the principles of Islam, especially the doctrine of monotheism which is the positive way for liberating mankind and putting into effect Islamic laws to establish human society on a foundation of justice, cooperation, integration and higher moral ideals' (ibid.: 23).

The state of Islam is a doctrinal or ideological state, i.e. it has ideological concepts and principles forming its basis and ensuring the application of its fundamental norms pertaining to human dignity, equality, the observance of Islamic legal edicts, the safeguarding of the principle of 'succession on earth' (*Istikhlaf fi al-Ard*) and fraternity in doctrine and faith (ibid.: 24-8).

Islam, however, does not impose a form of government that is well-defined and detailed. Rather, it represents 'general principles' and rules which constitute ideal goals that mankind aspires to achieve, leaving the details and practical applications that lie supported by these principles and rules for peoples' interpretation according to their various states, environments and circumstances (ibid.: 29, 52). The most prominent of these principles is the reference to the nation's opinion when instating a ruler or a head of state. It is for the people to determine the latter through a choice based on: a contract between them and the ruler; his acknowledgment of this; the commitment to the rules of Islamic law in matters where there are provisions and to interpretation ruled by shura where there is no provision; the principle of shura; the principle holding the ruler responsible before God and the people's right to judge, watch and criticise him; the principle of equality among people; justice; the rights of man, such as the right to protect oneself, one's honour, mind, possessions, morality and religion; the principle of mutual social responsibility; obedience to the ruler in exchange for his abiding by Islamic law and by whatever is of interest to the Muslims (ibid.: 29-50). Al-Mubarak's use of the term 'Caliphate system' to refer to the Islamic system of government should not be understood to mean more than a reference to the presidency of the state along Islamic lines, i.e. 'basic principles found in Islam in its two main sources: the Quran and Sunnah and whatever the learned Muslims in every age have deduced in the field of government and the state' (ibid.: 50).

Al-Mubarak mentions three component parts of the state: the authority or governmental apparatus over which the head of state presides; the people governed by this authority; and the territory within which the rule of this authority prevails. In dealing with the tasks of the head of state and the conditions for choosing him, he follows al-Mawardi as referred to by 'Abd al-Qadir 'Awdah. He adopts the modern distinction between the legislative, the judiciary, and the executive power (ibid.: 79-85). Then he follows Ibn Hanbal and Ibn Taymiyyah with regard to the question of the function of the state. He confines that function to 'ensuring internal security and external defence, establishing legal justice, achieving financial and economic sufficiency for the individual and society; spreading the doctrine of Islam through jihad and safeguarding it against any deviant behaviour' — that is what he calls 'the doctrinal-ethical' function — and installing men to run the affairs of the state who are characterised by ability and loyalty.

For al-Mubarak the nation, in the Islamic sense, is 'a human society based on common beliefs' (ibid.: 100). He affirms that this involves a 'humanistic concept' in contrast with the 'backward', 'static', nationalistic concept of a nation, one that perfectly agrees with the prevalent tendency in today's world to renounce nationalistic groupings in favour of ones based on ideas and ideological systems. Now, the nation as a basis for the state has rights protected by the state, for rulers simply 'speak for' or 'represent' the nation. And the nation, i.e. the people, holds the power, although it is not a legislative power except with regard to matters of opinion and *ijtihad* not determined by the original sources of Islamic law. As far as the individual is concerned, the state offers him the right to life and self-preservation, the right to own and profit, the right to equality, to personal freedom of belief, thought, opinion, criticism and to political freedom (ibid.: 115-24). These types of freedom remain limited for him by the principle prohibiting deviation from the ideology of the state or advocacy of a different and opposite ideology, for this would amount to an act of civil disobedience against the state and a call to rise against it and remove its Islamic character. Those who renounce Islam, its ideology and its law have no choice but to refrain from identifying with a state based on it and a society that believes in it and grounds its solidarity in it, and must identify instead with a different state and a different society (ibid.: 117). Any freedom practised in the Islamic state should not deviate from the criteria set by Islam nor should it conflict with the basic teaching which the state is entrusted with upholding, namely that of advocating Islam in all areas of social life.

With regard to the state territory, which is the third component of the state, al-Mubarak adopts the old distinction between *Dar al-Islam* and *Dar al-Kufr*, namely 'the home of Islam' and 'the home of disbelief' and considers the two mutually exclusive. People belonging to the latter are either in a 'state of truce or peace' with the Muslims because of some treaty they concluded with them, or in a 'state of war', thereby making their Dar al-Kufr *Dar-Harb*, namely 'the home of war'. Acquisition of territory by the Islamic state is effected by two means either the people of that territory convert to Islam, while remaining on it and thus transform the territory to Dar-Islam, or the territory is conquered by the Muslims and subjected to Islamic rule. The state and individuals have to protect the borders of this Dar by force, and Muslims have a duty to live within its boundaries and not to live in Dar al-Kufr except for accidental reasons (ibid.: 135-6).

Al-Mubarak concludes that the Islamic state has the following defining characteristics: the state in Islam is an ideology, as

131

well as a system of laws emanating from the latter. The Islamic state is not to be described as either religious or civil, but could be 'described as jointly religious and civil' or neither, since it is a unique system. The Islamic state is also a humanistic and moral state that does not aim to prevail over others or to accumulate wealth or military glory, but at liberating man from all forms of enslavement and binding him by a higher bond, namely 'submission to God alone and the upholding of justice for all people'. The Islamic state is, furthermore, a state of culture, engaging in various activities, of an educational, practical, material, intellectual and psychological nature. It is a humanistic and worldly state. Finally, it is a state with solid foundations and forms that evolve with the evolution of social and cultural conditions (ibid.: 137-44). One can, in fact, hardly distinguish between the position of 'political advocates' and that of the learned men of religion (Ghoshah, 1971).

The picture of religious radicalism we have been presenting would not be complete without considering the basic contributions made by an active Palestinian intellectual in Jerusalem in the early 1950s. This is Taqi ad-Din an-Nabhani, who founded a political party in the true sense of the word, aiming openly at establishing an Islamic state, restoring the Caliphate and declaring unrelenting war against all established political systems in the Arab world. The party he established is the Islamic Liberation Party (Hizb at-Tahrir al-Islami) which is, practically and theoretically, the counterpart of the Muslim Brotherhood.

Nabhani's early writings and pamphlets go back to 1952. His first book was entitled *ad-Dawlah al-Islamiyyah*, and was published one year after 'Awdah's book *al-Islam wa Awda'una as-Siasiyyah*. In it, Nabhani presented a preliminary and general outline for an Islamic system of government. The same year he published another book entitled *Nizam al-Hukm fi al-Islam*, in which he defined in complete detail the nature of this system in all its organisational aspects. No sooner had the latter appeared than he presented us with another, *Nizam al-Islam*, in which he went further by including a chapter devoted mainly to detailing the system's prospective constitution. This constitution contains ninety-nine articles, the first fourteen of which are general rules. The book in its entirety represents the first complete scheme for a state and its system, i.e. the first to appear in contemporary Islamic thought. It is one that agrees with most of 'Awdah's ideas, but it is better defined, more concise, clear,

132

complete and radical. Besides the fact that an-Nabhani's ideas have, since the 1950s, been the distinguishing ideas of the propagandists of his party which spread widely in the Arab Near East (Palestine, Jordan, Syria, Lebanon and Iraq), it is certain that these ideas also had a clear influence on a number of Muslim Brotherhood thinkers like Sayyid Qutb, al-Mubarak and others. This was so in spite of the differences between these two movements with regard to their methods. Whereas one sees the starting point for achievement of a renaissance in the transformation of thought and concepts through the establishment of a state, the other sees that starting point in a process of comprehensive moral, educational and religious transformation, i.e. in a behavioural transformation of the individual.

An-Nabhani affirms that Islam brought the word new concepts about the universe, man, life, and values which completely overturned old concepts. It imposed on Muslims not only the necessity of committing themselves to new concepts, but also of changing the old concepts of the rest of the people through the spreading of the doctrine of Islam. The primary task of Muslims, in fact, is the advocacy and furthering of the message of Islam, and the highest ideal is God's approval of their work. This approval can be obtained only if their work is directed at 'guiding the whole of humanity to Islam'. But that can be done only through domination or power based on it, and this power is the Islamic state. That is what

> the task of the Islamic state has been from the first moment of its inception and will be until the Day of Judgement: applying Islam and conveying its message to the world until it is universally accepted. It is this that makes Muslims the leaders of the world and the Islamic state, through Islam's fulfilment of the necessary requirements for worship and happiness, one which leads the world to good and happiness (an-Nabhani, 1952a: 36).

The states that rule the world today, according to an-Nabhani, whether capitalist or socialist, are grounded in a purely materialistic mentality, making it possible for the culture of materialism to dominate mankind. Because of this, mankind has undergone 'spiritual crises' that have caused destructive psychological misery and evil to spread everywhere. 'For this reason it is necessary, in order to save the world, to have a state established on a spiritual basis' combining spirit with matter, making it possible for the culture of spiritualism to dominate life. The Islamic state is the only way to achieve this great accomplishment, and herein lies the necessity of its establishment.

Moreover, Muslims today are in a state of backwardness, degradation and remoteness from the teachings of Islam, and they are 'subject to the system of Kufr in their own country. They are subject to its rulings, are controlled by the culture of materialism, and their Dar (home), from the perspective of Islamic law, is Dar Kufr and not Dar Islam.' Thus, it is 'imperative for them to bring about the Islamic state, to be subjected to the rulings of Islam' and to instate a Caliph as the head of state to fulfil what is required by Islamic law and reason.

> What has to be done in the way of setting limits and filling gaps cannot be done without the Caliph. Governing in accordance with the requirements of revelation as well as bringing what is beneficial to the people and warding off what is unbeneficial cannot be done without him (ibid.: 152).

Muslims are all sinners until they establish the Islamic state and officially inaugurate its head. What is meant here is not an Islamic state in name or in abstract, but one that applies the rulings of Islam in so far as it is a system emanating from the Islamic ideology and saturated with the Islamic idea, the Islamic spirit and the Islamic mentality. With this,

> life's motivating forces will be reborn from inside the soul, and a mental, psychological and social environment that can guarantee Islamic legislation and laws will exist and effect a total and not a gradual transformation towards a perfect Islamic existence (ibid.: 156).

Nobody can deny that Islam is a religion requiring a state or claim that the Islamic state is a purely spiritual one or that religion in Islam is something other than the state. Islamic law openly calls for the necessity of establishing a rule and a dominion. The verses of the Quran constitute straightforward evidence that Islam should lead to a state and that government ought to be in accordance with God's revelation. Further, the Quran has legislated matters pertaining to wars, politics, criminal behaviour and social and civil activities.

Islamic rule, in an-Nabhani's opinion, rests on four bases: the first is the predominance of Islamic law; the second, that government should be by the people; the third, that instating one Caliph for all Muslims, to represent the people in government, is an obligation of the people; the fourth, that the people have the right to ijtihad and to propose the legal rulings required to deal with the problems of life. But the right to legislate belongs to the Caliph and not to the people, for it is up to him 'to choose what legal rulings from among the statements of the practitioners of ijtihad should be binding on judges and rulers; it is up to him to deduce rulings through a correct ijtihad and make them binding on his followers' (ibid.: 83).

At any rate, shura is a right that the Caliph owes to all Muslims. He owes it to them to turn to them whenever consultation is necessary in matters concerning them (ibid.: 16). Given the extreme importance of shura, an-Nabhani considers the Council of Councillors (*Majlis ash-shura*) to which the Caliph refers concerning national matters, the first of the seven pillars of the state. The rest are: the head of state, the executive body (the assistants), the administrative apparatus, the rulers (*wulat*), the judiciary and the army. All of these, he asserts, were established by the Prophet himself as a part of his organisational structure of the Islamic state.

What attracts attention in this structure is that the members of the Council of shura should be elected and not appointed, for they 'speak for the people and represent individuals and groups in their countries and areas. Every citizen of the state, whether man or woman, Muslim or non-Muslim, may become a member of the Council of shura' (ibid.: 20). The functions of this council are: giving an opinion on legislation; acting as a check on the government, the rulers and the Caliph's assistants; discussing matters of government with the Caliph and judging the way he conducts these matters. The Muslim Council members have the power to nominate the Caliph whom the nation elects and instates. The head of state is the one

who rules and executes the law on behalf of the people. He is the one who puts legal rulings into effect, that is, makes them law. He is the one who runs and conducts the affairs of the nation. But he is neither the symbol of the latter nor the source of its powers; he is simply the executor of God's law.

His presidency is not to be recognised unless it is conferred on him by the nation. He ought to be obeyed only within the limits of the law (ibid.: 29).

The head of state has wide powers within the limits of the law: he is the one who appoints the members of the executive branch and all branches of government except the shura Council. He also renders legal rulings binding by adopting them. He prepares the state budget, and declares war, makes peace, concludes treaties and conducts all matters pertaining to foreign policy.

To give the head of state all these wide powers does not at all mean that he is sacred or has a divine right, for he does not rule on behalf of God but on behalf of the people, and all of the people have the right to judge him. To be a Caliph does not mean to be either a dictator or a saint (ibid.: 38-9).

His term of office is indefinite. He can, in fact, stay in office as long as he works at executing the law and does not violate it, otherwise he ought to be deposed. 'He can be deposed through a legal ruling issued by a legal body, namely the court dealing with injustices.' This court can rule on the question of whether or not he has adhered to Islam and can determine what is a sufficient basis for deposing him.

If he were not to submit to the ruling of this court, he would be considered disobedient to God and the Muslims would be required to depose him because their original approval of his instatement in office would no longer be binding on them (ibid.: 41).

An-Nabhani feels that the system of regency adopted by Mu'awiyah is contrary to Islam. Abu Bakr did not confer regency on 'Umar. The latter was elected by the people while the head of state was still alive and was then officially instated in office (ibid.: 115).

In dealing in detail with all important aspects of the state, an-Nabhani always draws inspiration from the Age of the Prophet and from *al-Ahkam as-Sultaniyyah*, and he uses some modern legal terms in the manner of 'Abd al-Qadir 'Awdah. His ideas on the state are crystallised in a proposal for a constitution whose articles are relative to the nature of the system of government and seven essential bases (articles 15-99); the social system of the state (articles 100-10); the economic system (articles 111-57); educational policy (articles 158-69); and foreign policy (articles 170-82) (ibid.: 80-113). He winds up by repeating that the system is founded on a spiritual basis: the Islamic ideology. Morals, then, are not the basis of society but the effects of the application of the system and Islam in general (ibid.: 114-15).

But how is the Islamic state to be established? The only way to resume the Islamic way of life, in his opinion, and to establish the Islamic state, is 'to transmit Islamic teachings' to all areas and societies, to educate societies in the right Islamic concepts and to have the advocates of Islam interact with their societies to create a general awareness of Islam among public opinion. This interaction can thus be transformed into a 'militant movement' aimed at establishing an Islamic state, exactly in the way the Messenger went about it when he established the first Islamic state. This means looking for a territory that can be used as a starting point from which to spread the doctrine to other Islamic areas and to develop the great Islamic state that is to convey the message of Islam to the world (ibid.: 162). Conveying this message requires bringing up an Islamic intellectual leadership that is at once strong, straightforward and daring, ready to challenge any situation or concept opposing Islam and relentlessly to apply Islam to the letter, with no sign of neglect or slackening or tendency to compromise with anybody on any matter pertaining to Islamic teachings (ibid.: 56).

The nation, which constitutes the practical means on earth of putting Islam into effect, by checking on and judging the ruler, needs to have a smaller group exhibiting a profound understanding of Islam and a strong fear of God, one that will work at providing the people with an intensive Islamic education aimed at building the Islamic character of the nation. This group is the 'party of principles' that arises on the basis of Islam, making advocacy its only task. Thus the real guarantee for the application of Islam and its advocacy and application is an Islamic political party (ibid.: 122). This leading party of the nation acts as a monitor to the state and as the advocate of Islamic principles, for the way to advocate the latter is through politics (ibid.: 121).

To achieve such a goal, the Islamic Liberation Party was established in 1952 and followed a radical line in its political advocacy of the re-establishment of the Islamic state. In its merciless criticism of the Arab political establishment, it brought on itself equally merciless harassment. Together with other reasons that cannot be detailed here, the party gradually weakened but did not totally disappear.

An-Nabhani's ideas had a substantial effect on the thought of a very prominent intellectual of the Brotherhood, namely Sayyid Qutb. Qutb began his career, after his initiation into the Brotherhood, by concerning himself with the question of social justice in Islam. He soon hit upon the role of the elite in bringing about the process of change. He also discovered that the principle of God's rule, on which the entire Islamic system is based, cannot be realised merely by upholding the creed and practising worship within 'the organic existence of the dynamic association of a pre-Islamic nature that in fact exists' (Qutb, n.d.: 65). What is required for its realisation is the actual existence of Islam. And this does not come about through individuals who are Muslims only in theory, but through 'the representation of the theoretical base of Islam, i.e. the creed, in a dynamic, organic association that is from the first moment ... separate and independent from the dynamic pre-Islamic organic association that Islam aims at abolishing'. The new association should be centered around a new leadership that will turn people to the divinity of God alone, to the fact that he is 'the Lord, the Prince, the Ruler, the Possessor of power and the Law-giver' and confine their loyalty to the new Islamic dynamic, organic association (ibid.: 65-7). The aim of this Muslim leadership is to put an end to any attempt at reconciliation with the pre-Islamic concepts prevalent on earth and the pre-Islamic countries existent everywhere and 'to move people from *jahiliyya* to Islam. The choice is between Islam or jahiliyyah, the rule of God or the rule of jahiliyyah.' However well-intentioned they may be, pre-Islamic societies cannot pursue solutions to their problems through Islamic law, because their society is not ruled by Islam.

Besides giving signs of the dissent within the Brotherhood as to how its advocacy should be carried out, a split also manifested by the *Jama'at al-Muslimin* group was unveiled in Egypt in 1980. Its ideas constitute a straightforward rejection of any 'moderate, middle ground' position, such as accepting the principles of Islamic law as a main source of legislation or the constitution. This is expressed by another radical writer, namely Yusuf al-Qardawi, when he states that the 'Islamic solution' aspired to specifically means the establishment of an Islamic state or purely Islamic rule which has in Islamic legislation its 'one and only guide' and 'reference' for all its rulings (al-Qardawi, 1974: 82). The Islamic solution is one 'that adapts all conditions and systems to the rulings of Islam and not one that adapts the rulings of Islam to conditions and systems' (ibid.: 95).

BETWEEN 'ABD AL-RAZIQ AND TWENTIETH-CENTURY *SALAFIYYA* IS A SYNTHESIS POSSIBLE?

From a dialectical perspective, thesis and antithesis cannot endure radical opposition for long. There must be a fresh starting point in which the two extremes are blended and possibly transcend their mutual contradiction. On the one hand then, there was the thesis of 'Ali 'Abd al-Raziq which reduced religion to the realm of spirit, pushing politics away from its domain. On the other hand, the opposite thesis conjoined politics with spirituality and went on to consider the restoration of the Islamic state and the Caliphate as necessary maxims not subject to compromise. A mediating synthesis inevitably emerged to overcome this opposition. It took two main lines, of which I call the first legislative and the other humanistic.

The seed of the legislative attitude goes back to 'Ali Abu al-Futuh who argued in 1905 that the established principles of Islamic shari'ah are appropriate for modern times, marked by civilisation and development. He held that the norms and precepts of modern secular law have counterparts in the fundamentals of Islam (al-Futuh, 1905: 5-6). 'Abd al-'Aziz Jawish laid emphasis on the same notion and professed, perhaps for the first time, that Islam is valid for every time and place (Jawish, n.d.: 45). This attitude matured in the hands of the famous professor of law, 'Abd al-Razzaq as-Sanhuri and appeared, in one respect, at odds with the radical theory of 'Ali 'Abd al-Raziq. One year after the 1936 treaty between Egypt and Britain, as-Sanhuri called for recourse to Islamic law in order to modify previous Egyptian legislation. The former was to be considered a source and should not be abandoned as had been the case a century earlier. He also stressed the fact that a

139

number of precepts in Islamic shari'ah go beyond Western laws. Professor as-Sanhuri seems to have no doubts that Islam is both religion and state and that the state must have a kind of jurisprudence upon which to depend in forging its own laws. He refers in this connection to Muslim *fiqh* which considers the Quran and prophetic tradition its higher sources. The cardinal principle chosen by as-Sanhuri for this proposed law is that it should be based on the fiqh in such a way that it accords with civilisation and the spirit of the age.

> It must be purely Islamic jurisprudence with regard to its logic, form and style, and not a mere imitation of Western law. It should not deviate from the shari'ah principles, assuming that evolution entails this departure. Hence, shari'ah being dependent upon ijtihad and consensus (*ijma'*), is fertile to the degree that it can meet all factors of evolution (Jadaane, 1981: 355-6).

In 1939, the lawyer Ahmed Husayn also called for the revision of constitutional laws in the light of Islamic shari'ah, maintaining that Islam is the source of legislation. Along this line, in 1940 the Iraqi 'Abd al-Rahman al-Bazzaz condemned those who disown shari'ah from the constitution of their country and confirmed the doctrine that Islamic legislation copes with evolution and does not deny canonical change. It is distinct from other modern laws and goes beyond them, thanks to its intrinsic merits. The way to overcome the inferiority afflicting the Arab-Muslim nation is by establishing a strong modern state that believes in Islamic morals: a Muslim state without priesthood; a socialist state without extremisms, like communism. It should be a consultative state, free of the hypocrisy of democratism and immune to anarchy (Jadaane, 1981: 361-2). Al-Bazzaz recognised that establishing such unity was difficult and that the position of the Caliph could possibly become similar to that of the Pope in Catholic Christianity, which would be unacceptable to the Muslim community. In addition, the Caliphate, despite its deep roots as an Islamic system, is among the precepts of religion which are liable to change and replacement by another system when agreed upon by the nation, for shura and the consensus of the nation form the basis in this question (ibid.: 363).

'Allal al-Fasi, the historic leader of the Istiqlal Party in Morocco, agrees in general terms with the thesis of al-Bazzaz. He condemns what he stigmatises as the new *Isra'iliyyat* which appeared when 'Ali 'Abd al-Raziq called for the isolation of the state from religion. Al-Fasi stresses that religion cannot be put outside the domain of socio-political life, for such a separation would imply the estrangement of 'the highest ideal which Islamic shari'ah lays down for people', and that is 'the realization of the divine will to build life on this earth and achieve justice among people' (al-Fasi, n.d.: 157). This means that legislation in the state necessarily stems from the spirit of Islamic shari'ah and its rules. In other words, the Muslim must produce the laws which he is to obey, making use, in particular, of the general rules of *istihsan* and *masalih mursalah* which open the door to legislative progress (ibid. 159).

The serious role in legislation assigned by al-Fasi to the Muslim individual is a counterpart to another role, no less serious, in the relationship between the state and nation. For if God enjoys the ultimate sovereignty and order in the ruling system, then it is equally true that political and practical sovereignty is left to the people who are entitled to elect and dismiss legislators and members of the government. In a word, ordinance is for God, power is for the nation. The constitution of the state must be in accordance with the principles and rules of the shari'ah (ibid.: 38, 315-16).

The state is Islamic when its laws conform to the shari'ah or when they derive, partially or totally, from its maxims and rules. This point was well discussed by 'Abd al-Hamid Mutawalli, a professor of constitutional law, when he confronted a controversial item in the Egyptian Constitution, namely whether 'the basic rules of the Islamic shari'ah are the only source of legislation' or 'are just a source among others' (Mutawalli, 1977).

Professor Mutawalli naturally addressed two other questions first, namely, is Islam a religion and a state as well, and is there a system of government in Islam: Caliphate or otherwise? His answer to the first question is a compromise between the two well-known contrasting opinions: firstly, that of 'Ali 'Abd al-Raziq holding that Islam is only a religion, and secondly, the doctrine which maintains that Islam is both a religion and a state. Mutawalli finds that both doctrines tend to exaggeration and inaccuracy. To put the question in the form, is Islam a religion and a state, is erroneous. To answer it negatively would lead to a fallacy and the denial of historical facts, whereas to give an affirmative answer would encourage the belief that Islam came with a complete ruling system and this is, in fact, uncertain. A valid question would be whether Islam contains the general basis for a ruling system in the state. There can be no dispute about this. The Quran professed shura, freedom, equality, justice and other principles pertaining to government. Such principles are valid for all humanity, irrespective of time and place. The Quran introduces them in general terms, i.e. they are pliable in form and content, susceptible to modifications according to the sort of milieu and age in which they are to be applied. In this connection, the Quran does not disclose details nor particular facts; there is no mention in it of the forms of principles, which could vary with time and place (ibid.: 104-5).

Thus, the final answer given by Mutawalli is that Islam is a religion and a state, not based on a specific system of government, but on general principles of government, applicable in various times and places. The Caliphate system is not a principle of government in Islam, but only one form, and particularly a form providing a head of state (ibid.: 153). Its concern is not with faith, but with temporal jurisprudence (ibid.: 152). The instatement of a Caliphate (in the form visualised by Islamic jurisprudence experts) is considered to be in our time, like consensus, a virtual impossibility. Moreover, the establishment of such a system in our day and age would lead to an embarrassment which Islam would rather see the Muslims spared (ibid.: 163).

But coming back to the question which aroused a good deal of argument, namely, whether the principles of shari'ah form 'the main source of legislation' or only 'one main source', Mutawalli finds that these principles are capable of development and can meet the needs of people and of sound government under varied temporal and geographical conditions. As sublime principles, capable of building up a great civilisation and of filling the needs of legislation and culture, they demand adoption as the basis for the constitution (ibid.: 245). Mutawalli finds that this formula leaves room for reference to other legal sources in planning legislation for the modern state. In my opinion, it is an inclination towards the legislative tendency which is an attempt to follow a middle course between the two sides in dispute: Islam as a religion and Islam as a religion and a state.

The other aspect of the thesis and the antithesis is what I call the humanistic aspect. This is represented by Muhammad Ahmad Khalafallah in a book published (in Arabic) in 1973 entitled *The Quran and the State*, and by Muhammad 'Amarah in his *Islam and Religious Power*. Both men are of the opinion that Islam does not carry a specific political system. The former believes that questions of government are left by God's authorisation to man and his commitment to public good. The latter calls for a distinction, not a separation, between religion and state in Islam and feels government should be left in the hands of man. Both opinions lead to the view that the state is national in nature, committed to the rulings of shari'ah, but that, in the human field, legislation is effected through the will and power of the community.

On the question of 'the Quranic state', Muhammad Ahmad Khalafallah has this to say:

> Concerning the formation of the nation and the establishment of the state, the Holy Quran draws only broad guidelines which safeguard against error and guide along the right path, the path of right, justice and public good. The Holy Quran has left to man the details and things affected by time and place (Khalafallah, 1973: 3-4).

The root of this opinion is that Islam is based on two major elements: religious faith and actual practice. The former is concerned with belief in one God, his Angels, Books, Messengers and the Day of Judgement. It is a permanent state of belief, not liable to change. Actual practice has two aspects: a religious life represented by acts of worship, performed in accordance with what God demanded of man after some deleterious aspects of earlier religions were abolished and the sound ones endorsed by Islam; and a civil life represented by matters that are changeable because they are connected with man who is not eternal or everlasting, but changeable (ibid.: 33).

The aim of Islam is to purify souls and rid minds of superstition, to liberate man from man, clearing the hearts of people to help them behave well in life and achieve perfection and happiness, so that the nation will be 'the best nation among mankind'. This depends on its ability to order the doing of good and the prevention of evil, i.e. the realisation of public good or the good of humanity.

Khalafallah asserts that the legislative institution set up by the Prophet was fully committed to the system of shura defined by the Quran ('and consult them in matters'). He also points out that

> in the time of the Prophet, there were two powers of legislation: that of the Creator, and that of the Prophet and the aldermen of Islam. Each of these powers had its own field of action. That of divine power was in portraying divinity, explaining religious beliefs and marking what is religiously taboo or otherwise; the field of human power, in the hands of the Prophet and his aldermen, dealt with questions of religion, politics, economics, administration, security and war (ibid.: 58).

Religious questions are a divine affair in which human beings have no say. Worldly questions, on the other hand, such as the policies of the nation, are delegated by God to Muslims on the basis of a consultative government committed to realising the public good in a framework of justice, equality and common interest: the shura system. By delegating this system to them, 'He has given us full freedom and independence in our worldly affairs and social interests' (ibid.: 68).

Legislative power lies with the councillors and aldermen, that is, the legislative body which the nation freely chooses on the basis of general elections, in which some members represent constituencies while others are chosen by technical and professional institutions. These free individuals, chosen by the nation, form a People's Council, which ought to be obeyed in matters of common interest. Its authority is limited to worldly affairs. As for questions of worship and religious beliefs, these matters concern God and his Messenger alone (ibid.: 75).

The question of choosing the head of state is left to the Muslim community to decide according to circumstances. That is to say, it is a question of ijtihad (ibid.: 134), which divine will does not touch. To Khalafallah's mind, the way of reaching the position of head of state is by election or choice, not appointment or regency in the manner of the Umayyads. The selection of the head of state by the majority of citizens in a public election is the best way to ensure stability of government. This would make revolt by the minority an unlikely event. To name the head of state Caliph or imam is a temporal consideration. It is our right to give the head of state whatever name we see fit in accordance with our own stage of civilisation. This is acceptable in religion, as it does not violate any text.

The Quranic state is a welfare state, concerned with directing the life of every member in the human community towards the achievement of public good, irrespective of sex, race, language or religion.

This is realised through land development and the use of its products to help the people. By changing the world and using it for the benefit of the people, it is possible to achieve a religious tie between God and man, represented from the beginning by the principle of Caliph delegation.

To say that the Quranic state is a welfare state also means it is a state based on equality, 'realising a large integration in the Islamic community at the expense of the rich for the benefit of the poor and needy' (ibid.: 173) and using the human mind and its readiness to build sovereignty and civilisation.

In the final analysis, how does Khalafallah's attitude differ from that of 'Ali 'Abd al-Raziq? Does he really make an attempt to mediate between 'Abd al-Raziq's thesis and its antithesis? It seems to me that there is a difference between the two which does not lie only in the peaceful, pious method of presentation which Khalafallah chooses, quite different from 'Abd al-Raziq's provocative method. The main difference lies in the face that Khalafallah recognises that the Quran laid out the guidelines of a government system and that God delegated to man the working out of the details. This is a new and novel idea, which cannot be found outside Khalafallah's thought. In all cases, it means that the rulings of the People's or Nation's Council, which represents the majority, are divine rulings and that the legislative body, whether we like it or not, speaks in the name of God. Perhaps this is the conciliatory point in Khalafallah's writings.

It is obvious that Muhammad Ahmad Khalafallah, in his *Quran and the State*, tried to avoid the pitfalls of 'Ali 'Abd al-Raziq's theory and did his best to get round them. Moreover, a close look at a later article by him, published in the *al-'Arabi* monthly, seems to indicate that he is aiming an answer at the new radical Islamic groups which demand a Caliphate system. This makes it difficult to see a real difference of opinion between the two men. In this article, Khalafallah frankly distinguishes between the system of prophethood and that of Caliphate. It is the same distinction previously made by Ibn Khaldun between Caliphate and kingship. Khalafallah considers prophethood a religious system, and asserts that it cannot in any way be a system of government: Muhammad the son of 'Abdullah was a prophet and a messenger of God and not a king or a head of state (an idea already presented by 'Ali 'Abd al-Raziq). The Caliphate is a system of government which can take forms that are suitable for modern times. But the Caliphate system cannot be a religious system since there is no text to support it. Its source is ijtihad, which means that the human mind is the author of the Caliphate system. If the government system in Islam has its source in ijtihad and not in a text, then the system is open to new ijtihad, since, as purely human reasoning, it is always liable to reconsideration. Therefore, religious groups should abandon the idea that the Caliphate is a religious system of government, and accept that the system of government in Islam is liable to new interpretations and ijtihad (Khalafallah 1984: 41-5).

Turning to Muhammad 'Amarah, we find that he is not far in his reasoning on this question from the ideas of Khalafallah. His main concern is to separate political power from religious aspects ('Amarah, 1980), to strip the ruler of the sanctity and infallibility implied in endorsing religious power (or the supremacy of the fiqh after the Shi'i style), and to emphasise the principle that power belongs to the nation only. He is adamant that the Islamic political heritage should distinguish between politics and religion, between a political group and a group of believers (ibid.: 111-12) and that anything beyond spreading the religious message is no longer religion but a form of politics, subject to reason, meditation and interpretation (ibid.: 131). He feels that Imam Qarafi decided upon this question by fully describing the distinction between the worldly and the religious, the judicial and the political.

He asserts that the theory of religious power is alien to Islam and that it penetrated Shi'i Islamic thought through the Persian Xerxian heritage (ibid.: 133). The new advocates of religious power among contemporary Muslims want the Islamic nation to inherit the backwardness, the despotism and the darkness which the Persians, the Byzantines and the Europeans suffered throughout the Middle Ages. Muhammad 'Amarah attacks the motto: rule is God's alone, saying that it deprives the nation of its political sovereignty (ibid.: 40) and Muslims of their human will. By offering rulers a divine right over them, it sets up a theocratic government, as desired by al-Mawdudi (ibid.: 46), and gives undue credence to the Shi'i vision of politics.

The real Islamic attitude, in 'Amarah's opinion, is that a separation of religion from the state is as much to be rejected as a union between religious and political powers. To draw a distinction between the two is a sound attitude. Islam, as a religion, has not specified a definite system of government for the Muslims, because that is left to be developed according to public interests and in the general frame of reference of the comprehensive rules set up by this religion (ibid.: 82). For him, the Islamic attitude boils down to two principles: the first is religion, revealed to us in the Quran, which we have to receive in a spirit of faith, with the help of the prophetic tradition and our own reason (which is God's agent in man); the second is what is worldly, judicial and political. These principles have to be dealt with through interpretation (ijtihad) and reasoning, provided the criterion and aim are the interests of the entire nation and the avoidance of possible harm, within the framework of the general directives and comprehensive rules prescribed by the Quran (ibid.: 17-18) and in the light of supreme human rules and ideals which may bring the Muslims closer to the achievement of the community they desire (ibid.: 18 and 83).

It is quite obvious that a rational human tendency influences 'Amarah's thought and that a preoccupation with the New Islam advocates who follow Khumayni and the Iranian Islamic revolution lurks behind his critique of religious power and his effort to disentangle Islam from any attempt to impose a uniquely radical religious character on its social and political systems and institutions. His view that reason is God's agent in man is comparable to Khalafallah's theory that God authorises man to implement worldly laws and systems.

In any case, one can finally say that the third alternative, generally speaking, is more acceptable to enlightened Muslims in modern times. It is an attitude which avoids the extremes of temporal radicalism, on the one hand, and saves Islam from slipping into the labyrinth of adventurous experiments on the other. It is also a natural attitude for states based on Islamic communities that cherish an Islamic heritage. Undoubtedly, radical Muslims may see in this attitude a type of leniency which should not be allowed. But the fact is that this question will always remain open to discussion and interpretation, especially when viewed in its highly complex framework, and when the paths of action taken are strewn with fatal dangers. I may finally add that what is more important than forming an Islamic state and what should come prior to any consideration is to provide the educational, spiritual, intellectual, economic and social conditions needed to implement the terms of humanistic Islamic life. The road to that objective is undoubtedly long, but to take a short cut preferred by our ideal desires may not be the best way to reach 'the cursed tree' and climb it. A union between the formula of 'no salvation except through the Islamic state' and the other formula of 'no salvation except through Islam' is, undoubtedly, a dangerous indication of impatience rather than a response to the real requirements of Islamic revelation.

6

Al-Watan and *Al-Umma* in Contemporary Arab Use

Said Bensaid

The appearance of new concepts at a certain point in time and in a particular scientific field constitutes an original event, usually foreshadowing the rise of a new scientific theory. This is true not only of the history of exact sciences, but also, to a considerable degree, of the history of political thought since the seventeenth century. The latter owes its modernity to the appearance of a set of concepts that were totally new, such as 'people' and 'citizen', 'social contract' and 'civil society', 'nation' and 'fatherland'.

In Spinoza's view (1981: 384), it was not possible for the notion of nation to take on the definite and permanent form which it has acquired in Western political thought since the beginning of the eighteenth century without first condemning and abolishing the notion of paternal royal authority, which regarded the king's subjects as legal minors. As Gérard Mairet (1981: 60) put it, 'the concept of nation was a revolutionary notion', perhaps because it meant the abolition of absolute monarchic power and its replacement by the power of the people.

This revolution not only marks the birth of contemporary political philosophy, but also gives the latter the characteristics which distinguish it from its previous counterparts up to the seventeenth century. By transforming the members of a society into subjects (i.e. totally submissive masses), the theory of divine right barred the notions of nation and fatherland from medieval political thought.

Parliamentary representation, political pluralism, and the various modes of sharing and controlling power constitute the main characteristics of political life in Western societies. The rise of this political life is to a great extent linked to and determined by the various meanings conveyed by such notions as nation, fatherland, citizen and so on. In fact, one might suggest that the Western mind operates within a well-defined philosophical-political framework of its own making, and that its evolution within that framework is to a great degree determined by the manner in which those notions correlate and interact with each other.

If this is the case with respect to contemporary Western political thought, what can we say with regard to its Arab counterpart? What can we say about the notions of citizen, fatherland, and nation in contemporary Arab use? Does the mere occurrence of these terms reflect some kind of crucial difference between the consciousness of the Arab in the past and his view of political life today?

THE NOTIONS OF UMMA AND WATAN IN CLASSICAL ARAB CULTURE

In his book, *Az-Zahir fi ma'ani Kalimat an-Nas* (fourth century AH), Ibn al-Anbari notes that the term *umma* (nation) occurs in the speech of the Arabs in eight different senses (as-Sayyid 1984: 43-4), which we may summarise as follows, because he mixes them up:
(i) the term umma may be used to denote:
(a) A community, or group of people, as in the following Quranic verse: 'And when he (Moses) came unto the water of Midian, he found there *a group of people*, watering' (XXVIII: 23).
(b) A religion, as the following Quranic verse illustrates: 'We found our fathers following a *religion*, and we are following their footprints' (XLIII: 23).
(c) Time, as in the following verse: 'And if we delay for them the doom until a reckoned *time*, they surely say: What withholdeth it?' (XI: 8).
(ii) The remaining five meanings of this term all involve one referent: the individual human being, denoting either physical characteristics (e.g. *al-umma* = *al-qama* = stature), or moral attributes (e.g. a godly man with exemplary behaviour), as can be read in the Quran: 'Abraham was an *umma* obedient to Allah, by nature upright, and he was not of the idolaters' (XVI:

120). Finally, the term umma denotes uniqueness (e.g. *ar-rajulu al-umma* = a man who is unique in his genre), or an original type.

This list, however, is not exhaustive. According to Ibn Manzur, the term umma can be used to denote a number of additional meanings which are unrelated to the notion 'man', such as 'way' or 'path'.

The task of exhausting the semantics of the term becomes even more complex and difficult when we attempt to survey its different uses in the writings of ancient Arab jurists, philosophers, and historians like al-Mawardi, al-Farabi, and Ibn Khaldun.

By contrast, the semantic field of the term *watan* (or fatherland, *patrie*), is much narrower than that of umma. On the one hand, the term watan occurs less frequently in ancient Arabic literature, and on the other hand, it has undergone no major semantic changes.

According to Ibn Manzur's (*Lisan al-'Arab*, Vol. XIII: 451), watan is 'the house in which you live; one's residence or native place; the home of sheep and cattle; the place where these animals lie down to rest'. In a strictly linguistic sense, the term watan refers to a 'place' which may be either for a human or an animal. In this sense, therefore, the term involves the notions of choice and voluntarism. As derivatives, the verb forms *watana* and *awtana* both denote the idea of choosing a place of residence; in other words to take up one's residence in a given place. The same meaning is conveyed by the verb form *istawtana*, thus the expression *istawtana al-ard* means 'to settle a country' or 'to live permanently in a place'.

There is a wide difference between the meaning of watan as used by Ibn Manzur and the meanings which the term conveys in contemporary Arab use, where both watan and its derivative form, *wataniyya* (patriotism), are highly charged emotionally. Besides referring to a national territory itself, in contemporary Arab use the term implies the existence of linguistic, racial and cultural ties between different groups and individuals living in the same geographical area.

As pointed out in Ibn Manzur's lexicon (al-Baghdadi, 1982: 270), the only strong bond which the Muslim Arab is ever conscious of is his sense of belonging to the land of Islam. In Ibn Manzur's view, the land of Islam is represented by 'the Muslim community' which necessarily constitutes one umma (or nation), which includes every country in which Islam is freely accepted as a religion and where Islamic law reigns over Muslim as well as over non-Muslim citizens who enjoy protection in return for paying *Jizya* (capital tax). In short, the land 'where the Sunnis are not oppressed by heretics', as the Muslim theologian, 'Abd al-Qahir al-Baghdadi, has put it.

NOTIONS OF UMMA AND WATAN IN THE CONTEMPORARY ARAB CONTEXT

A former Syrian leader, 'Abd al-Rahman ash-Shahbandar (Nassur, 1967: 141), noted that Ibn Manzur's concept of the term fatherland (watan) prevailed in the Arab individual's consciousness from the Middle Ages until the beginning of the twentieth century when such terms as 'caliphate' and 'imamate' had more appeal to people than the terms watan and *sha'b* (people). Hicham Djait (1972: 482) makes a similar observation with respect to the early stages of the Algerian resistance against French colonisation. He shows how the term *jihad* (holy war) proved to be the only slogan capable of mobilising popular forces to combat the French occupation at a time when the 'Algerian fatherland' was a totally new notion, as yet without emotional impact.

According to Adib Nassur (1967: 104-5), the Syrian Constituent Assembly, which met in Damascus in 1928, rejected the following oath-taking formula, 'I hereby swear by God and by my honour that I will be loyal to the fatherland and will defend and protect the rights and aspirations of the nation'. It did so on the grounds that the term fatherland (al-watan) was ambiguous, and that the fatherland to which they wanted to swear loyalty was still unknown: 'One does not take the oath to be loyal to a fatherland whose boundaries are unknown' (Nassur, 1967: 105).

This refusal to swear loyalty to the watan should be explained in terms of the semantic ambiguity of the term. This ambiguity reveals the Arab's emotional ambivalence between his desire to accept the notion of fatherland in its contemporary sense and his tendency to reject the idea of geographical division imposed by the advocates of this modern conception of the world. Acceptance of the modern concept of fatherland reveals an attitude which is contrary to the idea of one great nation, as realised under the Ottoman Caliphate. The notion of watan was used to justify rebellion against the Turkish occupation, even though the occupier professed the same religion as the occupied. Therefore, the Syrian deputy who refused to take the oath did not ask, for instance, 'What is a watan?' He simply said that the watan to which he was required to swear his loyalty was ambiguous and excessively vague. He did not recognise the boundaries established by the colonial West, and he still dreamed of the idea of one great Arab nation which, instead of yielding to Ottoman rule, would rebel against it. Nevertheless, the Syrian Constituent Assembly finally agreed on the following formula: to remain loyal to the *national cause*, to protect and defend *the rights of the umma*, and to realise its aspirations (emphasis mine).

The 'national cause' and the 'nation's rights', as well as 'nationalism', 'equality', and 'liberty', are all new notions, and the terms which express them are not familiar in classical Arabic rhetoric. Here one senses the influence of new ideas which have been introduced through student missions, and through Western colonisation.

This points to the importance of a diachronic approach in the study of such notions as umma and watan in contemporary Arab use. At the same time, the course of philosophical history in the Mashreq is different from that in the Maghreb. In Egypt, Iraq and Syria, there has been a kind of progressive evolution from religious awareness (pan-Islamic) to national awareness (nationalism), which culminated in Arab nationalism (or pan-Arabism). Adherence to pan-Islamism or to pan-Arabism has resulted in different conceptions of the notions of umma and watan. The situation is totally different with respect to the Maghreb, for while Turkish influence was either limited (as in Algeria and Tunisia), or non-existent (as in Morocco), there was no antagonism between the religious movement (pan-Islamism) on the one hand, and Arab nationalism (pan-Arabism) on the other. Nor was there any clash between these two and the national liberation movements.

In contemporary Arab thought, three major views underlie the systematic use of political notions: nationalism, pan-Arabism, and pan-Islamism. However, the distinction between the three is not always clear-cut. Furthermore, one finds exceptional uses of the notions of umma and watan, which cannot be included in any of the three views. However, given the fact that these exceptions are found in a large body of powerful texts, we believe that they should be fully taken into account.

With respect to the first difficulty, sometimes the writings of the same Arab thinker can fit into more than one, if not into all, of the three currents. For example, in his militant and patriotic writings, 'Allal al-Fasi appears as a nationalist thinker. Yet, the same author, and sometimes in the same work, appears as a pan-Islamist thinker whose views converge perfectly with those of Muhammad 'Abduh, or as a good example of a contemporary Islamist thinker, as in his work, *Maqasid ash-Shari'ah al-Islamiyya*.

In the same manner, we find that 'Abd an-Nasir (Nasser), who is commonly viewed as an eminent advocate of pan-Arabism, is no more than a local nationalist, especially in his *Falsafat ath-Thawra* (The Philosophy of Revolution). What seems to be an acceptable, practical solution is to consider a particular author not from the limited point of view of his use of umma or watan in a restricted context, insulated from its general orientation, but rather to consider the crucial question as posed by the author himself; in other words by taking into consideration the central problem in his work at the most crucial and influential stage in his thought process. What interests me most in 'Allal al-Fasi is the fact that he wrote the annals of national liberation movements in the Maghreb and that, furthermore, he presented a certain picture of his own watan as he saw it in the aftermath of independence. I shall therefore regard his Islamism as an addition to his nationalism, not the opposite.

Likewise, I am not interested in Nasser's insistence on watan in the sense of Egypt, or in the fact that Egypt was the focus of his thought (though this was perhaps the case), which fits him in the nationalist category. I am concerned with discerning how nationalism can constitute a specific type of pan-Arabism, distinct from the one represented by Michel 'Aflaq, for example. To overcome this difficulty, I propose to consider the general context in which the notion(s) under discussion occur(s) rather than considering just one specific aspect of the use of such notions.

With respect to the exceptional cases, all the texts which exhibit this difficulty belong to the nineteenth century. Essentially, this means that we are concerned with a period which is chronologically prior to contemporary nationalist, Islamist, or pan-Arab thought. A brief survey of those texts which best represent that period will bring to light the various senses in which a given political notion was used in the early days of the Arab renaissance. This will enable us to understand better how violently or spontaneously the notion passed into contemporary Arab use. Most scholars who have studied contemporary Arab thought and attempted some sort of classification have not found room for the authors of these texts, in spite of their great value.

This survey must necessarily begin with the work of Rifa'a at-Tahtawi. This Azhari scholar, who was appointed by Muhammad 'Ali as imam and religious guide of the first student mission to France, 'became one of the great channels through which the principles of the French Revolution and of its great thinkers passed into the Mashreq' (Khuri, 1943: 89).

Unlike ancient travellers who wrote down their fantastic experiences to thrill the reader, at-Tahtawi recorded his experience in France with the aim of inciting 'the land of Islam to acquire foreign sciences, arts and techniques' which were highly developed in France, while 'in Egypt, they are either insignificant or non-existent' (at-Tahtawi, 1973: 11-23). He was eyewitness to the events and riots which took place in Paris in 1830, when the King of France violated the pact which he had concluded with the French nation, and the French people rose to defend *la patrie* against the threats it was facing as a result of the king's conduct. During those events, Tahtawi was also able to acquaint himself with the writings of Rousseau and Montesquieu, reading extensively about the French Revolution and its aspects, both wonderful and horrifying. Readers of at-Tahtawi's works hear the echo of all this in his writings (especially in *The Paris Tour*) and are struck by the novelty of his language, characterised by the use of many new notions, such as fatherland, fellow-countrymen, citizen, patriotism, etc., expressing a new mode of thought. Its very resonance was totally new to the Arab ear.

Although at-Tahtawi does not seem to depart much from Ibn Manzur's lexicon when he writes, for example, that 'one's watan is the home in which one was born and brought up, the home of one's family and relatives, the land whose soil, food, and air have contributed to one's growth' (at-Tahtawi, 1973: 429), it is nevertheless possible to discern many additions. These constitute a clear demarcation line between two distinct views. Only since at-Tahtawi's time is it common to read that 'fellow-

155

countrymen are always united, sharing the same language system, having the same ruler, and obeying the same laws under the same political system' (ibid.: 433). Before him membership consisted in belonging to the Islamic community, or to the land of Islam, regardless of language and political differences. As ad-Duri (1984: 143) has pointed out, at-Tahtawi must have been influenced by the notion of the national state. It was simply impossible to read in earlier Islamic political literature anything similar to the view that the members of one fatherland are 'in relation to one another, like the members of one family, as if the watan were the home of their parents, the very place in which they were born and brought up'.

According to at-Tahtawi, provenance from one and the same geographical area is an important unifying factor. Also, the notion of watan becomes the basis for such derived attributes as *watani* (in the ambiguous sense of patriot, patriotic, national, nationalist), or in the sense of compatriot, or citizen. In ancient Arab epistemologico-political theory, neither the root watan nor the attributive adjectives derived from it had the meanings which they have today. In at-Tahtawi's view, the primary characteristic of a compatriot is that 'he/she enjoys the rights of citizenship, the most significant of such rights being *total freedom* in society'. Finally,

> the citizen will not be considered to be free unless he submits himself to *the law of the country*, and helps in its application. The individual citizen's submission to the national law necessarily entails that, in return, the country guarantees the citizen's *civil rights* as well as certain municipal privileges and services (at-Tahtawi 1973). (emphasis added).

What sounded totally new to the Arab ear in all this are not simply the expressions 'national law', 'civil rights', and 'municipal privileges', but also, and more importantly, the term freedom. According to Nicholas Ziadeh (1967: 14):

> The term freedom is used in Islamic religious literature in connection with fate, choice and unrestraint of man. But what reached our country at that time (19th century) was the *civil meaning* of the term: i.e. freedom in its socio-political sense, seen in terms of the individual's relationship with

authority and society, and also in terms of direct relationships between individuals themselves.

At-Tahtawi considers freedom to be a license to exercise a permissible activity in the absence of unpermissible prohibition or illegal opposition, whether such freedom is natural, behavioural, religious, or political (1973: 373). The notion of watan acquired a new dimension and became connected to nationalism and patriotism. At-Tahtawi writes that

> the devoted nationalist is the one who sacrifices everything, even his life, to protect his *watan* against any potential harmdoer, just as a father would protect his child from evil ... Therefore, the citizens' intentions regarding their *watan* should always be virtuous and honourable (1973: 433).

The difference is clear with the religious zeal which regards the individual Muslim as one who is attached to the home of Islam, wherever on earth that home may be, without taking into consideration linguistic, historical, or geographical ties. According to ad-Duri (1984: 144), 'At-Tahtawi's notion of nationalism is a combination of modern and ancient notions taken from the historical and cultural heritage'. However, the fact remains that at-Tahtawi makes use of a vocabulary which is totally modern with respect to his national cultural heritage. Duri's description of at-Tahtawi applies even better to a latter Arab thinker, Khayr ad-Din at-Tunsi, who re-employed many of at-Tahtawi's ideas (Hourani n.d.: 144-5).

At-Tahtawi was fully aware of the novelty of the notion of watan and its derivatives, especially with regard to his earlier education. His writings reflect the painful experience he had to go through in his attempt to subject the ancient Arabic vocabulary to his will in order to express new political notions. They also reflect his great interest in, and unreserved acceptance of, new ideas acquired through his personal reading.

Among authors using the notion of watan in a way which cannot be classified under any of the three suggested types (the nationalist, the pan-Arabist, and the pan-Islamic), we should also include Adib Ishaq. After listing the diverse manifestations of the 'winds of the French Revolution' in contemporary Arab political thought, consisting of the appearance of new political notions, Ra'if Khuri (1943: 127) concludes: 'We do not know of any leading Arab literary figure or thinker whose attempt to investigate the notion of watan can equal that made of Adib Ishaq'.

In Ishaq's writings, the Arabic language seems to have become more compliant and flexible in expressing political notions brought home by the 'winds of the French Revolution'. The notion of watan, for example, becomes more strongly linked to the notion of political freedom, and the author's handling of nationalism increases both in force and intensity. New and precise elements are added to make At-Tahtawi's definition of watan more accurate. 'It is the individual's place of residence. Traditionally, it is the country in which the great majority of a nation (umma) has struck roots and grown in number through the process of creation' (Ishaq, 1978: 74). The definition of watan as 'one territory with well-known boundaries' is replaced by an alternative definition in terms of 'territory in which the majority of a nation is firmly established'.

But the watan is not merely a home, or any dwelling place, as it is defined linguistically. Beyond that, it is, as political philosophers define it, 'the place you descend from, toward which you have well-defined obligations, in which you have sacred rights, and in which you, your kin and your property are secure'. The watan whose members are not respected is not worthy of esteem. In fact, such a watan is impoverished and despised. 'The least one can say of a habitation in which the inhabitant has no rights and feels insecure about his life and his property is that it is a refuge for the weak and the deprived, who have no alternative choice.' Quoting La Bruyère, Adib Ishaq writes: 'What use is it to me to have a great *watan*, if in it, I am unhappy, despised, living in perpetual humiliation, misery, and fear of imprisonment?' Consequently, a watan is meaningless unless it is a place where one can live with dignity and respect. This requires that the citizens be free, and that their freedom be assured both in theory and practice. As La Bruyère put it, 'there is no *patrie* where there is despotism'. Or, as the ancient Romans defined it, 'one's fatherland is that in which one enjoys political rights and performs political duties' (Ishaq, 1978: 66-7). This definition of the notion of watan has been taken up by many Arab philosophers. Muhammad 'Abduh, for example, adopted and publicised it through his writings.

There are three aspects of the use of the notion of watan for which we find no reference in either at-Tahtawi's or Ishaq's works or in the works of any of the other pioneers of contemporary Arab political thought. First, there is no mention of the watan which faces the threat of foreign occupation, or which is effectively under foreign occupation. Consequently, all that is said about nationalism by both at-Tahtawi and Ishaq is remote from the type of discourse which arouses citizens to resist a foreign enemy. The watan is seen simply as one's country of origin, whether it be Syria, Egypt, or Iraq. Secondly, there is no scope for a great watan expanding beyond the boundaries of one's province. Nineteenth-century Arab thinkers were familiar with the notion of *al-Watan al-'Arabi* (the Arab fatherland). This notion is referred to in their writings by the ambiguous term umma, without making clear, however, the distinction between the meaning of this term when it occurs unmodified, and its meaning when it is used with the pre-modifier Islam or Arab. The meaning of nation (umma) attributed by these authors is different from the meanings it acquires in the works of Rashid Rida and Sayyid Qutb, for example. In the former author's writings, it occurs essentially in the sense of fatherland (watan) which, though it apparently includes the ancient meaning conveyed by the expression Islamic nation, does not suggest any of the various meanings expressed by the notion Arab nation circulating since the beginning of the present century. It is the latter which constitutes the third aspect of use that is lacking in the writings of both at-Tahtawi and Ishaq.

The absence of these three aspects of the use of the notion fatherland can be explained by the lack of national, pan-Arab or pan-Islamic awareness in nineteenth-century Arab political thought. Because these three types of awareness determine both the different forms of use of the notions umma and watan and their different meanings, and since such types of awareness were alien to the pioneer Arab thinkers, the meaning conveyed by the notion of nation and fatherland in the writings of these pioneers remain unclassifiable.

THE NATIONAL TYPE

Our investigation of the use of the notions umma and watan has shown that the latter is by far the more prominent. The reason for this seems to reside in the fact that, while it sought its own course, contemporary Arab nationalist thought has had to resist two powerful currents, both striving to contain and subsume it. On the one hand, there was the pan-Islamist movement which called for a kind of Islamic renaissance, together with unification of political power around the exhausted Ottoman caliphate or around a central Islamic consultative system. In both cases, the movement's slogan was the Islamic umma. On the other hand, there was the pan-Arab movement which, whether seeking autonomy from Ottoman domination or calling the Arabs to resist Western colonisation, always brandished the slogan of the Arab umma. In resisting the two movements' attempts to encompass it, the nationalist movement held on to the slogan: watan. It follows, therefore, that Arab nationalist discourse brought out and reinforced the notion of watan. In fact, we may even make the assertion that the use of the notion of fatherland in its contemporary sense is to be found only in nationalist ideology (the expression Arab nation (umma) will be discussed later on).

According to Adib Nassur (1967: 43), 'About mid-nineteenth century, political thought in Egypt moved away from the atmosphere of religious fervor, broke with the Ottoman League, and shifted towards a regional type of nationalism'. He further observes that 'both religious and nationalist movements coexisted side by side for some time until the nationalist movement gained precedence just before World War One'. The Maghreb was alien to this ambivalence between religious sentiment which favoured allegiance to the Ottoman League, and the regional nationalist movement, which called for resistance against that same Ottoman League. In Morocco as well as in the rest of the Greater Maghreb, national unity was given priority over religious unity.

This priority constitutes one of the most striking features of contemporary Arab nationalism. Abdullah an-Nadim emphasised it just before the turn of the century. He once wrote in the al-Ustadh newspaper:

Sons of Egypt, let the Muslim among you turn to his Muslim brother in a spirit of religious solidarity. Then let the Muslim turn to the Copts and the Israelites and, together, create national unity. But let everybody be one man with one sole objective: to preserve Egypt for Egyptians.

He goes on to express his desire to see the Muslims and the Copts 'like members of one family, helping each other to submit, exchanging views on matters concerning their watan, and assisting each other to defend it against unexpected attacks'. When a Muslim charitable organisation opened a school for needy Muslim and Christian pupils, an-Nadim spoke at the opening ceremony, expressing his belief that the school would 'teach children how to be true patriots without being religiously or racially fanatic, and would also teach them how to love their watan and all of mankind' (ad-Duri, 1984: 145).

A new conception of the priority of national solidarity over Islamic solidarity was to be formulated half a century later by 'Allal al-Fasi. In his view, no action for the liberation of the colonised Arab countries could be undertaken within a pan-Islam or pan-Arab framework. On the one hand, the struggle for national independence requires special emphasis on and accentuation of national identity, whereas the advocacy of Islamic solidarity has the effect of submerging and suffocating such identity. On the other hand, the creation of an Islamic League necessitates religious reform and great effort in the field of legislation as well as close co-ordination between liberation movements, whereas pan-Islamism requires a kind of union within a league. This, however, makes linguistic, cultural and civilisational differences, which constitute the prerequisites of national identity, abstract. For these reasons, 'Allal al-Fasi (n.d.a: 136-7; b: 74) concludes that

> none of these things can be achieved under an Islamic government unless this new type of institution emanates from qualified deputies within a Council to be selected by the nation in such a way that it becomes the supreme legislative body. This means that it is necessary to adopt a constitutional form of government, based on the rule of the people through competent elected representatives. However, this goal will not be achieved unless Muslim countries are liberated from foreign domination, both physical and moral. Therefore, action for independence is a necessary condition for the recovery of freedom which is essential for assuming responsibility.

The view that national independence is a condition prior to any collective Islamic action, even though the country seeking such freedom belongs to the Islamic world, confirms in a different manner and under different circumstances, the emphasis on the priority of national over pan-Islamic action, which prevailed in Egypt at the beginning of the twentieth century.

Nationalism involves identity. It seeks to exhibit national characteristics, to emphasise them, and to deepen people's awareness of them. It is a response to a provocation, or to a series of provocations, aimed at dissolving the national personality and distorting its features. Therefore, nationalist talk contains a set of self-defence mechanisms developed to safeguard this personality, to assert its historical depth and authenticity, to demonstrate its homogeneity and strength and to prove its dynamism and effective presence in spite of all attempts to assimilate or destroy it. This identity, or personality, always bears the name watan. According to 'Allal al-Fasi (n.d. a);

> The second Phoenician war epitomises nationalism in its most modern form since all Mahgrebians became united around one national banner to defend a watan defined by its geographical boundaries. This watan was bounded by the sea on all sides, except the Sahara, which provided a link between this watan and the homeland of the Phoenician brotherhood, paving the way for Islam and the Arabic language.

The fatherland is also known by its moral personality. In al-Fasi's view, the Moroccan citizen has a deep sense of belonging to the Arab world; nevertheless, he does not accept being 'placed last in the Arab convoy'. Moroccans firmly believe in the strong ties which bind them to Islam and the Muslims, but their awareness of this moral personality (i.e. the fatherland) is much stronger. Speaking for Moroccans, al-Fasi writes: 'We Moroccans, for example, have never lived the experience of permanently following a spiritual power based outside our own country', pointing out that 'such is our character and our history. So it was during the pre-Islamic era, and so it has been over since we chose Islam as our religion.'

Another distinguishing feature is the link which the watan establishes among its citizens, namely the bond of nationalism or patriotism. 'Patriotism constitutes the noblest of all ties that can exist between individuals, and the firmest basis on which powerful states are founded.' As Mustapha Kamal (Khalafallah *et al.*, 1982: 87) put it, 'Europe's civilisation is the fruit of patriotism'.

This bond is the outcome of the effective interaction throughout national history of powerful and dynamic factors. According to 'Allal al-Fasi, such factors

consist of human interactions whereby worldly materialism blends with human spirituality so that the whole forms an abstract notion, the notion of genuine patriotism which values people not on the grounds of their racial, linguistic or religious differences, but rather on the basis of their individual ability to live in harmony within their watan on the one hand, and to adjust their outward behaviour to suit the environment in which they live (al-Fasi n.d., b: 95).

True patriotism is a passion which grows in the individual's psyche and whose flame flares up whenever a calamity befalls the fatherland. In al-Fasi's view (n.d., b: 95), love of the watan is not tied to one's childhood or even to one's racial or family relations since 'it is possible for any human to become a citizen of any watan provided that he frees himself not of his blood or religious ties, but of his mentality which has been shaped by the various environmental influences of the country in which he was brought up'. In fact, 'Allal al-Fasi becomes rather mystical, using such expressions as 'the spirit of the age', 'the spirit of the earth', 'psychological archetype', etc., which make his views coincide with certain contemporary German metaphysical theses.

Nationalist thought adds a new element to the significance of the notion of watan. This new element is partly the result of 'the winds of the French Revolution', and partly the outcome of the various implications of nationalism with respect to contemporary institutional studies. The notion of watan does not refer only to the patriotic bond, nor to the citizens who are proud of belonging to a given geographical area. As Adib Ishaq repeatedly pointed out, the worth of a watan resides in its citizens, that is, in the people who are 'equal in rights and duties before their watan'. The totality of these citizens constitutes the people. Mustapha Kamel, for instance, used to recite whole paragraphs from Rousseau's *Social Contract*, and his views regarding Egypt were similar to Rousseau's views regarding France. In fact, were it not for the fear of departing from the objective we have set ourselves, which is to discuss only the notions of watan and umma, we could demonstrate how the meanings and implications generated by the use of the notion of people in contemporary Arab nationalist thought have little or no relation with the original meanings of the term. The term people has a new impact on the Arab ear. Even its sound is unfamiliar to the collective Arab emotional and cultural memory. Consider, for instance, the following set of questions and answers by the Egyptian nationalist leader Mustapha Kamel:

> Who constitutes the army? The people. Who constitutes the police and preserves order? The people. Who produces the goods and riches of Egypt? The people. Who feeds the eminent personalities, the nobility and the princes of Egypt? The people. Therefore, *the people are the backbone of the watan and the source of its prosperity, its glory, and its happiness* (Khuri, 1943: 245-6) (emphasis added).

This conception of the notion of people is something new; indeed, it is unusual. 'The people are the only real power, to whose will even the greatest and mightiest men submit' (ibid.: 246).

THE PAN-ARAB MODEL

Nationalism focuses on the notion of watan, with all its positive dimensions which contemporary political thought has constantly emphasised. The pan-Arab model, however, both reduces the scope of this notion and diminishes its significance. In general terms, pan-Arabism gives much more importance to the notion of nation (umma).

In the nationalist model, the term watan is used to refer to a specific geographical area that constitutes the homeland of citizens bound to each other by legal and emotional ties, and who belong to a sovereign state, or to a state which is struggling to recover its sovereignty. In the pan-Arab model, however, the term watan is used in the sense of union, or league. Legally speaking, the notion watan refers to a league comprising a group of sovereign states, with their respective citizens being identified in relation to their respective fatherlands. Consequently, the meaning of watan loses its precision and becomes somewhat obscure and abstract. It refers to one or several emotional ties. As Az-Zahrawi describes it, 'Our watan is our union because we either happen to be neighbours, or speak the same language, or have the same aspirations and interests' (ad-Duri, 1984: 176). Therefore, what is meant by watan is not a given geographical province, but rather a group of provinces that share the same boundaries. In this type of use, the term watan is singular in form, but plural in meaning and reference.

In fact, whether we focus on the works of earlier pan-Arabists (such as az-Zahrawi, 'Abd al-Ghani al-'Uraysi, and Najib 'Azuri) which dominated the earlier twentieth-century period when pan-Arabism had not yet become an established ideology, or consider the works of the great pan-Arabist theoreticians of the 1950s and 1960s (such as 'Aflaq and Nasser), it is clear that the notion of watan, or Arab watan, signifies, basically a geographical area and reflects a desire for unity more than it denotes the idea of natural ties as in the nationalist model.

According to Marlène Nasr (1981: 182), what is meant by the notion of Arab watan in Nasser's writings is, in fact, 'a geographical space, stretching from the Atlantic Ocean to the Gulf'. Nasr further points out that, although Nasser uses the notion of Arab territory, the former notion does not refer to any territory in particular.

Because pan-Arabist thought finds the notion of watan rather troublesome, it treats it as an ordinary word, or as a static unit. On the whole, as Nasr puts it, the concept of watan either becomes marginal (as in Nasser's writings, for instance), or simply disappears from use (as in Michel 'Aflaq's work).

There is a clear difference between Nasser's earlier works (best represented by *Falsafat ath-Thawra*) and his later works (represented by *al-Mithāq*, The Manifesto), in the sense that there is a clear movement from a nationalist position in the former to a pan-Arab position in the latter. This progression faithfully reflects Nasser's view of the matter, but what concerns us here is not the change itself, but rather the effect of the change on the use of the term watan.

In Nasser's *Falsafat ath-Thawra*, the term watan is used frequently to refer to Egypt. What Nasser calls an early stage of consciousness is a reference to his presence in Palestine fighting in the ranks of Arab armies. 'We were fighting a war in Palestine, but our minds were in Egypt. Our guns aimed at the enemy

165

who was facing us, but our hearts were hovering around our distant watan which we had left to the care of wolves' (n.d. a: 13-14). Any action for the liberation of Arab land caused an outburst of nationalist consciousness, that is, awareness of the existence of a territory with well-defined boundaries as an entity distinct from all other political entities. When Egyptian army officers were under siege in the Faluja zone, they used constantly to remind each other of the fact that their watan, too, was besieged by problems and traitors. Nasser also establishes a comparison between Faluja and Egypt, his besieged watan. In his assessment of both the July revolution and the army's performance, he writes: 'I have always believed in military service. The latter gives the soldier one sole duty: to die on the frontiers of the watan. So, why was our army compelled to operate in the watan's capital instead of at the front?' (Nasser, n.d. a: 23).

Thus, the watan has well-defined frontiers and, consequently, it has a land and a national territory. Also, the watan has a national capital in addition to a national army and other symbols of sovereignty. If we return to Nasser's own expressions, we find that the term watan is used to refer accurately to the small fatherland. However, when he talks about the great fatherland, the term watan not only loses its expressive and referential meanings, but is replaced by a new expression, i.e. Arab nation.

Pan-Arabist thought is dominated by one sole and constant dream, the dream of a single Arab state, or Arab unity. Theories of Arab unity may well differ on the issues of relationships between unity and freedom, or liberty and socialism, or even on the relationship between national (or regional) action and pan-Arab action. In fact, similar differences of opinion may arise concerning the method by which such a united state can be achieved. However, behind all these differences, there is always one constant element: the notion of an Arab umma. Many concepts have been used to define this notion; its role in the history of humanity, its enemies and problems, as well as its characteristics. These attempts have given birth to a new conception of the notion of nation, which indicates that the term is used in a specific sense in connection with modern Arab life.

A nation is an idea, a matter of will. According to 'Aflaq (n.d. a: 74):

166

A nation (umma) is not a matter of numbers, but an idea embodied in the totality of its members or in part of them. Therefore, there is no relation between this idea and the increase or decrease in the number of individuals, because a nation does not perish when its population decreases in number. Rather, it dies out if the idea itself ceases to exist among the population. The total number of people is not holy in itself; rather, its holiness depends on its ability to embody the idea of umma in the present or in the future.

Consequently, every member of the nation's population bears his share of this idea in his mind because 'the idea exists like a seed in every single individual of the nation's population'. All those who belong to the same nation are tied to each other by a strong bond. 'The terms nation (umma) and mother (*umm*) prove by virtue of their being derived from the same root, that the notion of nation is an extension of one's family — indeed, it is the bond of brotherhood par excellence' (al-Arsuzi, 1958: 7).

In pan-Arabism, umma is conceived of as a living entity possessing all the conditions and assets for real existence. 'A nation is a uterine experience', says al-Arsuzi, meaning that it is an extension of fetal life. Therefore, a nation has its specific needs which vary and change according to the different stages in its life and development. As Michel 'Aflaq puts it (n.d. a: 202), 'At a given stage in its life, a nation reaches a point of extreme awareness and concentration and becomes capable of expressing its deepest needs'. Because it is conceived of as a living entity, the umma is therefore compared to a human being. Consequently, political leaders speak of its 'heartbeats', its 'pulse' as well as its 'wounds' and 'feelings', as Marlène Nasr (1981: 139) observes in her study of Nasser's conception of pan-Arabism.

However, a nation is unlike any other living entity. Each umma has its specific characteristics which distinguish it from other nations. Arab nationalist thought tries hard to identify the aspects and features of such specificity. However, it should be noted that the Ba'th Party's ideology is entirely based on an attempt to theorise identity. The specificity of the Arab nation would fit well as a sub-title for al-Arsuzi's *For the Sake of a Renaissance*, the ideological manifesto of the Arab Ba'th Party (Carré, 1978).

In addition to specific needs and its sacred mission towards humanity, the Arab nation also has enemies who wish it ill. These enemies are tied to each other by fierce and terrible alliances directed against the aspirations of the Arab nation. The tripartite alliance consists of 'coloniser and reactionaries on the one side, and of Israel on the other,' says Nasser (Nasr, 1981: 168). The enemies of the Arab nation are those who try hard to prevent it from realising its primary and vital dream: to achieve Arab unity. These enemies have one goal: to weaken Arab unity by all possible means.

All these specificities, which constitute the basis of Arab nationalist thought, have generated the rather unstable and ambiguous notion of the Arab umma. If the notion of watan is most recurrent and prominent in nationalist talk, the notion of Arab umma is the keystone of Nasser's Arab nationalism. It alone covers 24 per cent of the total space occupied by Arab nationalist terminology.

THE ISLAMIC FUNDAMENTALIST MODEL

It will be obvious to the reader of contemporary Arab thought that the fundamentalist trend is marked by extreme sensitivity regarding politics, in the sense that politics is considered a reference for understanding and explaining the progress/backwardness dichotomy which constitutes one of the central issues in that thought. While non-fundamentalist thinkers have different views regarding the factors behind the progress of Western Europe, as opposed to the backwardness of the Arab world, the fundamentalist movement is almost unique in regarding the dichotomy as being due mainly to political factors. All fundamentalist literature insists that the West owes its progress to the supremacy of liberty and law and to a system of government which treats all members of society on an equal basis. Fundamentalist thinkers are unanimous in attributing the backwardness of the Arabs to dictatorships which spread ignorance and suppress individual freedoms. We are thus faced with a model which is totally different from the previous two models — the nationalist and the pan-Arab.

Sensitivity regarding politics finds its justification in the tradition in which fundamentalist consciousness was nurtured by the theologians. We know that Muslims are brought up in the belief that religion and worldly matters are so interlinked that the Muslim cannot distinguish between the two even in matters concerning government and political power.

The fact of linking civilisation with justice and security is something that is not specific to Ibn Khaldun, for other ancient Arab historians anticipated him by establishing a close link between the rule of great kings and the reign of justice and democracy.

The Azhari scholar, 'Abd al-Rahman al-Jabarti, who was an eye-witness of Napoleon's Egyptian campaign, was amazed not only at the degree of progress which the Occident had achieved in the fields of science and arts, but also, and more importantly, at its superiority in the field of justice and application of law (Louis 'Awad, 1969: 95). Also, what most attracted at-Tahtawi's attention, as he noted in his *Paris Tour*, was the reign of justice and the absence of arbitrary judgements. At-Tahtawi does not hide his admiration for the French people who, anxious to respect the pact they concluded with their king, did not hesitate to rebel when he violated that pact (at-Tahtawi, 1973: 201-33).

Earlier Islamic thinkers not only establish a close link between progress and justice, but also admit that Arab thinkers in general have learnt a valuable lesson from the Occident. As Rashid Rida puts it, 'The most important lesson the Arabs have learnt from the Europeans concerns the system of government; that is, what a government should be like' (Oumlil, 1985: 165). The ordinary Arab Islamist would energetically reject the view that, during their earlier golden age, Muslims enjoyed the same type of political justice as that which prevails in Europe today.

Let no Muslim claim that this type of government has its origin in Islam, and that we have learnt it from the Quran and the caliphs' tradition. In fact, the type of government we aspire to is the result of our interactions with Europeans. Indeed, *had we not learnt such a lesson from the political life of these Europeans, it would never have occurred to us that political justice is part of the teachings of Islam* (Oumlil 1985: 165) (emphasis added).

It is amazing to note that the Islamist attitude towards the European political model is more open and positive than the pan-Arab attitude. The latter rejects the Occident and refuses to import foreign political notions that do not reflect the genuine authenticity which the Arab nation seeks to recover. Contrary to this introverted attitude, the Islamist (or fundamentalist) attitude is marked by openness and even a willingness to borrow from the Occident.

Hasan al-Banna, the spiritual father of the Muslim Brothers, also accepts the European conception of democracy. In his letter to the Muslim Brothers' Fifth Conference, al-Banna writes:

When one considers the principles that guide the constitutional system of government, one finds that such principles aim to preserve in all its forms the freedom of the individual citizen, to make rulers accountable for their actions to the people, and, finally, to delimit the prerogatives of every single authoritative body. It will be clear to everyone that such basic principles correspond perfectly to the teachings of Islam concerning the system of government. For this reason, Muslim Brothers consider that, of all the existing systems of government, the constitutional system is the form that best suits Islam and Muslims (al-Banna, n.d.: 172).

Islamist thinkers accept the basic principles of the constitutional system on the grounds that such principles not only agree with, but also derive from, Islam. Their criticism of the system concerns only certain details and minor points. Al-Banna, for instance, objects to the Egyptian Constitution on the grounds that some of its paragraphs are so ambiguous that they leave ample opportunity for subjective and whimsical interpretations which sometimes contradict even the Quran and the Sunnah. He also objects to the manner in which the constitution is implemented, and considers that competition among political parties over positions of power and parliamentary seats usually brings adversity and disaster to the nation.

In addition to his use of such modern notions as constitution, law and national sovereignty, al-Banna uses the notion of watan in the same sense in which it is used by modern Arab political thinkers. For him, the term watan denotes the notion of belonging to a specific country and to a definite people. Al-Banna's term for this sense of belonging is patriotism. According to him,

Every Muslim is required to fill a gap in the community and to serve the watan in which he was brought up. Therefore, the Muslim bears the deepest love for his watan and considers himself of the greatest utility to his compatriots because that is part of his religious duties. This applies most particularly to Muslim Brothers who wish their beloved country glory, prosperity and progress (al-Banna, n.d.: 175).

It is true that fundamentalist thought is characterised by its advocacy of Islamic unity, for, as al-Banna himself put it,

Islam does not recognise geographical frontiers and does not take into account racial differences. On the contrary, it considers all Muslims as one umma and regards all Muslim countries as one watan, regardless of the distance and boundaries which separate them (al-Banna, n.d.: 17).

This is a view which is capable of confusing all contemporary definitions of the notion of watan. However, it is worth noting that fundamentalist thought remains, in spite of everything, an offspring of modern political thought. This observation has been made by 'Ali Oumlil in his study, *Fundamentalist Movement and National State.* According to this scholar, al-Banna

adopts the notions of watan, umma, and constitution, but tries to translate them Islamically. Therefore, there is no inconsistency in al-Banna's view which considers that one individual can at the same time be a citizen of a watan like Egypt, for instance, and a member of the Islamic umma (Oumlil, 1985: 136).

In the writings of certain fundamentalists, notions such as nation, fatherland and nationality are used in a sense other than that in which they are used in al-Banna's works, thus giving rise to a new notion: *al-hakimiyya.*

In Sayyid Qutb's (1983: 10) view, 'The world today lives in a state of ignorance with respect to the source of life, its values and patterns'. The Occident, in spite of its progress, cannot alter this state of ignorance, because it is itself undergoing a sterile crisis in which 'it is unable to convince itself that it deserves to live after Western democracy has reached a state of bankruptcy' (ibid.: 5). On many occasions, this fundamentalist thinker reiterates certain fundamentalist theses that have been repeated since the time of Muhammad 'Abduh, except that the tone of his protest is louder, and his judgement more severe. He writes:

> The state of ignorance in which we live today is similar to, if not worse than, pre-Islamic paganism. Everything around us confirms this state: people's thoughts and beliefs, their customs, traditions, and cultures, including a large part of what we consider as Islamic culture. Even what we call Islamic references, Islamic philosophy, or Islamic thought are of pagan origin (ibid.: 10).

In fact, it seems that the notion of al-hakimiyya denotes a divine quality, a godly attribute: therefore the present state of ignorance in which the world lives today seems to be due to the fact that man has committed the unforgivable sin of comparing himself to God.

> People have become deities for other people, not in the innocent, primitive sense, but in a more dangerous sense. Man today claims the right to plan for the future of humanity, to create new values, to invent new laws, systems, and living conditions — all independently of God and His permission (ibid.: 10).

The least we can say of al-hakimiyya is that it is a strange word form. However, its use by Qutb seems to convey a sort of criticism directed against the view that the nation is the source of sovereignty, as modern political thought postulates.

From the fundamentalist point of view, there is no connection whatsoever between watan and territory. This has been the case since the dawn of Islam. 'Since that day, the fatherland of a Muslim ceased to be a portion of land. Instead, his watan became the home of Islam, the land in which Islam and Islamic law are the sole authority' (Qutb, 1983: 15). The question of overcoming geographical boundaries in order to establish a real (spiritual) link between Muslims all over the world is familiar enough in fundamentalist thought in general. Yet, in spite of his apparently extremist attitude, Sayyid Qutb defines the notion of watan in terms of contemporary international law which considers national territory and nationality as two basic constituents of any watan. In this respect, Qutb writes (158-9) that 'a Muslim's watan is not a piece of land, and his nationality is not that of a government'.

Our judgement might seem somewhat unfair, especially when it becomes clear that, in spite of the obvious differences in attitude between later fundamentalist thinkers and their predecessors, we have made an effort to establish some kind of link between them. However, we would still insist that, despite apparent differences, fundamentalist thinkers and modern political thinkers are guided by the same principles.

The history of fundamentalist thought began with the appearance of al-Afghani's doctrine. It has always been marked by a reactionary and recoiling tendency: nevertheless, in spite of the many changes that have occurred in the course of its history, fundamentalist thought has always preserved a number of constants. These unchanging elements make it a distinct model, which has to a large extent been responsible for the confusion that characterises the use of the notions of nation and fatherland as well as a number of other notions which modern political thought has created.

CONCLUSION

What is the significance of the polysemous character of the notions of umma and watan in contemporary Arab use? Why do these notions have only one simple meaning in Western political thought? How can we account for the hesitation between (a) accepting the clear meanings which the terms nation and fatherland have acquired in modern political thought, and (b) the tendency to revive the meanings which these terms used to convey before the birth of modern political thought? In this study an attempt has been made to show that these questions are relevant only in the twentieth century. During the nineteenth century, Arab thought was characterised by its interest in the Western political lexicon in its seventeenth-century form. One can easily establish a cause/effect relation between the absence of the image of the colonial West from the minds of Arab renaissance thinkers and their enthusiastic interest in modern political notions.

This interest took the form of attempts to translate and Arabise Western political terms. The works of Adib Ishaq and at-Tahtawi constitute concrete examples of such attempts. But it is not possible to establish a similar relation with respect to contemporary Arab political thinkers representing the nationalist, the pan-Arab, and fundamentalist models.

Contemporary Arab thought seems to be concerned mainly with the progress/backwardness dichotomy, i.e. why are they (the West, Europe) developed, and why are we (the East, the Arabs) underdeveloped? However, reactions resulting from contact occurred through direct colonisation and territorial partition, or in the form of attempts to distort national history and identity, or to create new entities, as in the case of Israel. This situation is capable of providing a plausible explanation of the state of emotional ambivalence which makes contemporary Arab thinkers' attitudes towards modern political thought waver between acceptance and rejection.

Part Three

7

Changing Perceptions of State Authority: Morocco, Egypt and Oman

Dale F. Eickelman

TRANSFORMATIONS IN AUTHORITY: PAST AND PRESENT

Since the early nineteenth century, most Middle Eastern countries have experienced three major transformations in the scope and intensity of state authority. An older vocabulary such as 'politics' (*siyasa*) and 'authority' (*sulta*) continued to be used in new contexts during the first transformation, which occurred at varying times throughout the region. As a result, attention was deflected from the extent of innovation in the concept and practice of state rule. Among Egypt's political elite, for example, politics shifted in meaning from an earlier usage denoting no more than the practice of governing to one signifying a distinct field of knowledge and practice concerned with 'the regulation, management, and supervision of men's affairs'. For intellectuals such as Rifa'a at-Tahtawi (1801-73), politics signified the discipline, order, control and well-being of both individuals and the state (Mitchell, 1984: 116-18; Gallagher, 1983).

The notion of politics as control, inspired in part by increasing European domination and a desire to emulate or contain the political successes of the dominating powers, was associated with that of renewed national identity under the aegis of Islam (at-Tahtawi, 1982).[1] In earlier epochs, the subjects of states were considered primarily in the aggregate. Henceforth, despite frequent resistance (e.g. Baer, 1969: 93, 107), they were individuals to be counted, policed, ordered, taxed, conscripted and inspected. Politics became 'the pivot on which the organization of the world turns' (at-Tahtawi, cited in Mitchell, 1984: 118, 120). At least such was the view of the elite.

By the 1860s, many of the ruling elite advocated a theory of progress in which they constituted the vanguard (*at-tali‘a*). Thus in 1866 Egypt's Foreign Minister explained that his country's Consultative Assembly of Deputies (*majlis shura an-nuwwab*), chosen from families of notables, was a school or 'civilising instrument' more advanced than the people, just as the government was in turn more advanced than the parliament (Mitchell, 1984: 120). Such 'trickle effect' (Fallers, 1973: 30-7) views are often echoed today by technocratic and political cadres infused with Western-style ideas of politics, organisation and progress not fully comprehended by the majority of the population. Cadres often draft legislation presuming that the intellectual level and commitment to the public welfare of agents of the state is superior to that of the rest of the population, or that a legislative act or decree suffices radically to reshape socio-political organisation (e.g. Ben Bachir, 1969: 16; Cigar, 1985: Hopkins, 1985; Lewis, 1979). Contemporary states of the Middle East frequently claim to represent 'the people' (*ash-sha‘b*) and 'the masses' (*al-jamahir*), but it is often difficult to know how the claims of a self-declared vanguard are understood in practice by citizens presumed to be less 'advanced'.

A second major transformation in state authority came with the independence and revolutionary movements that developed from the end of World War II through the late 1960s. Egypt's 1952 revolution set a pattern followed by neighbouring states. The state became much more pervasive than it had been in the pre-revolutionary period (Harik, 1974; Waterbury, 1983: 57-82). Educational opportunities, bureaucracy, governmental services, and centralised plans for infrastructure, industrialisation and economic development were expanded vastly over those of the *ancien régime*. Mass mobilisation, at least in theory, became the order of the day. In these specific respects, Egypt's experience paralleled that not only of revolutionary regimes, but also of conservative ones such as Morocco after independence in 1956 and even the Sultanate of Oman after its 1970 *coup*, in which Qabous ibn Sa‘id replaced his father as sultan.

The Arab world is now entering a third transformation in state authority, marked in part by a growing challenge to the legitimacy of the state by politically active Islamic groups. Ironically, a salient characteristic of these groups is that their most active members, persons now in their twenties and thirties, constitute the first generation to benefit from the greater access to educational opportunities offered since the second transformation in state authority.

As in other respects, developments in Egypt may suggest the shape of things to come elsewhere. Government policy since the 1952 revolution has been to expand educational opportunities vastly over what was available in the past, particularly to social groups that had earlier remained illiterate. Although the state preaches modernisation, Kepel (1984: 224-5) argues that schooling has failed to transmit its spirit and techniques. The ideas of Islamic utopia and resistance to the state as legitimate have had the greatest appeal to a younger, educated generation, primarily of rural origin but living in the peripheral quarters of major urban centres.

Even if the appeal of radical Islam in Egypt is not widespread, the existence of 20,000 independent (*ahli*) mosques in 1970 and double that number in 1981 (when in September Sadat ordered them placed under government control), as against only 6,000 mosques maintained by the state (Ansari, 1984a: 129) suggests the extent to which Islam is both a vehicle and a potential organising force for popular expression and activity. If a younger generation of radicals appeals to religious values to justify the overthrow of the 'pharaoh', the state in turn appeals to the same norms to seek to justify its conduct. What both militant and state appeals have in common is an attempt to convince a wider audience of citizens, or believers, that a given set of actions is legitimate in Islamic terms or — in the case of some state appeals — at least preferable to less legitimate alternatives (McWilliams, 1971: 430). Finally, the lack of overt challenges to state authority cannot necessarily be viewed as consent by the governed. It may be based upon no more than a recognition that the costs of resistance outweigh those of overt compliance (Asad, 1970: 242).

Several scholars have recently dealt at length with the nature of Islam in contemporary politics; for example, Ansari (1984a), Piscatori (1983) and Kepel (1984: 230) suggested that the Islamic political radicalism of the 1980s is likely to intensify. This prognosis can be questioned, none the less the common wisdom of an earlier decade asserting 'the growing irrelevance of Islamic standards and criteria in the issues, conflicts and policy processes of modern Arab politics and the diminishing influence of Islamic authorities in politics' (Hudson, 1977: 17)

179

is no longer acceptable. Each state of the region must contend with a citizenry with significantly varying interpretations of Islam, many of whom assert that Islam has direct practical application to political and economic affairs. It is ironic that the notion of holding rulers to an Islamic ideal of conduct, explicit in the jurist Ibn Taymiyyah's (d. 1328) claim that it is the duty of rulers to provide the material and spiritual conditions necessary for the existence of a truly Islamic life, has engendered widespread debate and significant popular support only in modern times (Rosenthal, 1962: 52, 82; Sivan, 1983).

The ideas of 'social actors less talkative than the elite' (Zghal, cited in Hopkins, 1983: 48) must be taken into account, even if their significance is denied, ignored or brutally suppressed by the state elite. Direct reliable evidence for the political sentiments motivating peasants and ordinary tribesmen in this period, as for later ones, is as difficult to obtain in the Arab world as elsewhere (Scott, 1976: 145). Shared notions of loyalty, responsibility, justice and authority often take the form of 'practical ideologies' (Eickelman, 1981: 85-7), incompletely systemised, largely implicit assumptions concerning basic aspects of the social order that are so much part of the 'natural' social world that they are seldom fully articulated by their carriers. Whatever the intentions of the state, its actions are constrained and shaped by, and interpreted within, the framework of these practical ideologies.

Such implicit assumptions also provide an organising framework for associations and networks, both covert (Sant Cassia, 1983) and overt, that parallel or limit the authority of the state. A gazeteer of contemporary Arab polities would reveal multiple instances of tribal, sectarian, ethnic and factional leaders with stable followings capable of circumscribing or in other instances of challenging state authority. Few states possess a complete monopoly on the use of force, and for this reason are often circumspect about expanding the scope of intervention in the affairs of their citizens. In some instances, shared notions of loyalty, trust and justice allow for a reasonably stable and predictable economic and social life independent of effective formal governmental and commercial institutions.[2] Despite the claim of most modern Middle Eastern states that loyalty to the state comes before other obligations, the loyalties of most citizens are significantly more complex. Politics is not necessarily coterminous with state authority.

This essay concerns contemporary non-elite perceptions of the state in three Arab states of significantly varying historical circumstances and scale: Egypt, with a population estimated at nearly 42 million in 1986, the most heavily populated Arab country and often considered to be an indicator of regional political and economic trends; Morocco, with a population of 22 million, the second most populous Arab state; and Oman, at the geographical antipodes of the Arab world from Morocco, with a population of 950,000, of which nearly 20 per cent, or 190,000, are foreigners.[3]

Egypt and Morocco can be considered 'production' states (see volume II in this series) which must secure revenues. Egypt's oil production was more than double that of Oman in 1979 and accounted for two-thirds of visible Egyptian exports. None the less, it contributed only 14 per cent to its GDP in the same year (Waterbury, 1983: 190, 198). Egypt's large population dilutes the impact of oil on national revenues and the overall standard of living. Oman, in contrast, is an 'allocation' state, dependent almost entirely upon revenues it receives from the rest of the world as a consequence of its oil resources.

Two of the three countries to be compared are monarchies, yet in many respects the exercise of political authority in them does not markedly differ from Egypt or the one-party states of the region. In recent decades, the Egyptian state has made only general claims to its Islamic identity, in part because of the presence in Egypt of a significant Christian minority. In contrast, the popular legitimacy of the Moroccan monarch is firmly rooted in Islamic tradition as it is locally understood; the Omani monarch must invoke religious tradition with more caution because of the country's multiple sectarian identity. Egypt was caught up in the secular pan-Arabism of the 'central' Middle East in the 1950s and 1960s, a movement that was never a significant political factor in Morocco or Oman despite the aid sporadically accorded by some Arab states to Omani exiles in the 1950s and 1960s.

The central concern of the ensuing comparisons, deriving in part from work in progress, is with the classical problem of legitimacy, how 'some men come to be credited with the right to rule over others' (Geertz, 1973: 317) and seek to maintain this 'accreditation' in the face of shifting popular expectations of what is politically just. This essay analyses how each of these states has sought to develop specific means, through elections and consultation, to widen or at least intensify support for its actions in the context of rapid economic and political change.

THE CONTEXTS OF CONTEMPORARY STATE AUTHORITY

Twenty years ago, some social theorists sought to formulate an Ur-model of Third World economic and political development. These 'modernisation' theories presumed a convergence of political expectations and forms correlated with changes in economy, scale, technology, and education. The postulate of a neat path between 'tradition', a category that obscures more than it clarifies by its global, all-encompassing nature, and 'modernity' has serious limitations. Overarching images of 'peasants' and the 'new middle class' often blocked analytical understanding when uncritically substituted for efforts to describe political processes in particular historical and economic contexts. The explanation of social events lies not in a gossamer search for logical 'closure' or universals, but in providing the best available account — consistent, plausible and in accord with known evidence — for the problem at hand. This goal is both realistic and attainable if one assumes that the comprehension of social action must always take into account unpredictable and contingent elements and that comparisons serve the purpose of sharpening the understanding of general processes at work in specific contexts. Brief profiles of major economic and political trends in Morocco, Egypt, and Oman suggest the contexts in which state authority must be made to appear acceptable and just.

Morocco

In 1948, one out of every 25 Moroccans was Jewish. With the Jewish community now reduced to 18,000 — still the largest Jewish population in the Middle East outside of Israel — the ratio is one out of every 1,400. Out of a population of 8 million in 1951, there was a European settler for every 22 Moroccan Muslims (Cerych, 1964: 321). Today Morocco's European population is numerically insignificant. The departure of both Europeans and Jews for many years provided an important outlet for the rising expectations of the Muslim majority, without major economic growth. Morocco's present rate of population growth is 2.7 per cent. There were 700,000 births in 1983, roughly equal to Oman's entire citizen population. Yet the only significant new employment for that year was created in the public sector — 10,000 new jobs, primarily for school-teachers (de la Guérivière, 1984). Unlike some allocation states, Morocco can no longer expand public-sector employment without regard for productivity.

Morocco is decidedly a 'production' state, especially since the precipitous decline in world prices for phosphates, its principal natural resource. The country depends significantly upon agricultural exports, tourism and remittances from emigrant workers to sustain a *per capita* GNP of $670. There are radical disparities in the distribution of the nation's wealth. According to a recent World Bank report, fully 45 per cent of Moroccans live below the level of 'absolute poverty' (Ramonet, 1984: 7). In a pattern common to the rest of the Middle East, the urban population has dramatically increased in recent decades, so that today an estimated 70 per cent of Moroccans live in towns. Of this urban population, 20 per cent lives in shantytowns (*bidonvilles*).

On the eve of independence, only 11 per cent of Morocco's school-age children had access to schools; today about half do. None the less, the country's estimated 1980 literacy rate was only 28 per cent. Despite impressive strides in expanding educational opportunities since 1956, over half of school-age children nationwide remain without schooling because population growth outstrips the resources allocated to education.

National politics in Morocco since 1960 have been characterised primarily by competition among the elite for the monarch's patronage and by an implicit tolerance of corruption as a means of ensuring the loyalty of key supporters and muting their possible objections to the conduct of the state (Waterbury, 1970, 1976). Demonstrations and violence have periodically recurred. Following ruthlessly suppressed riots in Casablanca in 1965, a state of emergency was maintained for five years. Subsequent serious urban riots occurred in 1981 and 1984, but the major threat to the monarch has been the military. Nearly successful *coups* took place in 1971 and 1972. A sequel to these *coup* attempts was a thorough reorganisation of the military and security services, and intensified efforts to strengthen the role of the rural notables, who since the early 1960s have been recognised as the monarchy's most reliable supporters.

Morocco's monarch, like Oman's, publicly stresses his unique vocation to guide the nation's destiny. In Morocco as in Oman, there is an explicit awareness on the part of both ruler and ruled of pressures for greater popular participation in decision-making and the exercise of authority. Hassan II's 'Revolution of the King and the People', a slogan reminiscent of that used by the late Shah, is considered banal by some educated Moroccans and hypocritical by others, but its very existence formally acknowledges that popular legitimacy today implies a ruler's affirmation of a desire to self-transform and widen the base of participation in government.

The monarchs of Morocco and Oman both place limits upon their willingness to effect greater popular participation. French-educated Hassan II (Vaucher, 1962: 70), citing the writings of Maurice Duverger, stated early in his reign that 'genuine' liberties such as those available in many European countries would be possible only 'after a certain standard of living and educational level' were attained. Since making this statement in 1961, Morocco has had parliamentary and municipal elections and two constitutional referendums. Yet, in contrast to the four years immediately following independence in 1956, party politics have been distinctly held in check.

Egypt

Egypt had an annual *per capita* income of $490 as of 1983. Only 3.5 per cent of the land surface is inhabited, giving the country an overall population density equivalent to those of Bangladesh or Java (Waterbury, 1983: 42); only 2.4 per cent of its total surface is cultivated. Roughly 10 per cent of the population is Copt. In spite of efforts to minimise sectarian strife, violent clashes have occurred in recent years, inadvertently encouraged by the state's occasional use of religion for political expediency, such as the enactment of shari'ah legislation in the Sadat era (Ansari, 1984b). Forty-five per cent of the population lives in urban areas, and only 40 per cent of the population is literate — double the literacy rate existing prior to the 1952 revolution. As in Morocco, remittances from emigrant workers provide a significant contribution to the national economy.

Soon after the Free Officers came to power in July 1952, they realised that Egypt's social and political life would not be transformed solely by removing the old regime. Whatever the intentions of the revolutionary government, Egypt's peasant masses remained inarticulate and inaccessible (Binder, 1978: 35-6) especially after the elimination of the country's one mass political movement, the Muslim Brotherhood. According to a 1968 village study, 21 per cent of adult males had not yet heard of socialism. Even in an age of state-controlled mass communications, there are limits to the diffusion of official ideologies (Harik, 1974: 185).

Although political life under Nasser and Sadat has been characterised as 'short-term maneuvering and manipulation, ... somewhat divorced from the currents of social and economic change the regime had released' (Waterbury, 1983: 307), the revolution slowly began to have an impact upon village life. One of the few available intensive case studies of the impact of the revolution at the village level suggests that it was minimal up to 1960, although conditions were created for subsequent higher levels of intervention (Harik, 1974: 56-7, 78-80).

At the level of formal political institutions, Egypt appears to have little in common with monarchic Morocco and Oman. Egypt's leaders since the 1952 revolution have been populist and charismatic. Yet in an ironic play on Weber's famous types of authority, Moore (1980: 120, 207) has characterised the post-revolutionary Egyptian state as 'sultanic socialism', characterised by 'both the concentration and expansion in scope of personal power'. The old social order of rural landowners was dispossessed through successive land reforms. The Muslim Brotherhood, another source of potential opposition to the regime, was crippled by a wave of arrests in 1954. Despite these changes, it has been estimated that class groups remained remarkably constant because of the ability of many families to 'transfer their socio-economic status, under changing institutional arrangements, to their children' (Moore, 1980: 110-11). In Morocco (Leveau, 1976) and to a lesser extent in Oman, the old social orders have also been a significant source of political stability.

Oman

Employment figures give some indication of the country's reliance upon foreign labour. Excluding the agriculture and fisheries sector of civilian employment, 30 per cent, or 61,000 of the 200,000-strong work force, were Omani in 1980. The work force has significantly expanded since then and is projected to reach 323,000 by 1985, of which 31 per cent, or 100,000 are Omani (World Bank, 1981: 75).[4]

Ninety-five per cent of government revenues derive from oil. Oman's *per capita* income, one of the lowest in the world prior to its first oil exports in 1967, was $5,780 in 1980. Prior to the 1970 *coup*, the country's revenues were not significantly applied to education or development. The excellent infrastructure and the proliferation of government services were created almost from scratch since 1970 (Townsend, 1977). Although 'absolute' poverty is now infrequent, thanks to a security blanket of social services, income distribution is highly inegalitarian. In 1980 the literacy rate was 20 per cent, up dramatically from 1970, when the country possessed only three modern schools. Most Omani youth now have access to schooling, either in civilian schools or, for army recruits from remote villages, through the army's highly effective adult literacy programme.

In contrast to Morocco and Egypt, Oman's small population has complex ethnic and sectarian identities. Ibadi Muslims constitute 55-60 per cent, Sunni 30-35 per cent and Shi'i no more than 5 per cent of the citizen population. Although Ibadi Muslims have only a slight majority, Ibadi notions of rule have historically figured significantly in the shaping of state authority.

Unlike Morocco, where there is a fusion of royal authority with Islam as it is locally interpreted, no such identity exists in Oman. The Ibadi notion of open selection for theocratic rule contrasts markedly with the ascriptive one of dynastic rule. Conflict between these two forms of rule has been basic to much of Omani political history. For much of the twentieth century (1913-55), the interior of northern Oman was in the hands of a popularly-supported Ibadi imamate, as it was before the eighteenth century when the present dynasty came to power. The basic political principle of the imamate was that the *imam*, the spiritual and temporal leader of the Islamic community, was the most qualified of available candidates, selected without regard to descent or tribal considerations through a consensus of the community's religious men of learning and notables. For this reason Ibadis are often referred to as 'the people of consultation' (*ahl ash-shura*).

Despite rapid economic and social change, the speed of

transformation in Oman's formal political institutions remains glacial. The country is engaged in 'segmental modernization' (Brennan, 1981); rapid transformation is formally encouraged in all spheres of economic and social activity except that of selection for rule at the top. Following the fall of the Shah in 1979, foreign and domestic observers commented increasingly upon the Omani monarch's insular reliance upon a small inner circle of advisers. Finally, a State Consultative Council (SCC) (*al-majlis al-istishari li ad-dawla*) was established in 1981 (Eickelman, 1984). The mandate of this appointive 54-member council is limited to providing advice to the ruler on specifically delimited issues. Matters related to petroleum and minerals, security and defence, and Islamic affairs are excluded from its scope. Its deliberations and recommendations are technically secret, so that its existence suggests no limitation upon the ruler's absolute authority.

In public pronouncements on Oman's political development, Sultan Qabous ibn Sa'id stresses a gradualist approach (*tahsin*). Political development, he has said, 'must take its place in the proper time'... It will be a very happy day for me when more people will take responsibilities from my shoulders. But we have to take into consideration the situation of our culture, our religious heritage and guidance, our traditions, and not to import a system that is already made and put in a package' (Qabous ibn Sa'id, 1983). At the outset of his reign, Sultan Qabous won considerable initial support simply by affirming that he would allow Omanis to enjoy the benefits of oil wealth in the same manner as the citizens of neighbouring oil states. Such material benefits are now taken for granted and many Omanis have a renewed interest in how their future is decided. This shift in expectations is in part an unintended consequence of the dramatic improvement in educational facilities since 1970.

Three concrete examples suggest how these respective programmes of revolution and gradualist development, or 'revolution from above', are popularly understood. The Moroccan example is Boujad (Eickelman, 1976: 65-88), a town of 28,000 located on Morocco's western plains, at the foothills of the Middle Atlas mountains, and its immediate region. The Egyptian one is Shubra al-Gadida, an Egyptian Delta village of 6,200 in 1966, studied by Harik (1974) in the mid-1960s. The Omani example is al-Hamra, a tribal oasis and provincial capital of 2,400 located in the country's interior (Eickelman, C., 1984; Eickelman, D., 1983a, 1983b, 1985) None of these communities can be taken as directly representative of larger aggregates in their respective countries, but each indicates how state authority is practically elaborated and experienced.

BOUJAD: ELECTIONS AND STATE AUTHORITY

At the outset of the protectorate (1912-56), the French appointed local notables throughout Morocco to positions of authority. In the colonial era they played a central role in facilitating the extension of state authority. In the countryside, taxes were exacted and pastoral movements and disputes were strictly controlled. In Boujad and other towns, a myriad of controls and regulations were elaborated and gradually intensified. Permits and regulations were established for many trades and crafts, building construction and land use.

For the duration of the protectorate, succession to local leadership was confined to the descendants or immediate relatives of those appointed at the outset. Privileged access to schools and military training gave the children of these notables the new skills necessary to preserve their status through to the present. Except for a brief interlude after independence, during which sweeping programmes of land and fiscal reform were proposed but never seriously implemented, rural notables have remained secure in their role as 'defenders of the throne' (Leveau, 1976, 1977).

After independence, expanded schooling provided one of the major new points of contact between the state and ordinary Moroccans. As diplomas became plentiful and academic standards declined, education no longer conferred the status and access to government sinecures that it did for an earlier generation. As the economy stagnated in the 1960s, emigration to Europe became increasingly attractive, although the necessary permits and passports, obtainable through local authorities, required clandestine payments. For all but notables, the state apparatus was perceived to be approached cautiously through intermediaries capable of securing favourable decisions on one's behalf.

The monarch himself was rarely held responsible for official abuses. At least up to the late 1960s, a common sentiment was that if the monarch only knew of the excesses of his subordinates, they would be checked. Tribesmen and many town-dwellers regarded the monarch as 'God's deputy on earth' (*khalifat Allah fi al-ard*), a phrase much more current than the Constitution's 'Commander of the Faithful' (*Amir al-Mu'minin*). Morocco's constitution also states that the person of the king is sacred, so that direct criticism is expressly forbidden. He is commemorated in popular songs and his actions are reported daily on radio and television. During Ramadan he appears nightly with the nation's leading official religious leaders and personally conducts some of the televised religious lessons. His behaviour is constantly associated with the nation's religious and material welfare.

In such an overall framework, it might appear that electoral politics are cosmetic. They decidedly have not provided a sustained central arena for determining national goals or in achieving nationwide power, however valuable they have been in allowing the government to assess the strength of various political groupings (Leveau, 1976; Rosen, 1972). None the less, since Morocco's first elections in the early 1960s, there have been modest yet significant changes in how electoral politics have been conducted and understood at the local level. An analysis of two elections in Boujad, the November 1976 municipal elections and the parliamentary ones held in 1977, together with brief comments on the more recent 1983 and 1984 elections, suggests the extent to which new understandings of political responsibilities have begun to emerge.

Morocco's post-independence elections were intended to symbolise the country's break with its colonial past. Soon after independence, Western-educated technocrats drew up economic plans and administrative reorganisations. A decree formally established rural communal councils (*jama'as*) in 1960. Urban councils had existed since the protectorate, but these were reorganised after 1959 (Ben Bachir, 1969). The legislative intention behind these councils was to replace the tribal units and leadership upon which the colonial power had relied with 'rational' local entities, much like the French communal system, appropriate for a modern Morocco.

In the Boujad area, communal councils remained moribund until 1976. Local representatives of the Ministry of the Interior in practice made all local decisions. The only initiative of this body up to 1970 was the purchase of chairs for the office of the local district administrator (*qa'id*). The conduct of local elections was derisory. In 1969, for example, large black rectangles were painted on the sides of several buildings for campaign posters that were never authorised. On election day itself, people who tried to vote at polling places were told that the government had already 'taken care' of the matter. Government-appointed shaykhs, like their predecessors in the protectorate, used their control over permits and the selective enforcement of regulations as levers to hold in check even the suggestion of opposition.

By the mid-1970s, the effects of earlier educational expansion were beginning to be felt in the form of a heightened political awareness on the part of younger, educated Moroccans and workers who had been to Europe. Following the 1972 *coup* attempt, restrictions on political parties were lifted.[5] In the Boujad region, three political groupings resumed activities: the Istiqlal party, the Union Socialiste des Forces Populaires (USFP),[6] and various groupings of 'independents', candidates often informally backed by the government.

A brief profile of the two organised parties shows significantly contrasting bases of local support. The local branch of the Istiqlal party dates almost from the party's national founding in January 1944. Locally, its leadership consists of key merchants, together with an older generation of artisans and craftsmen, most of whom joined the party prior to independence or in its immediate aftermath, when the party controlled government patronage. A distinctive feature of party recruitment prior to independence was that recruits swore an oath of support on the Quran. Those who took this oath, including youths of the time now in their forties and fifties, continue to vote for the party even after they have become disenchanted with its policies. New recruits to the Istiqlal are negligible.

Local USFP support is more complex. The party is strongest in the large coastal cities and includes an important component of organised labour. In the 1960s, the party leadership made few efforts to expand its base into small towns and rural areas (Waterbury, 1970: 198). Following the liberalisation of 1972, the USFP decided to seek recruits nationwide. A Rabat-based university instructor, the French-educated grandson of one of the more notorious Boujad-area qa'ids of the protectorate era, was entrusted with reorganising the party throughout the region.[7] In the still uncertain political climate of late 1972, his efforts concentrated upon the formation of clandestine cells (*khaliyyas*), each consisting of three to eleven persons, in which the local old guard of the UNFP was marginally involved.[8]

Local success among older merchants and artisans was minimal, since most of this group had sworn early allegiance to the Istiqlal party. Among the younger educated population, especially schoolteachers, the largest category of employment for educated persons available locally, party success was substantial. Efforts to recruit women were limited but significant.

By 1976, just prior to the municipal elections, the USFP had a local membership of 110 (Ma'ruf, 1978). These elections were the first practical test of USFP ability to influence people beyond the party ranks. The attitude of most Boujadis towards party politics was that they were a sham (*kizb*), masking personal interest with abstract slogans. Memory of the Istiqlal party's crude use of patronage and influence in the years immediately after independence was still fresh. Both the town and the countryside were divided into electoral districts, roughly determined by population units of 1,000-1,500 persons each. Each of Boujad's twenty-one districts provided a delegate to the municipal council. The Istiqlal and USFP each fielded twenty-one candidates, one for each district. There were an additional sixty-three 'independent' candidates.

The Istiqlal party sought votes through its locally traditional distribution of cloth and sugar cones to voters, a technique imitated by the wealthy 'independents'. Following a national directive, the USFP pointedly avoided material incentives. Although the party distributed its formal ideological platform in booklet form (*Al-Barnamij al-Intikhabi*) to its adherents, it decided to emphasise specific local issues, a major innovation in local party politics. The leaflets distributed for USFP candidates stressed an improved water supply to replace the overtaxed one installed by the French in 1920, construction of a new school, sewers, and an upgraded health clinic. These were all matters that could be decided or recommended by the municipal council, although some matters were clearly beyond their fiscal and technical means.

Local government attempts to manipulate the election suggest how the state seeks practically to manifest its authority. Government interference was most pronounced in the countryside, where fewer party cadres were present. One tactic was to convene tribesmen in mosques at the weekly markets, at which an administrator declared that the USFP was 'against Islam'. A USFP candidate was immediately told to desist on the one occasion when he used the same approach. The government was adamant against the use of religious symbols by the parties, although no such restriction applied to its own cadres. Although government spokesmen invoked Islamic values, they also clearly hinted that they could express displeasure by calling in agricultural loans, withholding government assistance or, in one instance, prohibiting a tribal group from making its annual collective 'visit' (*ziyara*) to a maraboutic shrine in Boujad. More subtle interference was prevalent in urban quarters.

Party workers quickly realised that mass rallies were ineffective. Few people understood or trusted the speakers, many of whom were little known. Public campaigning was an unfamiliar genre, viewed with singular interest. The USFP then decided to locate party members of local origin living elsewhere in Morocco and bring them back to talk with fellow tribesmen. This tactic proved successful. Indeed, all candidates extensively used ties of kin, neighbours, and clients to win votes, approaching voters whenever possible through trusted intermediaries.

In the town, candidates went from house to house, pointing out the correct colour to use in voting for them, an important consideration for illiterate voters. (In the 1977 parliamentary elections, the government switched colours at the last moment in crucial rural regions.) Women called on neighbourhood houses to explain voting procedures to other women. This tactic was especially important. Women have an equal franchise and the registration of women locally outnumbered that of men, many of whom work elsewhere in Morocco or abroad. Electoral rosters indicate long lists of 'Fatimas', suggesting that husbands or guardians frequently registered women, not revealing their names, and then voted for them by 'proxy', an illegal practice but tolerated by some electoral supervisors. Indeed, women officially cast 60 per cent of the votes in Boujad's 1976 elections (Ma'ruf, 1978). Of 5,501 registered urban voters, 3,683 votes were cast, a 67 per cent turnout. Comparable figures are not available for the rural regions. Since election days are not holidays, persons absent elsewhere in the country, such as students, servicemen, and workers, were unable to vote.

A significant distinction emerged between quarters in which long-time residents predominate and those composed of recent rural immigrants. A frequent pattern in the latter and in the rural vote was a tendency towards bloc voting (Ma'ruf, 1978). Tribesmen met among themselves prior to the election and decided how to cast their ballots. Split votes in these electoral districts directly mirrored prevalent local social divisions.

The urban election results surprised both the USFP and local officials. Nine seats of the municipal council went to the USFP, ten to the Istiqlal, and two to wealthy local merchants who were 'independents'. As a group, the USFP delegates were the best educated: five teachers, a university-educated engineer, a postal clerk and an electrician, ranging in age from twenty to forty. The Istiqlal delegate candidates were of an older generation, including four teachers, four merchants, and two illiterate workers. Because the USFP delegates had a better notion of how to formulate local issues, they took the initiative on most council matters over the next few years, the first time that any significant initiative had been taken in the seventeen years of the council's existence.

Government response to the defeat of preferred candidates in 1976 included the dismissal of some government-appointed shaykhs who did not sufficiently deliver the results which the government, formally neutral, expected. The message of these dismissals was presumably not lost on remaining cadres. In the 1977 parliamentary elections, government involvement was more pronounced.[9] Such interference contributed to the USFP's defeat in the local parliamentary elections, although the party none the less attracted substantial urban and rural support, winning 43 per cent of the total vote, in large part through its suggestion of an alternative to the politics of government-controlled patronage.

The rising educational level of Morocco's population and a tendency to hold the state to the letter of what it formally declares to be the rights of its citizens is beginning to alter the conduct of local politics. A decade earlier, rural youth identified local notables as a group as the principal representatives of the state, and not local officials (Pascon and Bentahar, 1971: 223). By the 1976 municipal elections, a younger generation that had known the colonial era only as small children had come of age. The educated members of this group had become increasingly disenchanted with the party politics of an earlier era and with the various political formations perceived to be 'preferred' by the monarch.[10]

Nationwide, the USFP won only 8.53 per cent of the official popular vote in the 1976 local elections and 16 seats in a 254-seat parliament in 1977 (Daoud, 1976; Marks, 1984). Moroccans widely acknowledged government manipulation of the elections and the election campaigns (Lamghili, 1976). None the less, most Moroccans consider the election results only in terms of the total political context. Despite government interference, the 1976 local elections offered significant choice. Until then, municipality budgets in smaller towns of the interior had for the most part been controlled by personnel from the Ministry of the Interior. Now they had their own budget and employees, and could control local patronage. A considerable latitude was created for the conduct of politics at a level below that of rule at the top.

The highest compliment that could be paid the USFP was that its most successful tactics were borrowed in 1983 by the Constitutional Union (UC), a new party perceived as inspired by the monarch. This party was formed a week prior to the 1983 municipal elections, the first to be held in Morocco since 1976. Its leader was the Prime Minister, Ma'ati Bou'abid, who was allowed by the king to resign in order to lead the party. The UC also made a predictably excellent showing in the September 1984 parliamentary elections. Unlike the USFP, local UC candidates could readily convince voters of effective connections with political leaders elsewhere to get things done locally. They even offered the hope to younger supporters of subsequent private employment.

Government interference in electoral politics is widely acknowledged, but so is the government's obligation to live up to its promise of delivering public services and acting in a predictable, just manner towards its citizens. This is a new expectation. The government recognises that political participation is wider than it was in Morocco's recent past. This widened participation may limit the appeal both of the extreme left and of Islamic fundamentalists, self-designated as 'the Islamists' (*al-islamiyyun*) in Morocco (Etienne and Tozy, 1979). The changing shape of elections and increased authority over some limited issues suggests one of the ways in which the state is actively and flexibly responding to long-term shifts in political expectations.

SHUBRA AL-GADIDA

The political mobilisation of the Nasser era promoted participation and free political choice at the local level, while progress-
ively narrowing such choice at the national level (Harik, 1974:
222), a use of elections not dissimilar from the Moroccan
experience. Harik's analysis of the 1968 local election for the
Arab Socialist Union (ASU), the one party permitted until
1972, suggests how Egypt's 'sultanic socialism' was experienced
at the village level. After the 1952 revolution, the official party
changed its name, character and leadership several times as the
regime changed policies. The result was to make local political
leadership roles insecure. As late as 1968, sixteen years after the
revolution, a single dominant family or coterie of wealthy
landowners could dominate elections in many villages. Recognising this, the government enacted measures to ensure that of
the ten local representatives to be elected for each ASU unit, no
more than one individual from a 'family', a term explicitly
defined, could be seated. Likewise, village headmen ('umdas)
and shaykhs were unable to stand as candidates unless they first
resigned their positions. Other strictly enforced regulations kept
candidates away from the election room, where each voter had
to declare orally the names of the ten candidates for whom he
was voting. Although interference was widely felt at the higher-
level elections in the ASU, especially in the election by regional
delegates to the Central Committee, the local elections were
regarded as the freest conducted during Nasser's rule (Harik,
1974: 224-6). In Shubra al-Gadida, twenty-four candidates
contested the ten local seats. In principle, ony ASU members
could vote, but no effort had been made strictly to define ASU
members or to collect dues. In practice, membership cards were
distributed to all adult male villagers, two weeks before the
elections in June. Seven hundred of 920 eligible voters cast
ballots (ibid.: 235-6).

All three political blocs active since the foundation of the
ASU in 1962 entered the race. One was a coalition centred
upon a family of resident landlords, the Kuras, who were led by
three brothers with modern education. Much of their effort was
invested in maintaining political connections outside the village.
Their leader, Muhammad, resided elsewhere, although he
returned to the village regularly. Another brother had earlier
served as mayor, although even he acted in the village primarily

through a buffer of supporters. The brothers had withdrawn from politics by the mid-1960s, but Muhammad sensed a renewed opportunity after the 1967 Arab-Israeli war and declared himself a candidate. His basic strategy was to run as a progressive and to make tactical alliances with other candidates so as to stress the unity of the village.

A second bloc of candidates was formed by peasants who participated in the agrarian reform co-operative. This group, generally of very modest origins, was antagonistic towards the Kuras and ran a united slate of four candidates. They also sought alliances that would win them votes from villagers other than co-operative members. Because of grudges held over from earlier periods when they were more politically powerful, they were not as successful in this respect.

The local ASU leadership formed the third cluster of candidates, although they did not run as a united platform. Their formerly powerful Youth Organisation was banned after the 1967 war and the party itself was in the throes of a national reorganisation, perceived locally as a rebuff to the party leaders. The party ended up running not as a slate, but as independents or in alliance with the Kuras.

The election results gave four seats to Muhammad Kura and his supporters, a lead but not an overwhelming victory. The land reform slate won two seats and the independents four. Without a clear majority, Muhammad Kura had to rely upon alliances with the independents for the conduct of local affairs. The election results suggest that the villagers rejected ideologically hardened positions and factional confrontations in favour of a local pluralism emphasising the maintenance of political ties with multiple groups (Harik, 1974: 238-41). As a means of preserving efficacious local leadership in the face of volatile national politics, this aggregate decision appeared to be a sensible choice. The rejection of appeals for votes based upon class divisions also suggests that villagers placed a high value upon candidates with demonstrable influence and working ties with provincial and national political leaders and officials (ibid.: 226-35).

Hinnebusch (1984) provides a wider context in which Shubra al-Gadida's experience can be interpreted. In post-revolutionary elections up to 1972, candidates were screened to eliminate overt opponents of the regime. Indeed, in the 1957 and 1960 elections, candidates from the rural notability were favoured over those from the extreme right or left. After Nasser's death in 1972, more than one party participated in elections, but the opposition was strictly controlled. In the 1984 parliamentary elections, considered to be relatively free from overt government fraud and intervention, candidates perceived as backed by the government still got an overall 75 per cent of the vote. The reason for this, argues Hinnebusch, is the competitive advantage of local notables. Ideology and issues signify less than the ability to demonstrate good connections with government authorities and the ability to secure benefits for the local community. Elections also provide a means by which acceptable members of the local community can be incorporated into the regime's political base. They channel opposition into manageable, tame forms, and provide a means by which the secondary elite (Binder, 1978) can be renewed and co-opted by the state.

AL-HAMRA: CONSULTATION IN AN ABSOLUTE MONARCHY

Like many of the other small towns and villages in which the majority of Omanis continue to live, al-Hamra preserves a relatively high degree of local autonomy, even as its economic and political importance declines in contrast to that of the capital. Until the mid-1950s, al-Hamra was part of the Ibadi imamate of the interior. Its tribal leaders none the less maintained contact with Sultan Sa'id bin Taymur (r. 1932-70) in Muscat.

The formal consensus among tribal notables in selecting an imam also served as a model for other forms of leadership, including that of tribes. Tribesmen distinguish between shaykhs who rule with the consent of the community or collectively (*jama'a*) and those who do not. Shaykhs who make illegitimate exactions or who fail to settle issues according to justice as locally understood are considered tyrants (*jabbars*).

The concepts of collectivity and consultation are crucial to understanding popular Omani notions of authority. Jama'as vary in composition. A jama'a can be constituted by any cluster of individuals who usually consult with one another before making major decisions. In tribal contexts, such consultations involve anything from an entire tribe to individual settlements or key members of the shaykhly lineage alone. The term jama'a is usually used regularly in non-tribal contexts to refer to any group of persons who habitually work or deliberate together.

After an uprising against his rule in northern Oman, the Jabal al-Akhdar war (1957-9), Sultan Sa'id left Muscat for Salala, the principal town of Dhufar, the inaccessible southern province, and never again returned to the north. With only one exception, he rarely consulted with tribal leaders, only with a handful of trusted subordinates. His decisions, backed by a foreign-officered army, were increasingly regarded as arbitrary.

Some very modest efforts at development, such as the introduction of a flour mill and motorised pumps for wells owned by local shaykhs, trickled through to al-Hamra. There were also two Land Rovers on the oasis, owned by tribal leaders, who alone had sufficient prominence to import vehicles, each of which required the sultan's personal authorisation. Permits to emigrate in search of employment were also strictly monitored, although many tribesmen evaded these restrictions.

Despite the deliberately glacial (if the term can be applied metaphorically to the Gulf) pace of development, by the 1960s Omanis began to acquire alternative expectations of what a just ruler should do. By the late 1960s at least 50,000 Omanis worked in neighbouring states. Even when not directly involved in overt political actions, these sojourners became aware of political movements elsewhere in the Arab world and of the more constructive attitude towards development of the rulers of some neighbouring states. The larger number of these emigrants, some of whom were able to return periodically to their villages in Oman, accelerated the transformation in popular conceptions of state authority. Maintenance of Sultan Sa'id's regime increasingly depended upon the threat of intervention by his small standing army and reliance upon an older generation of governors and tribal shaykhs who, like the sultan, were unresponsive to changing visions of social equity.

The change in ruler in 1970 was immediately felt through the lifting of numerous petty restrictions and Omanis again sensed momentum in their society. Tribal shaykhs, still the backbone of local administration in the early 1970s, were firmly assured of a place in Oman's 'new era'. A governor from a neighbouring tribe took up residence only in 1972, following a protracted local struggle over tribal leadership, but continued to consult with the local tribal leader on all issues of importance. Over a hundred tribesmen are employed in various capacities locally by the various ministries concerned with health, sanitation, land affairs and education. With the advent of funds to purchase motor pumps, the area of cultivable land has expanded considerably. A local committee, dominated by tribal notables, allocates 'vacant' land for new houses, commercial and agricultural use. The control over local resources and the ability to 'steer' government decision-making to its immediate benefit allows the tribal oligarchy to maintain its local pre-eminence, even if its investments have shifted to the more profitable area of the capital. None the less, the new wealth from employment elsewhere has lessened the authority of tribal leaders, so that townsmen now have considerably more personal latitude than they had in the past to operate independently of tribal shaykhs.

The sultan's word is in principle absolute, but agents of the state intervene in only a narrow range of affairs. From similar localities themselves, most are reluctant to execute unpopular government initiatives. The modern era has also reduced the scope of control that tribal leaders can exert upon their followers, although control or influence over the allocation of local resources provides them with a significant competitive edge.

The distance between the notables on the periphery and those at the centre is theoretically shorter in Oman than in Morocco or Egypt because of the country's smaller scale. A more important consideration, however, is the quality and style of perceived communications. Despite Oman's late developmental start, a major long-term consequence of its recently expanded educational system is an expectation among younger Omanis of a greater say in policy issues. A modest recognition of these changing expectations was the founding in 1981 of Oman's State Consultative Council (SCC), an institution which unfortunately remains peripheral to the perceived decision-making and even the advisory process, despite occasional general statements of praise for its work (Eickelman, 1984).

The notion of consultation (*shura*) carries a special meaning for Omanis who are Ibadi, as are all the Omani inhabitants of Al-Hamra, but the Omani adherents of other Islamic orientations are also aware of Ibadi usage and respect it. The circumspect comments of delegates appointed to the SCC suggest the implicit tensions between shura and royal authority (ibid.: 69). One delegate from the interior glossed the term as follows: 'Shura? It is like relations between a father and small children. The sultan is our father and tells us what to do. That is consultation.' Another poetically compared the sultan to the brightest star in the sky, the moon when it was full, making it clear that all initiative was with the sultan, who 'is bringing us more good things, one at a time'. Another delegate, also from the interior, compared the SCC to a child just out of the womb, which soon will walk, speak, and eventually, with His Majesty's guidance, act on its own. Some members see the SCC as the first step towards democracy (*ad-dimuqratiyy'a*), although they are aware that the sultan has never made such an allusion. Traditionally-educated Omanis emphasise the distinction between shura, which carries the suggestion of mutual consultation, and *istishara*, the one-way solicitation of advice which is at the basis of the SCC.

The prevalent Ibadi notion of consultation suggests why the sultan makes only general invocations of religion and 'our heritage' (*turathuna*) when discussing political development. Similarly, secondary school textbooks studiously avoid such subjects as discussion of the country's recent history, which would necessarily invoke discussion of the twentieth-century imamate. This avoidance of significant political and religious issues in formal schooling is not lost upon younger Omanis; the nature of state authority is not a topic for open discussion. From the vantage point of the late twentieth century, greater popular participation in decision-making might take considerable courage, but might also offer a firmer guarantee for long-term stability than a focus upon internal security alone.

CONCLUSION

It is increasingly apparent that secular nationalism, once a driving force in unifying the Arab world against colonial regimes and European domination, is a declining force. In the 1950s and early 1960s, political theorists advanced models of rational modernism and 'new men'. Religion was viewed as an increasingly personal affair devoid of immediate political implications. Yet one of the most salient features of contemporary Middle Eastern politics is the 'resurgence' of 'political' Islam, not necessarily as a replacement for secular nationalism, but as an integral component of personal and collective identity that has been ignored, suppressed or crudely manipulated by the state.

Many analysts have represented the emergence of militant Islamic groups as a major challenge to contemporary state authority, and to this end have focused upon recruitment to these groups. Published accounts suggest that their appeal is strongest among people from small towns and rural backgrounds, young, educated and politically aware, and living at present in areas that have experienced rapid urbanisation (for Egypt, see Ibrahim, 1980: 438; Kepel, 1984: 201-12; for Morocco, Etienne and Tozy, 1979). Their pattern of recruitment, through kinship ties and personal contacts, and lack of formal organisation, lend themselves to covert activity. Some authors argue that the majority of militants 'represent predominantly a special segment within the lower middle classes', although their leadership is composed of persons of a mixture of backgrounds, including members of the rural elite — that category of persons upon whom the central authorities have traditionally relied to keep the rural areas under control (Ansari, 1984a: 133-4).

There is a major dimension of contemporary Islamic political expression from which the extreme statements and acts of the militants have diverted attention. Islam is a vehicle for political expression difficult for any state to modulate, co-opt or control. Unlike the ideologies offered by secular nationalists of an earlier generation, appeals to Islam are understood by wide segments of the population, including those whose political voices have until recently been ignored or muted. Moreover, Islamic-oriented activities are one of the few domains in which most states intervene only with caution. Since most states seek to co-opt or suppress potential opposition, they are poorly attuned to shifts in popular expectations of authority. They are better prepared to handle threats such as dissident military, strikes, or equivalent forms of open and identifiable resistance. An emergent long-term factor in such shifts throughout the Middle East is the coming of age of the educated 'masses', beneficiaries of a schooling that emphasises the benefit of commitment to modern values. The effects of mass education, first organised in the 1950s in Egypt and Morocco and in the early 1970s in Oman, have become apparent with the passage of time.

The idea of social justice is not confined to the allocation of material resources alone. There is a growing expectation that a just government is an Islamic one, an expectation perceived to be at odds with the practical scope of the actual state despite state efforts to co-opt both religious values and leadership. In each of the three cases discussed in this chapter, the state has had to cope with social and economic change more rapid than that which has taken place in earlier eras. In Morocco, elections have emerged as part of a long-term strategy to accommodate shifting political expectations and realities. These are most apparent in Morocco, where continuity in leadership more readily permits comparisons over time.

In Egypt, as well, local elections suggest the importance of maintaining the support of effective, existing local notables in order to guarantee internal support for state authority. They also suggest that the state is able to accommodate new social forces. In Oman, the cushion of oil revenues and the lack, since 1975 — the year the insurgency in the southern province of Dhufar was formally declared at an end — of serious evident internal or external threats to the monarchy, has allowed to date the luxury of less accommodation of long-term changes in political expectations. An awareness and capacity to adjust to long-term change does not, *per se*, guarantee the longevity of any particular state formation. However, they ensure that such transformations will not threaten the state or necessitate the self-defeating use of repression, in itself a public acknowledgement of the lack of internal legitimacy. Perceived state flexibility and responsiveness to changes in non-elite perceptions of authority constitute a significant element of maintaining popular legitimacy in the late twentieth century.

'There can, at any time, be many legitimate systems or modes of conduct', all of which are relative to possibility and circumstances (McWilliams, 1971: 429-30). The same can be said of the contemporary Middle East. A capacity to maintain close, effective local ties, including the large body of citizens involved only peripherally in the political process, is a necessary component in recognising the changing contours of possibility and circumstance, and in facilitating the acceptance of existing state authority as more right and just than its alternatives.

NOTES

1. A significant development of the idea of 'order' (*nizam*) paralleling that of many Egyptian thinkers and in part derived from them took place in Morocco. One early twentieth-century scholar,

Muhammad al-Hajwi, who became Minister of Education in the early colonial era, argued that the Islamic community (umma) was strong and dominant in the first Islamic centuries because it possessed order, and that it would only regain its strength when Muslims once again achieved order through education and self-discipline. See Bensaid, 1983.

2. An outstanding pre-modern example is provided by Mottahedeh's study of political life in tenth and eleventh century western Iran and southern Iraq under the Buyid dynasty. See *Loyalty and Leadership in an Early Islamic Society*, Princeton University Press, 1980. A contemporary one is the Yemen Arab Republic outside of its major cities. See Dresch, 1983.

3. Population and GNP figures throughout this paper are derived primarily from Kimball *The Arabs 1984-85* (The American Educational Trust, Washington DC, 1985) and supplemented by the World Bank *Atlas* (Washington DC, 1984).

4. These figures exclude defence and security. Oman's military personnel stood at 23,550, of whom 3,700 are foreign. See A. Cordes, *The Gulf and the Search for Strategic Stability* (Westview Press, Boulder, 1984). Since about 1980, Oman has sought significantly to reduce its reliance upon British officer and foreign troops and to promote Omanis to command posts.

5. Other restrictions were also lifted. As Minister of the Interior until his implication in the attempted 1972 *coup* and subsequent demise, General Muhammad Oufkir, responsible for the suppression of the 1965 riots in Casablanca, revived in the late 1960s old protectorate policies of limiting migration from rural areas to towns and strictly regulating new urban construction. After 1972, these unpopular restrictions were quickly lifted and rapid urban expansion resumed.

6. Successor party to the earlier Union Nationale des Forces Populaires (UNFP), formed after a schism in the Istiqlal party in 1960 and led originally by al-Mahdi Ben Barka.

7. His father, however, was a merchant and early contributor to proto-nationalist causes such as the 'Free School' movement (J. Damis, 'Early Moroccan Reactions to the French Protectorate: The Cultural Dimension', *Humanoria Islamica*, *1*, 1973, pp. 15-31), which established schools independent of French control. Rural ties established by his father were successfully used by the son to muster local support.

8. One reason for the initial clandestine organisation was a temporary halt to political liberalisation following an abortive rural uprising in a neighbouring mountain village, Mulay Bu 'Azza, in 1973. By 1975, however, following the monarch's highly successful 'Green March' to mobilise support for reclaiming the Spanish Sahara for Morocco, political parties were again allowed to engage in local activities.

9. In the parliamentary elections, the USFP candidate easily carried the town and several rural regions, which possessed in the aggregate significantly more votes than the town itself. In the rural region with the largest number of votes, government interference was especially pronounced. On election day, gendarmes reportedly blocked

travel on roads to the region. Observers of election procedures permitted by law were consequently unable to reach the polling places to monitor balloting and the recording of results.

10. The first of these was the Democratic Front of Constitutional Institutions (FDIC), formed in 1963 by Ahmad Reda Guedira, a close confidante of the king. It was followed by the equally transparent Independent Assembly (RI) formed after the 1977 parliamentary elections.

8

'Strong' and 'Weak' States, a Qualified Return to the *Muqaddimah*

Ghassan Salamé

'The desert' (says the Hebrew Prophet), shall become a plough-land', so might all this good soil, whose 'sun is gone down whilst it was yet day', return to be full of busy human lives; there lacks but the defence of a strong government.
(Charles M. Doughty, *Travels in Arabia Deserta*, New York, 1936: 56)

There is, in contemporary political sociology, a clear reluctance to distinguish between 'strong' and 'weak' states. This 'habit' is thought to be restricted to limited circles, where 'some Weberian-minded comparativists started labelling states, especially modern national states, "stronger" or "weaker", according to how closely they approximated the ideal type of centralized and fully rationalized Weberian bureaucracy, supposedly able to work its will efficiently and without effective social opposition' (Evans, Rueschemeyer, Skocpol, 1985: 351). The distinction is therefore viewed as a mere 'temptation' (ibid.: 352) which is better avoided since 'possibilities for state interventions of given types cannot be derived from some overall level of generalized capacity or "state strength"' (ibid.: 353).

This reluctance is not general, however. Classic state-minded authors, from Hegel to Raymond Aron, could hardly avoid the strength/weakness distinction. The issue is not completely absent from contemporary sociology (Nettl, 1968). But, more important — at least for us here — is the fact that the issue has remained central in the political discourse, and more deeply in the political culture. One could see how American diplomats were busy rebuilding a 'strong state' in Lebanon in 1982-3, a natural alternative to several years of civil war. More generally, Arabic newspapers, Kuwaiti *diwaniyyas*, and Cairo cafés are so often places where the eternal comparisons between Syria and Iraq, Algeria and Morocco, North and South Yemen, and continuing arguments on their compared strengths, are feverishly made.

It is true that the concept is then used in a much wider meaning (which will therefore be adopted here) than the one used by political sociologists analysing the weight of the state *vis-à-vis* the society it pretends to control, i.e. its autonomy in dealing with other socio-economic actors and its capacity for influencing their behaviour. A more down-to-earth definition would certainly include this meaning, plus a view of Iraq or Syria as Arab countries, i.e., as relatively autonomous and implicitly competitive actors within the general regional framework. The state, then, means at the same time the apparatus in control of a particular society as well as the supposedly 'sovereign' international entity itself. It includes the state *per se*, plus all the resources this state can gather to compare well with other Arab neighbours.

This ambiguity in the definition partly explains why the necessary ingredients of a 'strong state' remain to be clarified, though the concept is widely used. What does it mean to say that Saudi Arabia is 'strong' or 'weak'? Its strength could easily be traced to its petro-financial resources, but also, at the same time, to the way these resources are used by one particular group of leaders. It would therefore be quite difficult, in a society which had not experienced a long democratic tradition, to explain to the 'man in the street' that the holders of political power could refrain from concentrating in their hands all the resources available to them. How to explain, for example, that an American president is at the head of a 'weak state' in a 'strong country'? How to explain the fact that in the Arab (and other Third World societies), the expansion of the state's role in society did not lead to its enhanced capacity in dealing with external challenges? How to explain that, unlike Beirut, Damascus, Baghdad or Riyadh, where political power automatically leads to the concentration of financial and economic activities in its fringes and to chaotic urbanisation, Washington and Bonn are not magnets attracting American and German bankers and industrialists. The distinction between the country and its leader, between the public budget and the resources at the dictator's disposal, or between national and praetorian armies, is yet to be fully made in reality as well as in perceptions.

One hypothesis runs through this paper: perceptions of the state's strength and/or weakness are substantially marked, in the Arab world, by a tradition of authoritarian rule, where the military *ghalaba* (domination) has preceded and practically made possible a generally unrestrained plunder of the society's available resources. These perceptions do not seem to have really adapted to modern times, where states are, more often than not, born dependent. They are generally blurred by centuries-old ideas on the privileges and vulnerability of states and a substantial amount of confusion between the national state apparatus and those who are manipulating it. This explains the current misperception of their (and other) states' strengths and weaknesses, in an era when Khaldunian views of political authority can no longer completely account for the situation of twenty-two (by any standard) weak Arab states in a highly integrated world system.

LESSONS FROM THE 'MUQADDIMAH'

A reader of 'Abd al-Rahman Ibn Khaldun's *Muqaddimah* would easily notice his inclination — almost an obsession — to discuss the strength/weakness dilemma. When he deals in the very first pages of the *Muqaddimah* with the problem of al-'Abbasa, al-Rashid's sister, Ibn Khaldun asks: 'How did al-Rashid lose his authority and how did the state of the Barmecides rise?' He seldom forgets the vulnerability of states throughout the *Muqaddimah* and is clearly fascinated by the regular succession of dynasties.

Ibn Khaldun asserts that the rise of the state is based on the necessity of deterrence (*wazi'*) and is therefore equivalent to the appearance of a leader who enjoys superiority (*ghalaba*) over others. The persistence of that leader in power is based on the strength of blood ties (*'asabiyya*) among the people, whose defence and protection are successful only if they are a closely knit group with common interests. This strengthens their stamina and makes them feared since everybody's affection for his family and group is more important than anything else (Ibn Khaldun, 1967: 97).

Ibn Khaldun then gradually uncovers the components of

207

state power. The first is related to the division of society into several parts. The 'natural' state must possess the means to control each part on its own, and it in turn must recognise the state's power over it. This is because leadership (*ri'asa*) exists only through superiority (*ghulb*) and superiority only through group feeling (*'asabiyya*). Leadership over people, therefore, must, of necessity, derive from a group feeling that is superior to each individual group feeling. Each individual group feeling that becomes aware of the superiority of the group feeling of the leader is ready to obey and follow him. However, the superiority of the leaders' 'asabiyya over all other individual group feelings is not sufficient to build strength. Following that, the whole society must be coalesced (*iltiham*) in accordance with the new authority:

> Natural authority is derived from a group feeling through the continuous superiority over competing parties. However, the condition for the continuation of this authority is for the subservient parties to coalesce with the group who controls leadership (Ibn Khaldun, Arabic: 139).

Thus, Ibn Khaldun judiciously distinguishes between two ingredients of the state's strength. There are, on the one hand, the actual capabilities of the state and, on the other, the recognition by others of these capabilities. Their recognition of this strength will make them accept it, obey it and shift their political loyalty to its possessors. This central concept of iltiham makes Gramsci's 'hegemony' have clear Khaldunian connotations, if not an identical meaning. As well noted by G. Fiori (1970: 238):

> Gramsci's originality as a Marxist lay partly in his conception of the nature of bourgeois rule (and indeed of any previous established social order), in his argument that the system's real strength does not lie in the violence of the ruling class or the coercive power of its state apparatus, but in the acceptance by the ruled of a 'conception of the world' which belongs to the rulers.

The iltiham is then the ultimate form of hegemony in its insistence on social integration by and around the ideology professed by the ruling 'asabiyya.

The larger the new iltiham the stronger the state. Ibn Khaldun does believe that strength is related to the numbers of the state's supporters. Iltiham remains necessary, however; Ibn Khaldun clearly postulates that societies which are formed of one group are always stronger than those composed of different tribes and consequently several 'asabiyyas: 'A dynasty rarely establishes itself firmly in lands with many different tribes and groups. This is because of differences in opinions and desires. Behind each opinion and desire there is a group feeling defending it.' At any time, therefore, there is much opposition to a dynasty and rebellion against it. Ibn Khaldun then points to the ease with which Egypt could be governed; because in Egypt 'Royal authority is most peaceful and firmly rooted, because Egypt has few dissidents or people representing tribal groups. Egypt has a sultan and subjects' (Ibn Khaldun, 1967: 130). The crisis is therefore inevitable when a ri'asa proves to be unable firmly to dominate other group feelings and to draw them to accept its domination now formalised into 'state power'.

Luxury and procreation are linked. Ibn Khaldun distinguishes two stages: at the inception of the state luxury adds to its strength, because it leads to more procreation. The group grows in numbers and in strength. In addition, a greater number of clients and followers (*mawali*) are acquired. But during the state's final days luxury becomes the sign of weakness and senility, owing to its negative demographic consequences, because it is sought for itself, not to strengthen the group. It is in this vein that Ibn Khaldun discusses the sensitive issue of Banu Quraysh's claim to legitimate authority. He treats a matter overloaded with clear ideological implications, in a dispassionate way: 'If we try to understand the *raison d'être* of this condition (that the Caliph should be a qurayshi), we shall find that it is based on the 'asabiyya which allows protection and ambition. This is its foundation and not — as many authors have claimed — the Qurayshis' closeness to the Prophet through direct lineage' (Ibn Khaldun, 1967: 195). In other words, the Qurayshis possess the political legitimacy not forever, but as long as they constitute a strong 'asabiyya. Ibn Khaldun could not accept the idea of a 'divine right' to rule.

Compared with these pivotal blood links, attachment to the land is much less important. The preference of a group for national or religious ties over those of patriotism (i.e. attachment to a territory) would be a self-inflicted weakness. Ibn

Khaldun could not contradict a respected Caliph: 'Umar said: learn your lineage and do not be like a commoner, if somebody asks him of his origin he would say from such and such a village.' Ibn Khaldun rules that belonging to a locality is something which is historically alien to Arab culture and which would threaten blood ties and consequently the very existence of the state. If some Arabs have been known by their locality, this was due to superficial and passing reasons, because for them lineage remains a more important base:

It happened not because the Arabs rejected genealogical considerations, but because they acquired particular places of residence after the Conquest. They eventually became known by their places of residence. These became a distinguishing mark, *in addition to the pedigree* (our emphasis), used by the Arabs to identify themselves in the presence of their Amirs. Later on, sedentary Arabs intermingled with Persians and other non-Arabs. Purity of lineage was completely lost, and its fruit, the group feeling, was lost and rejected (Ibn Khaldun, 1967: 100).

In another part in the *Muqaddimah*, Ibn Khaldun criticises Abu al-Walid Ibn Rushd (Averroes), for deciding that long residence in a territory would be an ingredient in one's identity: 'I should like to know how long residence in a town can help (anyone to build loyalties to his person), if he does not belong to a group that makes him feared and causes others to obey him' (Ibn Khaldun, Arabic: 135).

STATE BUILDING IN SAUDI ARABIA

Saudi Arabia, as a state has many reasons to attract Khaldunian attention, beginning with the desert, enclaved environment in which the state was born. Of no less interest is its continued survival at a time when so many other states in the same region have perished. In two instances, vigour indeed returned to this state following severe defeats. The first was after the Ottoman-inspired Egyptian invasion of the Arabian Peninsula and the second following a bloody civil war in which brothers fought each other and in the process destroyed their father's state. The rise of the third Saudi state at the dawn of this century, and its domination, in less than a quarter of a century of military campaigns, of four-fifths of the Arabian Peninsula, in addition to its victorious entry into the age of the modern nation-state at the beginning of the 1930s, probably transcends in importance the power of the financial and oil factors that were discovered and exploited years after the establishment of the Saudi state's political-military structure (Salamé, 1980).

One major factor in the emergence of a Saudi state undoubtedly lies in *a religious call*. Following the death of Prophet Muhammad, the history of the Arabian Peninsula was characterised by tribal and regional dispersion. The *da'wa* of Muhammad ibn 'Abd al-Wahhab (1703-92) carried, in addition to the fundamental principles attached to the Hanbali ideas, a call for unity among competing and conflicting factions. Thus al-Muwahhidun, the self-given name of the movement, had two meanings. The first was explicit: to re-assert the unity of God in the face of the idolatrous practices to which most of the inhabitants of Najd used to resort. The other was implied: it aimed at the unity of (at least) the Arabian Peninsula by the iltiham of the various tribal attachments, around a new tribal ri'asa.

What could this unifying link be other than religion? In the middle of the eighteenth century nationalism as a modern ideology formulated in Europe was scarcely known to the inhabitants of this area and even if it had reached them, it would have required generations before it became entrenched and before its proponents could answer a basic question, that remains open to this day: the nationalism of which nation — Saudi Arabia, Arabia, the Arab or the Muslim world?

Islam was actually the only available unifying factor. All Najdis also spoke Arabic, but language is an element of cultural unity and would hardly be useful here as a tool of political mobilisation. Through a religious revival movement, the new call would eventually be able to mobilise the majority of the area's inhabitants, i.e. Sunni-Muslims, Bedouins and settled, Hasawi and Najdi, 'noble' and not. Its political strategy was consequently to differ from that usually followed by neighbouring religious minorities, such as the Zaydis in Yemen, the Ibadis in Oman's Green Mountains or the Shi'a in Bahrain and Hasa. These minorities' objective was to survive as schismatic groups united around specific interpretations of the Book and hence with a built-in group solidarity. It was therefore natural to

211

see them entrenched in islands (Bahrain) and mountains (Oman and Yemen) as an antidote to the continuous (and generally hostile) pressure of the Sunni/orthodox majority on Islamic minorities and other *milal.* For these minorities, the strategy was basically that of self-defence, and an obstinate rejection of the calls for political or cultural integration into the prevailing majority.

Wahhabism, as its enemies usually called it, had another purpose, and a much wider potential audience. Its strategy was based on offence. Its implied premisses were that the whole world should adopt Islam and that all Muslims should go back to earlier orthodox religion, as interpreted by the Wahhabi reformer along Hanbali lines. Therefore it was a call directed towards all without exception, and the movement was eager to see it adopted by every tribe, in every oasis and village, either by persuasion or coercion, or usually through a combination of the two. Thus, the internal dynamics were those of attack, invasion and intervention, without which the movement could hardly have survived. The call was for the re-establishment of 'true Islam'. It did not claim to offer a minority interpretation of Islam, it was not based on a new religion, but on a fundamentalist interpretation embodying a strong nostalgia for the supposedly original Islam: simple, aggressive and victorious. This interpretation was to prove attractive to many eighteenth-century Arabians.

One could hardly be surprised to read in a British traveller's diary of 1784: 'When I arrived at Basra, the Ottoman Wali of Baghdad, his delegate in Basra as well as other Turks, were all worried by the activities of the leader of the Wahhabis. This is because they knew that Ibn 'Abd al-Wahhab's strict interpretation of the Quranic texts was the purest and most abiding by it' (Rentz 1972: 57). While two centuries later the Lebanese traveller Amin ar-Rihani described King 'Abd al-'Aziz by saying: 'Sultan 'Abd al-'Aziz is the Saudi people's *imam* in every sense. He recognises the courageous, fearful, patient, sane and foolish among them, while he is also capable of ruling over them and thus placing them in the service of God and the Kingdom of Ibn Saud' (Ar-Rihani n.d.: 87).

This duality (God and Ibn Saud) embodies another component of the state's 'strength'. A geographic region (Najd) falls under the control of a coalition led by a ri'asa. The Saudi family's rule is established over other tribal alliances in the hinterland of the Arabian Peninsula. In other words, a superior 'asabiyya was able to defeat other group feelings and later to coalesce them into one greater group feeling. The religious call acted as a cement to make this coalescence (whatever its depth) possible in such a highly segmented tribal society.

Ibn Khaldun is fond of repeating Prophet Muhammad's famous saying: 'God sent no prophet who did not enjoy the protection of his people'. He relates the story of Ibn Qasi, a sufi shaykh who rebelled in Andalusia without any tribes or group feelings to support him. He was soon forced to surrender to another Andalusian call. This is what the Wahhabi call knew how to avoid by attaching itself, a few years after its inception, to a strong tribal 'asabiyya, that of the Sa'ud family. This new, by now 'ideologised', group feeling was brought about through the adoption by the Amir of Dir'iyyah, Muhammad ibn Sa'ud, and following him, by his son 'Abd al-'Aziz, of the religious reformer's views. Both father and son, and the Amirs of the family who succeeded them, embraced that call. Thus an element of strength resulted from the blending of a religious call and a group feeling, in a way Ibn Khaldun would have considered ideal. Since according to him:

> prophets in their religious propaganda depended on groups and families, though they could have been supported by God with anything in existence. If someone who is on the right path were to attempt [religious reforms] in this way, his isolation would keep him from [gaining the support of] group feeling and he would perish (Ibn Khaldun, Arabic: 159).

He adds, with obvious sarcasm, 'Many deluded individuals took it upon themselves to establish the truth. They did not know that they would need group feeling for that.' He compares those who are not supported by a group feeling to the foolhardy who deserve to be ridiculed:

> They did not realise how their enterprise must necessarily end and what they would come to. Toward such people it is necessary to adopt one of the following courses. One may either treat them as if they are insane, may punish them either by execution or beatings when they cause trouble, or may ridicule them and treat them as buffoons (Ibn Khaldun, 1967: 124).

The Sa'ud family skilfully used the idea of equality among believers in order to mobilise the Bedouin as an aggressive force against rivals and enemies. And they were to use the politically *status-quo*-oriented jurisprudential school of Ibn Hanbali to strengthen the basis of their authority, once it was established. There is no doubt that the decision (*fatwa*) issued by Shaykh 'Abd al-Latif Ibn 'Abd ar-Rahman on lending political and religious legitimacy to the strong party in any civil war, is the best example of the use of the religious Wahhabi *da'wa* in strengthening the Sa'ud authority (Helms, 1981: 76-126). The bearers of the religious call were also instrumental in collecting taxes and then redistributing them in a way which was gradually to strengthen the 'legitimate' political authority, by cementing subtle forms of economic dependence among Bedouins (bounty) and the settled population (by ensuring stability and encouraging trade).

STRATEGIC IMMUNITY AND LEGITIMACY

Engaging now in geo-strategy, Ibn Khaldun makes what he considers as a central distinction between the state's core and its more distant periphery:

> This may be compared to light rays that spread from their centres or to circles that widen over the surface of the water when something strikes it. When the dynasty becomes senile and weak it begins to crumble at its extremities. The centre remains intact until God permits the destruction of the whole dynasty. Then the centre is destroyed. But when a dynasty is overrun from the centre it is of no avail to it that the outlying areas remain intact. It dissolves all at once (Ibn Khaldun, 1967: 128-9).

In other words, the degree to which the centre is immune in the face of external challenges and threats plays a pivotal role in the emergence of the state and later in its persistence and unavoidable decay. It is not an accident that the Saudi state happens to have been born in the heart of the Arabian Peninsula. In the mid-eighteenth century, during the state's formative years, it was neither easy nor very alluring to invade such a desert space and even less to colonise it. When the British and before them other naval powers (the Portuguese, Dutch and French) circled the Arabian Peninsula, they landed in Aden, Muscat or Hudayda, but refrained from entering Arabia Deserta. They certainly realised the difficulty of the task involved and underrated its usefulness. Similarly, the Ottomans used to move from the north to the south along two axes: the first originated in Damascus, passed through Hijaz and ended in Hudayda; the second originated in Mosul, went on to Baghdad and Basra and reached al-Hasa via Kuwait. In both cases the Ottomans avoided entering the Arabian Peninsula's heartland. They seemed content merely to encircle it along the coasts of the Gulf and the Red Sea, leaving its rugged barren centre undisturbed. Muhammad 'Ali's was the first army of modern times to invade the Arabian Peninsula, cutting across it from the Red Sea to Hasa and destroying in the process the first Saudi state. However, the Egyptian ruler was soon obliged to pull back and retreat, providing an opportunity for the re-establishment of the Saudi state, in spite of the destruction of its capital, ad-Dir'iyyah, and the presence of many Amirs in Cairo as Muhammad 'Ali's captives.

A state whose centre is located in a region like Najd would benefit from a long period of time to develop and expand without being immediately threatened by external interference. This was the case with the first Saudi-Wahhabi state, which for a period of eighty years was hardly challenged. It was located in a remote region far outside the reach of strategic naval bases or important overland routes, in the midst of an inhospitable desert, the penetration of which, even by 'legitimate' Ottoman troops, was considered utterly senseless. One might even assume that the *wali* of Basra could not easily assess the strength of the new state or the ambitions of its leaders, except after a long lapse of time. For who in the Middle East was then capable of concluding that a new powerful state had been born, and not just a new vulnerable coalition of tribes which, a few months or a few years later, would naturally disintegrate.

This asset is clearer when one compares the Egyptian experience of Muhammad 'Ali at the beginning of the nineteenth century with that of the Sa'uds, two state-building processes taking place in roughly the same era. There is no doubt that the ambitious and highly organised Albanian soldier possessed enviable instruments of power, in contrast to those at the disposal of the Amir of Najd. Egypt under Muhammad 'Ali

215

enjoyed a surplus in agricultural production, relatively well organised and well equipped military power, openness to the outside world, not to mention the experience Muhammad 'Ali himself already had in leadership and international affairs. Paradoxically, because of all these factors, Egypt did not enjoy Najd's immunity. It was permanently in danger of being conquered and occupied precisely because it was so open to the outside world and strategically located on the road to India, and on that strip of the south-eastern coast of the Mediterranean.

Galal Ahmad Amin has accurately observed that the degree of Western pressure over the different parts of the Arab world varied with the strategic importance of the country or with the raw materials it provided. Thus, while Egypt, Syria and Iraq were connected to the Western economy by the middle of the nineteenth century, the relative unimportance of the Libyan desert allowed the spread of the Sanusiyya movement. This movement survived until 1911 when the Italian occupiers destroyed it. Similarly, it was only at the end of the nineteenth century that Britain became interested in developing the agricultural resources of Sudan. Thus in the second half of the nineteenth century, Sudan experienced the rise of an independence movement similar to the Sanusi and Wahhabi movements. This was the al-Mahdiyya movement, which ruled over Sudan for thirteen years (1885-98), during which it unified the greater part of the country, eliminated the slave trade and enjoyed great popularity not only in Sudan, but also in Egypt where many Egyptians pinned great hopes on it to save them from British occupation. The strategic importance of the coastal regions overlooking the Arabian Gulf made Britain impose on their tribal shaykhs consecutive defence pacts during the last two decades of the nineteenth century. However, the unattractiveness of the economic and strategic conditions existing in the Arabian Peninsula and Yemen allowed this region to be left on its own until the discovery of oil after World War I (Amin, 1979: 97).

Galal Amin suggests that the failure of Muhammad 'Ali's Egypt and the relative success of a state such as Japan in modernisation, industrialisation and development during the nineteenth century are to a great extent due to the relative geographic seclusion of the latter in comparison with the former's geographic centrality, depriving it of a necessary level of immunity to foreign pressure. It is indeed agreed that the location of a strategically situated state represents a source of weakness rather than of strength, when this state is not powerful enough to defend the resources and/or the services which it provides.

The relative seclusion of Najd led to yet another ingredient in the young Saudi state's strength. Abdallah Laroui points to the way nationalist forces with a fundamentalist outlook have viewed the rational reforms which the colonial powers brought to the heart of the traditional Arab state:

> it was probable or actually expected that the nationalist movement would give birth to a theory of the state, completely different from the ulama conception of authority. However, the foreign domination of authority ... forced the nationalists to adopt the fundamentalists' view whole-heartedly. The legitimate imamate which was a utopia when authority was in the hands of Muslims, became a double utopia when real authority was controlled by Europeans while claiming the application of justice and declaring the dispensability of the revealed divine law. During the modern age the instruments of state were reformed and the economic conditions, even those of the lower classes, improved. However, the state remained alien and the society miserable (Laroui, 1981: 139).

The refusal of anything European was indeed stronger in nationalist circles than the acceptance of these modern 'benefits' of domination. Foreign powers' domination consequently had negative effects on the legitimacy of the local forces which agreed to co-operate with them. When the British Empire was helping a state such as the Amirate of Bahrain or the Sultanate of Oman to survive it was at the same time weakening these states' legitimacy. Foreign support seemed to produce an ambiguous reaction in which admiration for the ruler's crafts-manship in securing a great power's support was mixed with the idea that his rule could not survive this power's change of mind or its departure. Hence the necessity of securing the ruler's legitimacy through bureaucratic, Western-inspired achieve-ments such as an improved health service, a modern education system, or organised police and military forces which compared favorably with neighbouring emirates' forces.

In clear contrast to the Gulf shaykhdoms or Transjordan, the

Saudi state was certainly not the product of a foreign intervention, and its legitimacy was hardly based on the kind of support it was getting from Britain. Quite to the contrary, the *imara* was established despite the opposition of the external powers (the Ottoman Empire and Britain) and at their expense. Thus its legitimacy was based not so much on the Western-inspired services it offered to its citizens as on a mixture of local nationalism and religious fundamentalism which embodied a definite chauvinism. In such Arab states as Bahrain, Kuwait, Jordan and Morocco the colonial powers penetrated the local authority and, in a mimetic drive, created the structure of a modern local bureaucracy. Whether through a military governor, a *Haut-Commissaire*, or a Political Resident, the British and French Governments directed, commanded, discussed and rationalised from within the local authority either as 'employees' of the prince or as his advisers. External power became a basic element in the local equation of power, which in the process restructured the local administration and increased its adaptability.

This osmosis between the two powers weakened the legitimacy of the local power, though it provided it with the ability to control its citizens and expand its bureaucracy, thereby enabling it to maintain authority in a more 'modern' way. The Saudi state, at least up until World War I, did not go through this process of penetration/satellisation which was spreading from the capital of the Ottoman Empire in Istanbul to such tiny Amirates as Bahrain. The Saudi state (like the Sanusi state up until the Italian conquest, or the Madhist state until it was militarily defeated by Gordon) remained largely outside the colonial realm and to a great extent secured a 'nationalist-fundamentalist' legitimacy. The institution-building process was much less the result of Western-inspired 'expertise' than an authentic attempt to meet the challenge of foreign forces beyond the borders of the Saudi nucleus.

A comparison with one or two other Arab states will clarify the concept of legitimacy in relation to the early contact with international powers. In his book on the rise of the Saudi state in the period between 1910 and 1926, Gary Troeller observed that relations between Britain and 'Abd al-'Aziz ibn Sa'ud barely existed, since the former did not believe that Ibn Sa'ud posed any threat to its regional interests, while 'Abd al-'Aziz was still reluctant to engage in foreign relations which could undermine his 'asabiyya. The *rapprochement* was basically dictated by the necessities imposed by World War I. This *rapprochement* did not cause Britain to intrude into this nascent desert country as was the case with Sharif Husayn ibn 'Ali in al-Hijaz. Rather, it led to an agreement specifying borders and later to Britain's gradual acceptance of the continuous Saudi expansion. Ibn Sa'ud was able to go beyond the red lines that Britain specified for him, having imposed himself on Britain as an independent and ambitious leader. This was to help strengthen his authority substantially *vis-à-vis* his Arabian rivals since, as Stinchcombe has put it, as far as legitimacy is concerned, 'The person over whom power is exercised is not usually as important as other powerholders' (Stinchcombe, 1968: 150).

In comparison, things were radically different in a country like Jordan, where Britain played an essential role in the very creation of the state. This could be explained by Britain's prior attachment to the Hashemite family and by the continuous presence of a number of British officials and soldiers in Amman. To 'legitimise' the deep British penetration of the newly established state there was the League of Nations mandate, an experience which Saudi Arabia has never been compelled to undergo. And in Amman, 'given the impoverishment of the new kingdom, both the British envoy and the financial counsellor in the administration of finance were given the right to supervise all financial affairs ... Then the details of the general budget were submitted to the British envoy, who in turn transferred them to the British High Commissioner in Jerusalem and then to the Minister of Colonies in London to approve them' (al-Mahafdha, 1973: 38).

In this respect one could consider Lebanon, for example, as falling somewhere between the Saudi and the Jordanian examples. Meir Zamir's dual conclusion is accurate: modern Lebanon is the product of the evolution of the centuries-old Druze imara into a Maronite-dominated entity as well as of French colonial designs. His study of the state's formative years (1920-6) clearly shows that the geo-social nucleus of a state was well-entrenched in the area when the French were given the mandate over Lebanon and Syria. They played a central role in defining the new state's borders, but they did not create it (Zamir, 1985; Salibi, 1965; Harik, 1968 and in this volume).

Saudi Arabia stands out in a positive way, when compared to these two and other examples, at least as far as legitimacy based

219

on 'authentic', non-Western-induced state-building is concerned. But should these credentials lead to the conclusion that the regime's legitimacy is endowed with a resilience that is beyond erosion?

INTEGRATION IN THE WORLD SYSTEM: THE EFFECTS

Legitimacy, when it exists, is certainly not resilient to all kinds of challenges. The first among them is the largely unsuccessful attempt at compulsory social integration. The Saudi leaders have tried to create an integrated society by bringing together different tribes whose men were militarily trained and drawn into a religious 'asabiyya. By this means, each was to become the 'brother' of the other, in spite of differences in their tribal allegiances. It has become clear that this experience did not actually succeed, as the various *hijra* (intended to mix tribes together) continued to be characterised by the domination of specific tribal cleavages. True iltiham is indeed very difficult to trigger, despite the combined and intensive use of two supra-tribal cleavages: first, the Wahhabi da'wa and then the allegiance to the modern Saudi national state.

When the creation of this state became the conqueror's exclusive endeavour, the clash with the religious zealots and the feared soldiers of the *Ikhwan* became inevitable. This clash was indeed to be a watershed in the Kingdom's history for several reasons. 'Abd al-'Aziz had first to mobilise troops to fight against the rebellious Ikhwan and to do this he cleverly used tribal cleavages as well as the settled population's fear of Bedouin extremism, thereby acknowledging the disintegration of the inter-tribal coalition between the Bedouin and the settled population which made possible the re-emergence of Saudi rule.

'Abd al-'Aziz also had to call for (or at least to accept) external help in order to crush the rebellious Ikhwan. Hence the utopia of an 'authentic' state, built outside the reach of foreign powers and at their expense, was seriously undermined. The West was no longer a *kafir* enemy, but an ally in the fight against those groups who most clearly embodied the traditional religious-chauvinistic legitimacy. British financial aid was rapidly to follow military support, and the Saudi ruler's position came gradually to resemble that of his previously deposed neighbours, such as the two Hashemite kings of Jordan and Iraq or the Gulf shaykhs, surviving under, and thanks to, British protection. This integration into the world system had huge implications for the state's vision of its own capabilities and for the ways in which its survival could be secured. 'Abd al-'Aziz was to trade his imam title for a secular royal one; the country was to sign border treaties and thereby accept an imposed limitation on the spread of the da'wa; the idea of coexisting with differently-minded neighbours and with foreign colonial powers was to prevail and, last but not least, oil explorers were to be tolerated in the Kingdom.

The Bedouin were to be the designated victims of this shift in the King's political strategy:

Although the alliance of the al-Sa'ud and the Badu in the early twentieth century had fulfilled specific functions, especially the military expansion of the kingdom, it was not practical. While the al-Sa'ud emphasized the unity of 'church' and 'state' as well as the legitimacy of their own authority, they were eventually forced because of external influences to define their state on a territorial basis (Helms, 1981: 272).

The Saudis were indeed to witness a clear concentration of power within the now-royal family, and eventually within one exclusive 'House', that of 'Abd al-'Aziz (Salamé, 1982). Largely similar movements of power concentration took place in Bahrain, Kuwait or Qatar. In these shaykhdoms, however, politics were traditionally dominated by a ruling coalition between the Amir and the leading trading families. But, with oil, the Amirs were able not only to settle the ruling families' debts to the merchants, but also collectively to buy them off. 'As a result, trading families in both states rose economically, but declined politically' (Crystal, 1985: 27).

Swords and British help were to defeat the Bedouin and oil was to cut the appetite of the settled population for political participation. Studying the Iranian case, Skocpol (1982) has concluded that huge and sudden oil revenues can render states more autonomous vis-à-vis domestic social and political actors, but more vulnerable in moments of crisis. In Saudi Arabia and the Gulf shaykhdoms at least the first part of this proposition can be verified. And this trend is not restricted to oil countries, but has a special significance in those where extractive industries

221

are central in the economy (Evans in Evans, Rueschemeyer and Skocpol, 1985: 119-226).

This state 'autonomy' on the domestic level, coupled with a deepening integration in the world economic system, naturally leads rulerships to seek other bases of legitimacy, other definitions of strength: a welfare state, a skilful redistribution of resources, some form of co-optation within the new elites. While the process is taking place, these countries' political evolution remains largely unpredictable, because it is very hard to measure, at a particular moment, the extent to which these new elements of the state's legitimacy have been integrated into the political culture. Political socialisation is by definition a long-term process, and even longer in these countries where, in contrast to Iran, the ruler is reluctant radically to depart from his traditional bases of legitimacy, or to trade them completely for his new role as head of state. He will hesitate before operating such a radical shift, correctly recognising that, among his 'subjects', identification with the abstract concept of a national state remains vulnerable. The society indeed remains vertically disintegrated and rival groups may use any shift in policy to organise along old tribal or geographic cleavages, around a new ri'asa.

LEBANON: A STATE IN A SOCIETY AT WAR

For the individual, this shift is certainly not an easy process, and this can not be ignored even by the 'modernisation' school of analysis. Lucian Pye has noted that 'the stable modern state cannot be realized without a clear feeling of identity: that is, without solving the problem of the co-existence of traditional cultural forms with modern practices and factional allegiances with cosmpolitan lifestyles. It is as if the individual is torn between two worlds without having roots in either of them' (Pye, 1962: 63).

Erich Fromm is more explicit in the description of this new psychological dilemma (1960: 29):

> The identity with nature, clan, religion, gives the individual security. He belongs to, he is rooted in, a structuralised whole in which he has an unquestionable place. He may suffer from

hunger or suppression but he does not suffer from the worst of all pains: complete aloneness and doubt.

The rise of the modern state represents a real challenge to the individual, a challenge to his feeling of belonging to a group and to the security of having a defined place within it. The transfer of loyalty from the traditional group to the modern state can not be easily completed, and anyway takes place in a clearly alienating manner. It is doubly alienating when not only the form of the state is unfamiliar but when those commanding it are strangers as well. This could be due to the leader's allegiance to an external power (during the period of colonialism), or to his membership in another traditional group (much as a Shi'i would look at a Sunni-dominated state or a Berber at a state dominated by the Arabs), or to his belonging to a social group that is unfamiliar to the rest of the citizenry (such as technocrats or professionals).

Thus, suddenly the citizen is given an identity card or a passport specifying for him a new exclusive identity. He is either Lebanese or Syrian, Tunisian or Libyan, Qatari or Bahraini. Yet a real identity crisis exists underneath this change in outward form. To quote Fromm again (1960: 177):

The loss of the self and its substitution by a pseudo-self leave the individual in an intense state of insecurity. He is obsessed by doubt since, being essentially a reflex of other people's expectations of him, he has in a measure lost his identity. In order to overcome the panic resulting from such loss of identity, he is compelled to conform to seek his identity by continuous approval and recognition by others.

The Lebanese war has harshly revealed the fragility of the state within the society, due, among other factors, to the failure of (Ibn Khaldun's) iltiham and to the lack of (Fromm's) 'continuous recognition'. The most revealing fact of this situation is the survival of the state itself, not through the strength of its internal structures but for much the same reasons as those explaining its weakness.

With the prevailing international system not favouring any geographical reformulation of existing political entities, whether through partition and division or through integration and unity, any state is in a way guaranteed its existence. And this is all the more so in sensitive regions like the Middle East because here a challenge to a state's existence might lead to a reformulation of the political map and consequently to wars that are not necessarily desirable. Regardless of internal wars, the state remains intact as a form through the support and recognition of regional and international powers. The Lebanese state, at least since 1975, is to a great extent a form without a substance.

Some Lebanese have felt that they were alien to the Lebanese identity and that this was imposed upon them by external powers. Before Lebanon's independence in 1943, Muslims often expressed their desire to be part of Syria instead of being 'artificially' attached to Mount Lebanon. And when the domestic balance of power shifted after 1975, many Maronites felt that remaining in Greater Lebanon was becoming too heavy a burden for them, and was no longer the asset it had been in the days when — thanks to their higher level of education, their advanced 'asabiyya and the support France was providing to them — they had greater control over the country. Most of the Muslims before 1943 and some Maronites after 1975 think therefore that, to use Clifford Geertz's distinction, their attachment to Lebanon is not 'primordial', is not 'given', and could consequently be negotiated or even radically repudiated.

But these people also feel that they cannot really alter a *status quo* which is beyond their power. Identity is indeed a cultural product which is not exclusively shaped by those who are going to bear it. David Laitin has successfully shown that foreign powers have been able to intervene substantially in this process. Their success could be measured by the extent to which 'locals' viewed as 'authentic' and 'primordial' a cleavage which was previously identified and supported by the hegemonic power (Evans, Rueschemeyer, Skocpol, 1985: 285-316). Berber identity indeed depended on the Berbers' and Arabs' views as much as on the French strategy concerned with political cleavages in North Africa, and the determination with which this strategy was pursued. Ian Lustick has convincingly demonstrated how Israel has pursued a policy of direct control over the Arabs living within the pre-1967 borders through a mixture of segmentation, co-optation and economic dependence. The following words by an Israeli anthropologist, quoted by Lustick, should conseqently be viewed more like a government programme than a mere description:

Arabs in Israel do not constitute a united, integrated community. They are divided on many lines which tend to overlap, rather than cut across each other. There is the broad division into Bedouin, village dwellers and townsmen, with hardly any links between these divisions. Furthermore, each of these divisions is divided internally, etc. (Lustick, 1980: 82).

As far as Lebanon is concerned, it is difficult to believe that the war has suddenly unleashed all these competing loyalties, thus leading to the collapse of the state. The Lebanese have generally known how to live 'outside the state'. Their wealth and most of their cultural and political trends have been imported. Their press was often established and/or subsidised by foreigners. The economy has been restricted to the private sector, and only with great difficulty can a popular trend be found supporting state intervention in the economy and society. Actually it was very easy for the mercantile right to destroy the only attempt aimed at giving the state a social, economic and security base: President Fuad Shihab's regime (1958-64) which vanished during the second half of the 1960s under the attack of the representatives of radical Lebanese individualism, and later under the parallel attacks of militarised sectarian forces and the Palestinians.

The Lebanese state did not fall in 1975, it continued outside society by means of the external recognition it still enjoyed. Following the failure of the Shihabi initiative which was based on some *sens de l'état*, the problem of identity was exacerbated and went on to destroy the basis of the society. States are in need of suitable political cultures which they can adopt as legitimate legal frameworks. Under Shihab, the Lebanese state, as in other Third World countries, attempted to develop this same political culture through political socialisation focusing on such concepts as national unity, religious sectarian co-existence and Lebanon as a final indisputable entity. Yet the war was also to reveal the failure of Lebanese iltiham, which was meant to rise within the modern state in defence of its borders and institutions.

The war also led to the strengthening of sectarianism as a central political cleavage. But its victory was never complete. Many Lebanese were too accustomed to 'the Lebanese idea', or too opposed to sectarianism, to be born-again Maronites or Shi'a. And sectarianism itself remained ambiguous, since the new warlords were continuously changing their strategy, stressing one day the sectarian cleavage (Maronites-Sunnites-Druzes, etc.) and the religious binary cleavage (Muslim/Christian) the next (Salamé, 1986).

The Lebanese case is extreme but not exceptional. Indeed, the Arab state seems to be caught between the combined fire of sub-state and supra-state forces. Hanna Arendt points to the crisis of states in the face of greater nationalities transcending their limits (a good example being German nationalism). This is why, for example, pan-Germanist Schroener was among the bitterest enemies of the state, as was pan-Slavist Rozanov. Both looked with disdain at modern international political entities and considered them obstacles in the way of a nation's self-fulfillment. Both can inspire (and have inspired) the propagators of the Islamic nation, or those championing the unity of Greater Syria, and most importantly, the modern Arab nationalists. A 1985 editorial of *Al-Mustaqbal al-'Arabi*, probably the best scholarly journal to appear in Arabic, included the following evaluation:

> All appearances point to the spread of the phenomenon of the state in the Arab world. But, in spite of these appearances, the failure of the Arab state — despite its slogans, flag, national anthem, university, plan and national museum — in achieving true independence and in eliminating all kinds of dependence, or in liberating the occupied Arab territories in Palestine, not to mention the failure to accomplish national security on the part of all states, will sooner or later strengthen the Arab citizen's conviction that the state has failed to achieve the major objectives it has set for itself. Consequently, this same Arab citizen will be inclined to work at a national [pan-Arab] level and transcend the local state phenomenon (Hasib, 1985: 7).

The above statement approximates the idea of the state to a mere 'local phenomenon'. Any acceptance of such an attitude is a blow to the legitimacy of existing Arab states. The writer of this article, like other Arab nationalists, seeks the achievement of precisely this aim. The need to fulfil this objective is stronger among Arab nationalists than it is among proponents of the Islamic *umma* who generally seem to accept the independent existence of the current Islamic states, as long as they adopt the

226

Islamic *shari'ah* and its laws, and seek active 'solidarity' with other Islamic countries. The aim of Arab nationalism is the elimination of all existing states and their integration into one Arab state. Twentieth-century Islamism (Al-Banna, Qutb, 'Awdah) is more interested in domestic politics than in bringing about the unity of the world's Muslims into one state.

Whether Arab nationalists, propagators of Greater Syria or of the Islamic unity, like it or not, they are working alongside other enemies of existing states that are also intent on undermining their legitimacy. These enemies are sectarian, tribal and ethnic movements which, in turn, also aim at reformulating the existing political map. While Arab nationalists regard contemporary states as too small clothes for the Arabs to wear, others find these same states too large or completely unsuitable. The Kurds, for example, may well believe that borders were drawn with the specific intention of dispersing them into a number of states.

Whether Kurds, Maronites, Berbers or south Sudanese, these groups often reject the states in which they find themselves. Even when they adopt a more rational and realistic attitude and recognise that existing states cannot be easily destroyed, they prefer them to be weak and fragile, allowing ethnic groups the largest possible autonomy. This autonomy must also be expressed geographically, that is, self-rule in specific regions in which these groups enjoy a demographic superiority, or as the euphemism goes in Lebanon 'de-centralisation in security and development matters'. Foreign interference is rendered easy and attractive by these separatist trends.

A short-cut remedy to all these problems is 'unity'. Anyone following the Lebanese war will recall that it was continuously said that the solution lay in the unity of the Maronites or of the Shi'a, unity of Muslims or Christians, national (Lebanese) unity, unity with Syria, or Arab unity. Too often 'unity' appears as a panacea, whatever the political cleavage. This reveals this 'remedy's' highly ideological nature and hence its extreme vulnerability. In so far as the identity remains debatable, in so far as those in control of the state have not established a strong social iltiham, unity remains an empty shell. This widespread obsession with unity is so 'tribal' (Arendt) that it becomes a sort of 'political religion' (Apter), with no real impact on the society. It probably also hinders a more rational search for state strength, outside the old Khaldunian realm.

HOW IMPORTANT IS THE ECONOMY?

Yet where does the source of strength lie? Is it found in a strong economy? Among the interesting elements in Ibn Khaldun's thinking is the place given to economic activity, as he describes the five stages of the state: the first stage is that of success; the second is the one in which the ruler gains complete control over his people. The fourth is one of contentment and peacefulness and the fifth is one of waste and squandering. The economic stage is the third:

> It is the stage of leisure and tranquillity in which the fruits of royal authority are enjoyed: the things that human nature desires, such as acquisition of property, creation of lasting monuments and fame. All the ability (of the ruler) is expended on collecting taxes; regulating income and expenses, keeping books and planning expenditure; erecting large buildings, and constructions, spacious cities and lofty monuments; presenting gifts to ambassadors of nobility from (foreign) nations and tribal dignitaries; and dispensing bounty to his people. In addition, he supports the demands of his followers and retinue with money and positions. He inspects his soldiers, pays them well and distributes their allowances fairly every month. Eventually, the result of this (liberality) shows itself in their dress, their fine equipment and their armour on parade days.

Even more interesting is his conclusion, when he says: 'this stage is the last during which the ruler is in complete authority' (Ibn Khaldun, 1967: 141-2).

Why should the economic stage be in the third position and yet be the last stage during which the ruler is in complete authority? Ibn Khaldun points out two basic factors. First, that the economy (actually economic capability) is related to actual political and military strength; thus, when superiority is achieved and the authority of the ruler is established, wealth comes as a natural bonus to whoever is in control. Second, that economic activity is not so much related to production as it is to spending. This is why this stage does not lead to more strength, but actually leads to the stage of senility. *Iqtissad*, in contrast to the usual meaning of the word (that is, to cut down on expenses), is based on spending. Its political result is not so much derived from the strengthening of the economic and then the political structure of the state, as it is from giving both supporters and enemies the indisputable impression of luxury and of an unlimited capacity to spend. This will enhance the state's authority since it is capable of buying loyalties and paying the military.

For anyone who has travelled in the Arab oil countries, this view can hardly be surprising. But one could get an identical impression in other poorer countries, as this conclusion on Syria's industrial efforts, drawn by Michel Seurat shows:

> It is not necessary to be an expert in economic anthropology to discover that a factory in the public sector there does not function like a similar one in France, as the real reason behind its presence is not the achievement of profits, as much as it is to provide a means for spending. This spending represents a part of the strategy of the political authority and provides it with a new source of strength (Bourgey *et al.* 1982: 35).

If this analysis holds in Syria, it is all the more relevant in Arabia where, historically, stable powers used to persuade long-range caravan tradesmen to take their routes through their areas. One could hardly say that this long-range caravan trade 'created' states, since it was vulnerable and therefore dependent on the level of security that was established along its routes. Hence the weakness of the vulgar 'Marxist' theory that conquerors, ambitious Amirs or established tribal leaderships were the mere tools of these merchants. These leaderships were certainly affected by this trade and very much relied on the mixture of protection and racketeering which they exercised over it. Without it, a military-political tribal power would have had less control over its troops, or would have been less influential with the area's smaller tribes, but it would not have disappeared altogether.

In modern Kuwait and Saudi Arabia no ideologised economic nationalisations took place, as was the case in Syria or Iraq. But are the consequences any different? In the Gulf countries political leadership is clearly based on 'asabiyya. This leadership has ruled from the outset that the oil is state property. But what is the state? The state was then more a cover for a ri'asa than an 'autonomous' apparatus. Money, which

229

essentially means immense oil revenues, was controlled by the governing families, by small groups of brothers and cousins who head the ruling families and rule the rest of the people. Since oil is itself the revenue that is extracted by means of the help of external Western technology, it is not really subject to the laws of production. And one is often tempted to compare the relationship in the 1940s or 1950s between the new Saudi state and the international oil companies with the one binding its ancestors with long-range tradesmen. An enclaved economic activity was merely paying the dues for a continued peaceful expansion. For the state, the issue is not about the means of production or its actual development, nor about the identity of those controlling it. Rather, it is about the way the oil revenues are distributed, about the identity of those controlling this process, about the amount of money that is being distributed and the identity of the beneficiaries.

If this is how things stand in such countries, then it is no wonder that a country like Saudi Arabia did not and could not provide a sufficient political cover for a number of American political projects in the region. A country's capabilities do not lie only in the extraction of millions of barrels of oil per day, nor in the fact that a quarter of the world's oil reserves are found under its deserts, nor in receiving billions of dollars of revenues or, finally, in the possession of huge financial reserves. These assets would have constituted a real 'power' if they had been found in a fully developed country like Britain or France. But Saudi Arabia is a country with a small population. It is technologically underdeveloped, unable to integrate women into the work force, dependent on millions of foreign workers and possessing only one almost exclusive and exhaustible source of revenue: oil. In addition to all this, Saudi Arabia continues to be militarily weak in a region characterised by intense conflicts and the emergence of strong military forces (Iraq, Iran, Israel). Given all these facts, it cannot limit itself to the immense oil revenues if the 'asabiyya is in danger or if the ri'asa is threatened. It might even be that the present state of oil revenues is not the last stage in which these gulf ri'asas are in control. Is not the ease with which money is procured a sign of senility?

Arab political culture is rarely tuned to stock market indicators. Although there are Arab economists, the existence of Arab economic thought and its influence on society remains an open question ('Abd al-Fadil, 1983). The Arab renaissance was not

230

characterised by a clear interest in economics. Even a figure known for his great openness to 'modernity', such as Ahmad Lutfi as-Sayyid, was not concerned with this topic. As noted by Albert Hourani, 'industry is not, in his opinion, the basis of national strength. All his emphasis is on a strong national consciousness' (Hourani, 1983: 181). In a more general summary Hourani had observed that

the content of nationalism in this period included few precise ideas about social reform and economic development. This may have been a result of indifference, or of the fact that most of the leaders and spokesmen of the nationalist movements either belonged to families of standing and wealth or had raised themselves into that class by their own efforts. But it can also be explained by the liberal atmosphere of the time ... To be independent in the language of the time, was to have internal autonomy and be a member of the League of Nations (ibid.: 344).

Did this interest in the economy develop after World War II? It certainly increased for a variety of reasons, among them being: the growth of socialist thought, the process of nationalisations and socialist practices adopted in more than one country, not to mention the establishment of economics departments in a number of Arab universities. There is an increased coverage of economic affairs in the media and the establishment of a number of specialised journals and newspapers in the field. A quantitative development has certainly taken place. Yet economic 'power' as an important factor to be dealt with remains largely absent from the works of political activists. For a long time, economic journalism in the Arab world was the work of foreigners or local Christians and mainly directed towards them. This was the case with *Le Commerce du Levant*, Beirut or with *La Bourse*, Alexandria. Following these came *Al-Ahram al-Iqtissadi*, published in Arabic, as well as *Al-Bayan*, *Al-Masarif* or *Al-Iqtissad wa al-A'mal*.

Yet one cannot conclude that the economic question has become an integral part of political culture. One might compare, for example, the reactions to a contemporary event such as the 1979 Iranian Revolution. At the time of its occurrence, many Western observers began to question what type of economic and international economic relations the new regime would adopt, while Arab commentators, both supporters and critics, were almost entirely concentrating on personalities, parties, or even the theological-political debate. The thousands of pages written on the nature of the 'Islamic economy' are in large part boring and scarcely informative and the reader may eventually reach the conclusion arrived at by Samir Amin, that the 'Islamic economy, in the real sense of the word, outside of a number of fundamental slogans and measures, can hardly be regarded as Islamic' (Amin, 1982: 181-98).

Arab political culture is to a great extent the reflection of a centuries-old reality: economic and financial resources did not play a central role in the establishment of political power in the Arab world. Consequently, people still refrain from viewing them as being necessary elements of power. Wealth is the reward received by the powerful and not the source of this power. One could argue that such an un-economic political culture is the most suitable local complement to foreign economic domination.

THE (ARAB) MAN ON HORSEBACK

Ri'asa is basically achieved by military means. Following the 1967 defeat, Nasser said: 'What has been taken by force, cannot be claimed back except through force'. Did not Max Weber himself describe the Arab as 'a warrior more than anything else'? Was not Saudi authority established on the basis of repeated military campaigns initiated by a small group of armed men in their bid to control Riyadh in the mid-eighteenth century, with similar attempts being made in the nineteenth and twentieth centuries? Similarly, was not the independent Algerian state established through a popular liberation war that expelled the French *colons* and established a national state? Did not the military dominate the Arab state, with the aim of endowing it with more strength and rationality, and with an organised, modern and effective military spirit? Is it not easy to link the yearning for the great Islamic conquests and the ambitions of certain current officers in their attempt to build a better future through power? Only a few years back, the parents of a would-be bride were accustomed to say that the bridegroom had to be an officer or he would not do (*Mulazim* or *mu lazim* in a Damascene accent).

Arab culture presents us with contradictory images of the military. On the one hand, there are the glorious conquests and the great military leaders, such as Khalid ibn al-Walid, 'Uqbah ibn Nafi' and Tariq ibn Ziyad, the great victories of the wars of *Ridda* (apostasy) and conquests stretching from Khurasan to Andalusia. However, this bright image of the Arab military was to a large extent replaced by another: the image of foreign mercenaries who, through the adoption of Islam, were able to become an integral part of authority and consequently transformed the Caliphate into a formal instrument in their hands. This transformation most probably began in the ninth century less than two centuries after the establishment of the empire. Turkish soldiers played an important role in the dismissal of Caliphs and the designation of their successors. They also took part in the suppression of rural and urban insurrections. A clear separation took place between the Arabs and the military, with the latter's transformation from conquerors of new lands into mere protectors of those in power.

This historical development is probably central in understanding the present ambiguity in the Arab's view of the soldier. As noted by Claude Cahen, 'The armies of conquest were for the most part composed only of Arabs'. But in the Umayyad period, the great distances separating warriors and their tribes made conquests more difficult to carry out than before. Following their successful uprising, the Abbasids formed their main army from Khurasani troops. This meant that they put an end to the role of Arabs in war and their claim to war booty. Distrust of Arabs grew and intensified during the reign of al-Ma'mun, when he rejected any military volunteers of Arab origin. A substantial number of Arabs who used to form the army of conquest were forced into misery and returned to a Bedouin way of life. Matters deteriorated further when al-Mu'tasim imported slaves and through them created a separate force with a Turkish majority. Cahen believes that the creation of this settled army in Samarra' meant in practice the forsaking of all fighting outside the country.

All things considered, the soldiers were aliens to the nation and their conflicts were unrelated to the problems of the people. Hence, the army was perceived as an alien system and the system which provided this army with political cadres was also an unfamiliar one and unwillingly accepted by the people. As for the army, it perceived that the Caliphate was incapable of doing without it and thus became even more aggressive (Cahen, 1977: 164).

There is no doubt, that the first Islamic conquests still stir up a yearning for them. Yet we should also take into consideration the intervening centuries of alienation between the people and the military, in the professional, political and ethnic realms, for al-Mu'tasim's example was adopted on an even larger scale in the centuries that followed. The Saljuks, in their time, became the victims of the same slaves that used to form the bulk of the army, until the Mamluks established control in the thirteenth century under the leadership of Buyides. Following them, the Ottomans, through their domination of most of the Islamic world, fully achieved the surrender of form (the Islamic Caliphate) to the content of power (the militaristic ethnic group feeling). The two examples of the Janissaries and the foreign military aristocracy, which continued to rule Egypt in one form or another until 1952, point to the continued elimination of Arabs from the military and to the division of society into two groups: the military and the civilian population (al-'Askar:al Ra'iyya).

It is therefore not difficult to understand why the image of the military in the political culture was shaken. A number of those who studied Egyptian society (Edward Lane, Husayn Fawzi) concluded that there are reservations among all parts of Egyptian society about joining the army. Henry Ayrout concentrated on the inclination of the Egyptian peasant towards peacefulness and his distaste for revolution and bloodshed. In one of his moving productions, the Egyptian film director Salah Abu Seif portrays the image of an officer (Omar Sharif) who is unable to attain his position except through the help of his sister who becomes a prostitute for this purpose. In the end, however, when he discovers this, the officer kills his sister.

Leaders and intellectuals of the period prior to 1945 were rarely interested in developing the military. Al-Afghani was only concerned with finding the source of the early Muslims' strength in confronting the enemies of Islam. Muhammad 'Abduh's negative reaction towards the insurrection of 'Urabi comes as no surprise. 'Abduh's analysis of this incident remains on the personal and psychological level. He believes that 'Urabi was an Egyptian officer who revolted for the simple reason of the preference of Circassian officers over him in the military hierarchy. As for 'Urabi's later interest in the idea of calling the parliament to convene and introduce political reform, 'Abduh believes that it was only an attempt to legitimise his movement. 'Abduh's discussion of 'Urabi's movement is full of sarcasm; he portrays the Egyptian officer as a naive reader of newspapers and magazines, taking superficial political ideas from them but lacking the capacity to understand them.

Similarly, it is very difficult to find among the intellectuals of the next period such as Constantine Zuraiq or Sati' al-Husri any real interest in the problem of the establishment of Arab military potential. It seems as if the well-established remoteness between the intellectuals, attempting to speak in the name of the people, and the military continued to exist.

The picture began to change in the 1930s. In Iraq, through Bakr Sidqi and Rashid 'Ali al-Kaylani, the military entered politics by force. In Syria, Husni az-Za'im began a long series of military *coups*. In Egypt the revolution of 1952 entrenched its authority on the basis of a new military-based form of legitimacy. In Algeria, after three years of Ben Bella's rule, the military seized political power. The toppling of the royalist regime in Iraq led, among other things, to the elimination of the civil factions that had contributed to bringing down the previous regime.

The Iraqi experience prior to 1958 had embodied a novel development capable of integrating military officers — even older officers of the Ottoman army — into the new Arab political context. Of the prime ministers who succeeded each other in Iraq, many were officers who graduated from the high military academy in Istanbul: Ja'far al-'Askari, 'Abd al-Muhsin as-Sa'dun, Yasin al-Hashimi, Nuri as-Sa'id, Jamil al-Midfa'i, 'Ali Jawdat al-Ayyubi, Taha al-Hashimi and Nur ad-Din Mahmud. All the above played an important role in Iraqi politics from the creation of the state until the 1958 revolution. This made the participation of Bakr Sidqi and al-Kaylani and, after them, others such as 'Abd al-Karim Qasim, 'Abd as-Salam 'Aref and Ahmad Hasan al-Bakr, in the leadership of the state, more acceptable. Hanna Batatu counted around three hundred Ottoman officers who had entered Iraqi politics during the 1920s.

In the 1950s, the intervention of the military in politics was expanded and generalised and, consequently, its image was considerably improved. Specifically, there was a growing conviction in public opinion that the military might bring new blood into the structure of the state and in the process endow it with new momentum. The memoirs of 'Adel Arslan are full of almost continuous demands for the arming and training of the armies in all the Arab countries in which he was politically involved, particularly Syria and Iraq (Arslan, 1984). Arslan is obsessed with Ataturk and Turkey, for he perceives Ataturk as an active military man who dared to side openly with modernity and to adopt Western methods. Loyal to his people, he continuously sought to increase his country's strength. Arslan compares him with Arab rulers lacking in perception and concerned only with their own interests. He views Turkey as a model, and not once does he forget that the source of all this strength was a modern and reconstructed army.

However, Arslan remains at the level of generalities. Interestingly enough, Arslan was to become the foreign minister of Husni az-Za'im, the first military ruler of contemporary Syria. Much as Muhammad 'Abduh viewed 'Urabi's revolt, so does Arslan explain az-Za'im's rise to power. Arslan even goes further in his criticism of Husni az-Za'im, accusing him of high treason for plotting with the Americans to conclude a separate agreement with Israel. Az-Za'im came to power with a platform of army reform, following the scandals of the first Arab-Israeli war, yet he considered doing what no Syrian civilian dared to do.

The Arab military came to power with the slogan of liberation and its publicised capacity to confront the enemy. Bakr Sidqi was inclined to emphasise his role in maintaining national unity by means of his bloody suppression of the Assyrian rebellion in the north of the country. Husni az-Za'im and his allies in Damascus as well as 'Abd an-Nasir (Nasser) and his colleagues in Egypt, came to power as a consequence of the devastating results of the first Arab-Israeli war. Those who succeeded them also upheld the same slogan of liberation.

But this positive development in the image of the strong, patriotic and liberating military was accompanied by a historical deterioration in the field of liberation itself, for the military establishment did not have much success in its battle with external powers. Many examples can be mentioned: the devastating 1967 defeat against Israel, Somalia's failure in its confrontation with Ethiopia, and the failure of more than one Libyan military adventure in Africa. It is as if the Arab armies were committing themselves to the achievement of objectives greater than those they had previously set themselves, but they seemed to suffer from at least an equal incapacity to achieve them. Iraq's performance in the war with Iran is yet another example, and one might even mention here India's victories over Muslim Pakistan.

Nor is it possible to say that the politicisation of the military led to the strengthening of the state *vis-à-vis* other states or within society. There has been a slight improvement in image. There is no doubt that the Libya of Mu'ammar al-Qadhafi appears to be stronger than the Libya of the Sanusi king. The same thing can certainly be said about Syria under Hafiz al-Assad. But the question remains open. To what extent does an Arab feel that this or that state is stronger because its leaders come from the military? To what extent does he believe that the price of the presence of the military in power is comparable with what the state has gained in strength?

To what extent is this military authority identified as a patriotic and popular one? The military's rise to political power did not mean that it was being purified from all the maladies of civil society. As a matter of fact, it can be said that the maladies have survived with the military and at times have even grown in proportion. To what extent can we consider the Sudanese, or Libyan, or Somali or Syrian or Iraqi armies to be ruling their respective countries, without regarding the ethnic, sectarian or tribal 'asabiyyas looming behind them? It appears as if a number of neo-Mamluk regimes have arisen in some Arab countries. These regimes are based on old group feelings that now dominate the state and society through the army, behind the mere façade of modern institutions.

WHERE DOES STRENGTH COME FROM?

In 1905, the Arabs were amazed by the victory of Japan over Russia. How could a small underdeveloped Asian country defeat a great country that was threatening the territorial integrity of the Ottoman Empire? The Egyptian politician Mustafa Kamel found time to write a book on the subject. This war also inspired the Algerian thinker, Malek bin Nabi, to daring ideas. He compared the Arabs who approached European civilisation as consumers with the Japanese who approached it in quest of knowledge. The Japanese imported

237

ideas, while the Arabs limited themselves to the importation of commodities. The interest in Japan which filled the pages of Arab newspapers for years after 1905 was only a reflection of the deep and basic questions that occupied the Arabs/Muslims of the *Nahda* concerning their own weakness and the strength of other nations. 'Why Japan?' asks Charles Issawi (Issawi, 1983). Why did Japan alone among the countries of Asia, Africa and Latin America 'make it' in the nineteenth and early twentieth centuries? Why not the Arabs? Why not, for instance, Iraq, whose potential was, and still is, so great? Or why not Egypt, with its homogeneous population, centralised government, substantial agricultural surplus, excellent internal waterways, long-established fiscal tradition and, by contemporary standards, urbanised society?

Galal Amin's answer is based on geo-strategic factors. Amin argues that Egypt failed in this endeavour owing to its (too-enviable) geographical location, the proximity of the European powers, and because the Suez Canal had to be established. These factors enabled the West to penetrate Egypt, tame its will and fetter it militarily and financially, with the aim of preventing it from developing on its own. Issawi's answer is based on culture: he explains that Japan is the best example of the active and successful khaldunian group feeling. However, the Japanese were able to preserve a double standard of moral superiority and of cultural inferiority, *vis-à-vis* the West. The Arabs, on the contrary, combined a feeling of moral superiority with a false feeling of cultural superiority. According to Issawi, this false feeling resulted in the absence of the 'spirit of curiosity' among the Arabs and Muslims regarding other cultures.

As the Arabs sense their senility, the modern models of power (Europe, the USA, Japan, the USSR) grow in front of their eyes. Questions relating to the reasons behind this discrepancy in power still remain. If Issawi's opinion is valid, then the current period, which is characterised by a return to fundamentalist religious slogans, is moving away from, rather than approaching, the solution he prescribes. The emphasis on the religious-cultural superiority of the Islamic religion could hardly be stronger than it is today. The 'spirit of curiosity' that Issawi looked for among Arabs to no avail is sometimes condemned as 'cultural alienation'. Why should we seek others, when the solutions to our problems are found in our Holy scripture, religion and culture? Is not the interest in the culture of others, according to the fundamentalists, the reason for our plight?

They say this while having in mind the example of Israel, which is the closest to them and the most violent and destructive. Israel appears as a supreme military power and a strong actor in international relations, rejecting all red tape and possessing a capability for continuous brinkmanship. Was not Israel established specifically by stressing its religious personality? Was it not right to do so? Israel, at least as viewed by the Arabs, is the ideal of the religious state. It contradicts all the ideologies that call for the separation of religion from the state. According to the fundamentalists, these ideologies have weakened the Arab state despite Abdallah Laroui's warning that 'the expression: *al-Islam din wa dawla* (Islam is a religion and a state) implies a co-existence and not an integration between religion and the state ... Islam ... means the civilisation which developed throughout history in the Islamic nation, and not the ideology ... the state did not transform Islam into a state religion, and Islam did not transform the state into a religious institution' (Laroui, 1981: 122).

This quotation from Laroui represents the exact contradiction of the fundamentalist attitude towards the community and the enemy (particularly Israel). It seems that a new dynamism, almost materialising in a 'war of religions', may have been established in the region. Israel is as Theodor Herzl dreamt it to be in *The Jewish State*: 'A state in the full meaning of the word, having its territories and laws, ruled and administered by Jews'. Herzl thought along two lines: that of the political system and that of the financial company supporting it, to which Herzl devotes the longest chapter in his book. Consideration of Israel as an example to be followed in an attempt to establish a strong state is growing in the writings and practices of Arabs. Are the continuous Arab defeats by Israelis driving them to adopt the ideas and terminology of the victors, as was the case with other peoples at different periods?

Despite many recent theories on the 'communalisation' of the Arab-Israeli conflict, it is still possible to believe that this conflict has and will continue to have tremendous effects on political culture. Its seeming transformation into a mere war among religions, a war of the True God against the Old One or the False One, is a frightening prospect. Arabs and Muslims may be tempted to consider the historical conditions in which Israel was created as marginal, and to view it basically as a 'religious

239

product', despite Herzl's laborious financial planning. The idea of a gradual identification of strength with faith should not be dismissed; each side can gird on its sword and join the battle, chanting: 'How can we be defeated when God is on our side?'

References

Abadha, F. (1975) *Al-Hukm al-'Uthmani fi al-Yaman: 1872-1918*, Al-Hay'a al-Misriyyah al-'Amma li al-Kitab, Cairo

'Abd al-Fadil, M. (1983) *Al-Fikr al-Iqtissadi al-'Arabi wa Qadiyyat at-Taharrur wa at-Tanmiya wa al-Wahda*, (Arab Economic Thought and the Problems of Liberation, Development and Unity), Center of Arab Unity Studies, Beirut

'Abd al-Rahim, A. (1975) *Ad-Dawlah as-Sa'udiyya al-Ula, 1745-1818*, Al-Jami'ah al-'Arabiya, Cairo

'Abd al-Raziq, A. (1925) *Al-Islam wa Usul al-Hukm*, Egypt Press

Abu al-Futuh, A. (1905) *Ash-Shari'ah al-Islamiyyah Wa al-Qawanin al-Wad'iyyah*, Cairo

Abu-Hakima, M. (1967) *Tarikh al-Kuwait*, Lajnat Tarikh al-Kuwait, Kuwait

Abun-Nasr, J. (1975) *A History of the Maghreb*, Cambridge University Press, London

'Aflaq, M. (n.d.I) *Fi Sabil al-Ba'th*, Dar at-Tali'a, Beirut

'Aflaq, M. (n.d.II) *Al-Ba'th wa al-Wahda*, Al-Mu'assasa al-'Arabiyya li ad-Dirasat wa an-Nashr, Beirut

'Amarah, M. (1980) *Al-Islam wa as-Sulta ad-Diniyyah*, Beirut

Amin, G.A. (1979) *Al-Mashriq al-'Arabi wa al-Gharb*, Center for Arab Unity Studies, Beirut

Amin, S. (1970) *The Maghreb in the Modern World*, Penguin Books, London

Amin, S. (1982) 'Y a t-il une économie politique du fondamentalisme islamique?', *Peuples Mediterranéens, 21*

Anonymous (1976) *The Role of the State in Socio-Economic Reforms in Developing Countries*, Progress, Moscow

Ansari, H.N. (1984a) 'The Islamic Militants in Egyptian Politics', *International Journal of Middle East Studies, 16*, 123-44.

Ansari, H.N. (1984b) 'Sectarian Conflict in Egypt and the Political Expediency of Religion', *The Middle East Journal, 38*, 397-418

Antonius, G. (1955) *The Arab Awakening*, Khayat, Beirut

Arendt, H. (1982) *L'impérialisme*, Fayard, Paris

Arslan, 'A. (1984) *Mudhakkarāt* (Memoirs), Yusif Ibish (ed.), ad-Dar at-Taqadumiyya, Beirut

Al-Arsuzi, Z. (1958) *Al-Umma al-'Arabiyya: Mahiyyatuha, Risalatuha, Mashakiluha*, Dar al-Yaqdha al-'Arabiyya, Damascus

Asad, T. (1970) *The Kababish Arabs: Power, Authority and Consent in a Nomadic Tribe*, C. Hurst & Company, London

'Awad, L. (1969) *Tara'iq al-Fikr al-Misri al-Hadith: al-Khalfiyya at-Tarikhiyya*, Dar al-Hilal, Cairo

'Awdah, 'Abd al-Qader (1951) *Al-Islam wa Awda'una as- Siasiyyah*

Al-'Aziz, M. (1969) *Al-Idarah al-'Uthmaniyyah fi Wilayat Suriyyah, 1864-1914*, Dar al-Ma'arif, Cairo

Baaklini, 'A. (1976) *Legislative and Political Development: Lebanon*

241

1842-1972, Duke University Press, Raleigh, North Carolina

Baer, G. (1969) *Studies in the Social History of Modern Egypt*, University of Chicago Press, Chicago

Al-Baghdadi, A. (1982) *Usul ad-din*, Matba'at ad-dawla, Istanbul

Baker, R. (1979) *King Husain and the Kingdom of Hejaz*, Oleander Press, Cambridge

Bakhash, S. (1984) *The Reign of the Ayatollahs*, New York, Basic Books

Al-Banna, H. (1981) *Majmu'at Rasa'il al-Imam ash-Shahid*, Al-Mu'assasah al-Islamiyyah, Beirut

Al-Banna, H. (n.d.) *Rasa'il al-imam ash-shahid*, Al-Mu'assasa al-Islamiyya li at-tibaa wa al-nashr, Beirut

Barakat, H. (1984) *Al-Mujtama' al-'Arabi: Dirasa istitla'iyya*, Center for Arab Unity Studies, Beirut

Barbour, M. (1965) *Morocco*, Thames and Hudson, London

Batatu, H. (1978) *The Old Social Classes and the Revolutionary Movements of Iraq*, Princeton University Press, Princeton

Béji, H. (1982) *Le Désenchantement national*, Maspéro, Paris

Ben Bachir, S. (1969) *L'Administration locale du Maroc*, Imprimerie Royale, Casablanca

Ben Dor, G. (1983) *State and Conflict in the Middle East*, Praeger, New York

Bensaid, S. (1983) 'Al-Muthaqqaf al-Makhzani wa-tahdith ad-Dawla: Bidayāt as-Salafiyya al-Jadida fi al-Maghrib', *Al-Mustaqbal al-'Arabi*, 58, 27-38

Bernard, C. and Khalilzad, Z. (1984) *The Government of God*, Columbia University Press, New York

Berque, J. (1962) *Le Maghreb entre deux Guerres*, Editions du Seuil, Paris

Beydoun, A. (1984) *Identité confessionnelle et temps social chez les historiens libanais*, Université Libanaise, Beirut

Binder, L. (1964) *Ideological Revolution in the Middle East*, Wiley, New York

Binder, L. (1978) *In a Moment of Enthusiasm: Political Power and the Second Stratum in Egypt*, University of Chicago Press, Chicago and London

Bourgey, A. *et al.*, (1982) *Industrialisation et changements sociaux dans l'Orient arabe*, CERMOC, Beirut

Bozeman, A. (1960) *Politics and Culture in International History*, Princeton University Press, Princeton

Brennan, L. (1981) 'A Case of Attempted Segmental Modernization: Rampur State, 1930-1939', *Comparative Studies in Society and History*, 23, 350-81

Brown, L. (ed.) (1963) *State and Society in Independent North Africa*, Middle East Institute, Washington, D.C.

Brown, L. (1974) *The Tunisia of Ahmed Bey, 1837-1855*, Princeton University Press, Princeton

Buheiry, M. (ed.) (1982) *Intellectual Life in the Arab East, 1890-1939*, American University of Beirut, Beirut

Bull. H. and Watson, A. (eds.) (1984) *The Expansion of International*

Society, Oxford University Press, Oxford

Cahen, C. (1977) *Tarikh al-'Arab wa ash-Shu'ub al-Islamiyya Mundhu Dhuhūr al-Islam Hatta Bidayat al-Imbaratoriyya al-'Uthmaniyya.* (The History of Arabs and Islamic Peoples since the Rise of Islam and until the Beginning of the Reign of the Ottoman Empire), Dar al-Haqiqa, Beirut

Carnoy, M. (1984) *The State and Political Theory*, Princeton University Press, Princeton

Carré, O. (1978) 'Utopies Socialisantes en terre arabe d'Orient', in *Revue Tiers-Monde*, Vol. *29*, No. 75

Cerych, L. (1964) *Européens et Marocains, 1930-1956*, De Tempel, Bruges

Chabry, L. and Chabry, A. (1984) *Politique et Minorités au Proche-Orient*, Maisonneuve et Larose, Paris

Cigar, N. (1985) 'State and Society in South Yemen', *Problems of Communism, 35*, 41-58

Crystal, J. (1985) 'Coalitions in Oil Monarchies: Patterns of State-Building in the Gulf', paper delivered at the 1985 Annual Meeting of American Political Science Association, New Orleans

Ad-Dabbagh, M. (1962) *Qatar*, Khayat, Beirut

Daoud, Z. (1976) 'Analyse des résultats électoraux', *Lamalif, 84*, 22-9

Dickinson, J. (1983) 'State and Economy in the Arab Middle East: Some Theoretical and Empirical Observations', *Arab Studies Quarterly*, Vol. *5*, No. 1, pp. 22-50

Dictionary of Political Thought (1982) R. Scruton (ed.), Macmillan Reference Books, London

Divine, D.R. (1979) 'Political Legitimacy in Israel: How Important is the State?', *International Journal of Middle East Studies, 10*, pp. 205-24

Djait, H. (1972) 'Problématique et critique de l'idée de Nation arabe', in A. Abdel Malek *et al.* (eds), *Renaissance du Monde Arabe*, Editions Duculot, Belgium

Dresch, P. (1983) 'The Position of Shaykhs among the Northern Tribes of the Yemen', *Man* (N.S.), *19*, 31-49

Dumont, L. (1983) *Essais sur l'individualisme: Une perspective anthropologique sur l'idéologie moderne*, Seuil, Paris

Ad-Duri, A. (1984) *At-Takwin at-Tarikhi li al-Umma al-'Arabiyya*, Center for Arab Unity Studies, Beirut

Eickelman, C. (1984) *Women and Community in Oman*, New York University Press, New York and London

Eickelman, D.F. (1976) *Moroccan Islam: Tradition and Society in a Pilgrimage Center*, University of Texas Press, Austin

Eickelman, D.F. (1981) *The Middle East: An Anthropological Approach*, Prentice-Hall Inc., Englewood, Cliffs, N.J.

Eickelman, D.F. (1983a) 'Omani Village: The Meaning of Oil', in John Peterson (ed.), *The Politics of Middle Eastern Oil*, The Middle East Institute, Washington D.C. pp. 211-19

Eickelman, D.F. (1983b) 'Religious Knowledge in Inner Oman', *Journal of Oman Studies, 6*, 163-72

Eickelman, D.F. (1984) 'Kings and People: Oman's State Consultative

Council', *Middle East Journal, 38,* 51-71

Eickelman, D.F. (1985) 'From Theocracy to Monarchy: Authority and Legitimacy in Inner Oman, 1935-1957', *International Journal of Middle East Studies, 17,* 3-24

Enayat, H. (1982) *Modern Islamic Political Thought,* University of Texas Press, Austin

Etienne, B. and Tozy, M. (1979) 'Le Glissement des obligations islamiques vers le Phenomène associatif à Casablanca', *Annuaire de l'Afrique du Nord, 18,* 235-59

Evans, P., Rueschemeyer, D. and Skocpol, T. (eds) (1985) *Bringing the State Back In,* Cambridge University Press, Cambridge

Falk, R., Kratochwil, F. and Mendlovitz, S. (eds) (1985) *International Law: A Contemporary Perspective,* Westview Press, Boulder, Col.

Fallers, L.A. (1973) *Inequality: Social Stratification Reconsidered,* University of Chicago Press, Chicago

Al-Fasi, 'A. (n.d. a) *Maqasid ash-Shari'ah*

Al-Fasi, 'A. (n.d. b) *An-Naqd adh-Dhāti,* Dar al-Fikr al-Maghribi, Tetouan

Fiori, G. (1970) *Antonio Gramsci, Life of a Revolutionary,* New Left Books, London

Fried, M. (1968) 'State: The Institution', *International Encyclopaedia of the Social Sciences, 15,* Macmillan and Free Press, New York, pp. 143-50

Fromm, E. (1960) *The Fear of Freedom,* Routledge and Kegan Paul, London

Gallagher, N.E. (1983) *Medicine and Power in Tunisia, 1780-1900,* Cambridge University Press, Cambridge

Geertz, C. (1963a) 'The Integrative Revolution: Primordial Sentiments and Civil Politics in the New States', in C. Geertz (ed.) *Old Societies and New States,* Free Press of Glencoe, New York pp. 105-57

Geertz, C. (1963b) (ed.) *Old Societies and New States,* Free Press of Glencoe, New York

Geertz, C. (1973) 'The Politics of Meaning', *The Interpretation of Cultures,* pp. 311-26

Ghoshah, A. (1971) *Ad-Dawla al-Islamiyyah, Dawlah Insaniyyah,* Amman

Goldschmidt, A. Jr. (1983) *A Concise History of the Middle East,* Westview Press, Boulder, Col.

Guérivière, J. de la. (1984) 'Derrière une façade d'une belle ordonnance: La lente montée des périls', *Le Monde,* 21 February

Haim, S. (1962) *Arab Nationalism: An Anthology,* University of California Press, Berkeley

Harbi, M. (1980) 'Nationalisme algérien et identité berbère' *Peuples Mediterranéens,* June, p. 36

Harik, I. (1968) *Politics and Change in a Traditional Society: Lebanon, 1711-1845,* Princeton University Press, Princeton

Harik, I. (1974) *The Political Mobilization of Peasants,* Indiana University Press, Bloomington

Hasib, K. (1985) 'Kalimat al-Mustaqbal al-'Arabi', *al-Mustaqbal al-'Arabi, 73*

Helms, C.M. (1981) *The Cohesion of Saudi Arabia*, Croom Helm, London

Hermassi, E. (1972) *Leadership and National Development in North Africa: A Comparative Study*, California University Press, Berkeley

Hill, N.L. (1976) *Claims to Territory in International Law and Relations*, Greenwood Press, Westport, Conn.

Hinnebusch, R. (1984) 'Parties and Elections in Post-Revolutionary Egypt'. Paper delivered at the Eighteenth Annual Meeting of the Middle East Studies Association of North America, San Francisco, 30 November

Hinsely, F.H. (1963) *Power and the Pursuit of Peace*, Cambridge University Press, London

Hollist, L. (1985) 'An International Political Economy' in F. Tullis (ed.) *International Economy Yearbook, 1*, Westview Press, Boulder, Col.

Holsti, K. (1967) *International Politics: A Framework for Analysis*, Prentice Hall, Engelwood Cliffs, N.J.

Holt, P. (1966) *Egypt and the Fertile Crescent, 1516-1922*, Longman, London

Holt, P. (1980) *The History of the Sudan from the Coming of Islam to the Present Day*, Westview Press, Boulder, Col.

Hopkins, N. (1983) *Testour ou la transformation des campagnes maghrébines*, Cérès Productions, Tunis

Hopwood, D. (ed.) (1972) *The Arabian Peninsula: Society and Politics*, Allen and Unwin, London

Hourani, A. (1954) *Syria and Lebanon: A Political Essay*, Oxford University Press, Oxford

Hourani, A. (1962) *Arabic Thought in the Liberal Age*, Oxford University Press, London

Hourani, A. (1983) *Arabic Thought in the Liberal Age — 1798-1939*, Cambridge University Press, Cambridge (new edn)

Hourani, A. (n.d.) *Al-Fikr al-'Arabi fi'Asr an-Nahda*, Dar al-Nahar, Beirut

Howarth, D. (1964) *The Desert King: Ibn Saud and his Arabia*, McGraw Hill, New York

Hudson, M. (1968) *The Precarious Republic: Political Modernization in Lebanon*, Random House, New York

Hudson, M. (1977) *Arab Politics: The Search for Legitimacy*, Yale University Press, New Haven

Al-Husri, S. (1985) *Al-Mu'alaffat al-Qawmiyya al-Kamila*, Center for Arab Unity Studies, Beirut, 17 volumes

Hussain, A., Olson, R. and Qureshi, J. (eds) (1984) *Orientalism, Islam and Islamists*, Amana Books, Brattleboro

Ibn 'Ashur, M. (1344 A.H.) *Naqd 'Ilmi li-Kitab al-Islam wa Usul al-Hukm*, Cairo

Ibn Khaldun — Arabic (n.d.) *Al-Muqaddimah*, Al-Muthanna Library, Baghdad

Ibn Khaldun, (1967) *The Muqaddimah*, (translated from Arabic by Franz Rosenthal), Princeton University Press, Princeton

Ibn Taymiyyah (1951) *As-Siyasa ash-Shari'yyah fi Islah al-Ra'i wa ar-*

Ra'iyyah, Ali Sami an-Nashshar and Ahmad Zaki 'Atiyah (eds), Dar al-Kitab al-'Arabi, Cairo, 2nd edn

Ibrahim, S.E. (1980a) 'Anatomy of Egypt's Militant Islamic Groups', *International Journal of Middle East Studies*, *12*, 423-53

Ibrahim, S.E. (1980b) *Iltijahat ar-Ra'i al 'Amm al-'Arabi nahwa mas'alat al-wahda*, Arab Public Attitudes Toward the Question of Unity, Center for Arab Unity Studies, Beirut

Ibrahimi, L. (1978) 'The Crisis of Democracy in the Arab World', (in Arabic) *al-Mustaqbal Al-'Arabi*, Vol. *1*, No. 6, pp. 116-34.)

Ismael, J. (1982) *Kuwait: Social Change in Historical Perspective*, Syracuse University Press, Syracuse

Ishaq, A. (1978) *Al-Kitabat as-Siyasiyya wa al-Ijtima'iyya*, Dar at-Tali'a, Beirut

Issawi, C. (ed.) (1966) *The Economic History of the Middle East, 1800-1914*, University of Chicago Press, Chicago

Issawi, C. (1983) 'Why Japan?' in Ib. Ibrahim (ed.) *Arab Resources*, Croom Helm, London

Issawi, C. (1984) *An Economic History of the Middle East and North Africa*, Columbia University Press, New York

Al-Jabiri, M.A. (1982) *Al-Khitāb al-'Arabi al-Mu'asir*, Dar at-Tali'a, Beirut

Jadaane, F. (1981) *Usus at-Taqaddum 'inda Mufakkiri al-Islam fi al-'Alam al-'Arabi al-Hadith*, Al-Mu'assasah al-'Arabiyyah li ad-Dirasat wa an-Nashr, Beirut

Jadaane, F. (1983) 'Al-Mu'tayat al-Mubashira li al-ishkaliyya al-islamiyya al-Mu'asirah', in *Dirasat Islamiyya*, Yarmuk University, pp. 9-26

Karpat, K. (ed.) (1968) *Political and Social Thought in the Contemporary Middle East*, Praeger, New York

Kazancigil, A. (ed.) (1985) *L'Etat au Pluriel*, Economica and Unesco, Paris

Keesing's Reference Publications (1982) *Border and Territorial Disputes*, Alan J. Day. (ed.), Gale Research Company, Detroit

Kepel, G. (1984) *Le Prophète et Pharaon: Les mouvements islamistes dans l'Egypte contemporaine*, Editions La Découverte, Paris

Khadduri, M. (1960) *Independent Iraq, 1932-1958*, Oxford University Press, London

Khadduri, M. (1963) *Modern Libya: A Study in Political Development*, Johns Hopkins University Press, Baltimore

Khadduri, M. (1981) *Arab Personalities in Politics*, The Middle East Institute, Washington D.C.

Khalafallah, M.A. (1973) *The Qur'an ad-Dawla*, n.p., n.d.

Khalafallah, M.A. *et al.* (1982) *Al-Qawmiyya al-'Arabiyya wa al-Islam*, Center for Arab Unity Studies, Beirut

Khalafallah, M.A. (1984) 'Text, Interpretation and Government in Islam', *Al-'Arabi (Kuwait)*, *307*, pp. 41-5

Khalid, K.M. (1950) *Min Huna Nabda'*, Cairo, p. 47

Khalifa, M. (1979) *The United Arab Emirates: Unity in Fragmentation*, Westview, Boulder, Col.

Al-Khatib, A. (1963) *Al-Khilafa wa al-Imama*, n.p.

Khuri, R. (1943) *Al-Fikr al-'Arabi al-Hadith: Athār ath-Thawra al-Faransiyya fi Tawjihihi as-Siyyasi wa al-Ijtima'i*, Dar al-Makshuf, Beirut

Khuri, F. (1980) *Tribe and State in Bahrain: The Transformation of Social and Political Authority in an Arab State*, Chicago University Press, Chicago

Kirk, G. (1952) *A Short History of the Middle East from the Rise of Islam to Modern Times*, Methuen, London

Korany, B. (1983) 'The Take-Off of Third World Studies', *World Politics*, Vol. XXXV, No. 3, pp. 465-87

Korany, B. and Dessouki, A.E.H. *et al.* (1984) *The Foreign Policies of Arab States*, Westview Press, Boulder, Col.

Lambton, A. (1981) *State and Government in Medieval Islam*, Oxford University Press, Oxford

Lamghili, A. el-Kohen (1976) 'La "boulitique" d'une élection', *Lamalif, 84*, 32-6

Landen, R. (1967) *Oman since 1856: Disruptive Modernization in a Traditional Arab Society*, Princeton University Press, Princeton

Laroui, A. (1973) *L'idéologie arabe contemporaine*, Maspéro, Paris

Laroui, A. (1980) *Histoire du Maghreb*, Maspéro, Paris

Laroui, A. (1981) *Mafhum ad-Dawla*, Dar at-Tanwir, Beirut

Lazreg, M. (1976) *The Emergence of Classes in Algeria: Colonialism and Socio-Political Change*, Westview, Boulder, Col.

Leveau, R. (1976) *Le Fellah Marocain: Défenseur du Trône*, Presses de la Fondation Nationale des Sciences Politiques, Paris

Leveau, R. (1977) 'The Rural Elite as an Element in the Social Stratification of Morocco', in Van Nieuwenhuijze (ed.), *Commoners, Climbers and Notables*, E.J. Brill, Leiden, pp. 226-47

Lewis, I. (1979) 'Kim Il-Sung in Somalia: The End of Tribalism?', in William A. Shack and Percy S. Cohen (eds), *Politics in Leadership: A Comparative Perspective*, Clarendon Press, Oxford, pp. 13-44

Longrigg, S. (1956) *Iraq: 1900 to 1950*, Oxford University Press, London

Longrigg, S. (1958) *Syria and Lebanon*, Oxford University Press, London

Louis, W.R. (1984) 'The Era of the Mandate System and the Non-European World', in Bull and Watson (eds) *The Expansion of International Society*, Oxford University Press, Oxford, pp. 201-13

Lustick, I. (1980) *Arabs in the Jewish State: A Study in the Control of a Minority Population*, University of Texas Press, Austin

Machiavelli, N. (n.d.) *Il Principe*

Al-Mahafdha, 'A. (1973) *Tarikh al-Urdun al-Mu'asir: 'Ahd al-Imara 1921-1946*, Amman: Jordan University

Al-Mahafdha, A. (1985) *Mawqaf ad-dual al-Kubra min al-Wahda al-'Arabiyya*, Center for Arab Unity Studies, Beirut

Mairet, G. (1981) 'Peuple et Nation' in F. Chatelet and G. Mairet (eds), *De Rousseau à Mao, Vol. 3*, Les Editions Marabout, Belgium

Marks, J. (1984) 'All Systems Go for Morocco Elections', *The Middle East*, August

Ma'ruf, 'A.A. (1978) 'Taqrir hawla al-Intikhabat fi Abi al-Jad', unpublished manuscript

Al-Mawdūdi, (1967) *Nadhariyat al-islam wa Hudiuhu fi as-Siyasah wa al-Qanun wa ad-Dustur,* Dar al-Fikr, Beirut

Mazrui, A. (1984) 'Africa Entrapped' in Bull and Watson, (eds.) *The Expansion of International Society,* Oxford University Press, Oxford

McWilliams, W.C. (1971) 'On Political Illegitimacy', *Public Policy, 19,* 429-56

Mitchell, T. (1984) 'As If the World were Divided in Two: The Birth of Politics in Turn-of-the Century Cairo', Ph.D. Thesis presented to the Department of Politics and the Program in Near Eastern Studies, Princeton University

Moore, C.H. (1980) *Images of Development: Egyptian Engineers in Search of Industry,* MIT Press, Cambridge, Mass.

Al-Mubarak, M. (1975) *Ash-Shari'ah al-Islamiyyah Ka-Masdar Asasi li ad-Dustur,* Alexandria

Al-Mubarak, M. (1981) *Nizam al-Islam fi al-Hukm wa ad-Dawlah,* Dar al-Fikr, Beirut

Musa, M. (1964) *Nizam al-Hukm*

Mutawalli, A. (1977) *Mabadi' Nizam al-Hukm fi al-Islam*

Al-Muti'i, M. (1344 A.H.) *Haqitat al-Islam wa Usul al-Hukm,* Maktabat an-Nahda al-Haditha, Cairo

An-Nabarawi, F. and Mehanna, M. (1984) *Tatawwur al-Fikr as-Siyassi fi al-Islam* (The Evolution of Political Thought in Islam, Dar el-Ma'arif, Cairo

An-Nabhani, T. (1952a) *Ad-Dawlah al-Islamiyyah,* al-Manar Press, Damascus

An-Nabhani, T. (1952b) *Nizam al-Hukm fi al-Islam*

Naff, T. (1984) 'The Ottoman Empire and the European State System', in Bull and Watson, (eds) *The Expansion of International Society,* Oxford University Press, Oxford

Naff, T. and Matson (eds) (1984) *Water in the Middle East,* Westview Press, Boulder, Col.

Nasr, M. (1981) *At-Tasaww'r al-Qawmi al-'Arabi fi Fikr Jamal 'Abd an-Nasir: Dirasa fi 'ilm al-Mufradāt wa ad-dalala,* Center for Arab Unity Studies, Beirut

Nasser, Gamal 'Abd al- (n.d. a) *Falsafat ath-Thawra,* Dar al-Masira, Beirut

Nasser, Gamal 'Abd al-(n.d. b) *Al-Mithaq* Dar al-Masira, Beirut

Nassur, A. (1967) 'Muqaddima li-Dirasat al-Fikr as-Siyasi al-'Arabi fi mi'at 'am', in Fuad Sarruf *et al.* (eds), *Al-Fikr al-'Arabi fi Mi'at 'Am,* American University of Beirut, Beirut

Nazmi, W. (1984) 'Malamih min al-Fikr al-'Arabi fi'Asr al-Yaqdha', in Sa'dun Hammadi *et al., Dirasat fi al-Qawmiyya al-'Arabiyya wa al-Wahda,* Center for Arab Unity Studies, Beirut

Nettl, J.P. (1968) 'The State as Conceptual Variable', *World Politics,* Vol. *20,* No. 4, pp. 559-92

Northedge, F.S. (1976) *The International Political System,* Faber, London

Oumlil, Ali (1985) *Al Islahiyya al-'Arabiyya wa ad-Dawla al-*

Wataniyya (Arab Reformation and the Nationalist State), Dar at-Tanwir, Beirut

Pascon, P. and Bentahar, M. (1971) 'Ce que disent 296 jeunes ruraux', in Abdelkebir Khatibi (ed.), *Etudes sociologiques sur le Maroc.* Bulletin Economique et Social du Maroc, Rabat, pp. 145-287

Peterson, J. (1982) *Yemen: The Search for a Modern State*, Johns Hopkins University Press, Baltimore

Petran, T. (1972) *Syria*, Ernest Benn, London

Phillips, W. (1967) *Oman: A History*, Longmans, London

Piscatori, J.P. (ed.) (1983) *Islam in the Political Process*, Cambridge University Press, New York

Pradelle, P. De(1982) *De la Frontière: Etude de Droit International*, Les éditions Internationales, Paris

Pye, L. (1962) *Politics, Personality and National Building: Burma's Search for Identity*, Yale University Press, New Haven

Qabous ibn Sa'id (1983) 'How the Sultan sees the Tasks Ahead', *Financial Times*, Oman Survey, p. II. January 13

Al-Qardawi, Y. (1974) *Al-Hall al-Islami: Farida wa Darurah*, Mu'assasat ar-Risalah, Beirut

Qasim, J. (1966) *Al-Khalij al-'Arabi: Dirasa li-Tarikh al-Imarat al-'Arabiyya, 1840-1914*, Ayn Shams University, Cairo

Al-Qawmiyya al-'Arabiyya fi al-Fikr wa al-Mumarasa (Arab Nationalism: The Thought and the Practice), Center for Arab Unity Studies, Beirut, 1980

Quandt, W. (1969) *Revolution and Political Leadership: Algeria, 1954-1968*, MIT Press, Cambridge, Mass.

Qutb, S. (n.d.) *Al-Islam wa Mushkilat al-Hadara*

Qutb, S. (1983) *Ma'alim fi at-Tariq*, Dar ath-Thaqafa, Casablanca

Rabbath, E. (1973) *La Formation historique du Liban politique et constitutionnel, Essai de synthèse*, Université Libanaise, Beirut

Rafiq, 'A. (1974) *Al-'Arab wa al-'Uthmaniyyun, 1516-1916*, Damascus

Ramonet, I. (1984) 'Maroc', *Le Monde Diplomatique*, January, pp. 7-11

Rentz, G. (1977) 'Wahhabism in Saudi Arabia', in Hopwood (ed.), *The Arabian Peninsula*, Allen and Unwin, London

Ar-Rihani, A. (n.d.) *Muluk al-'Arab*, Dar ar-Rihani, Beirut

Rida, M.R. (1938) *Al-Khilafah aw al-Imamah al-'Uzma*, Dar al-Manar, Cairo

Rosen, L. (1972) 'Rural Political Process and National Political Structure in Morocco', in Richard Antoun and Iliya Harik (eds), *Rural Politics and Social Change in the Middle East*, Indiana University Press, Bloomington, pp. 214-36

Rosenau, J. (1985) 'The State in an Era of Cascading Politics', paper presented at the International Political Science Association Congress, Paris, July

Rosenthal, E.I.J. (1962) *Political Thought in Medieval Islam*, Cambridge University Press, London

Rousseau, J-J., (n.d.) *Du Contrat Social*

Ruedy, J. (1967) *Land Policy in Colonial Algeria*, California University Press, Berkeley

Rustow, D. (1971) *Middle Eastern Political Systems*, Prentice Hall, Englewood Cliffs, N.J.

Said, E. (1978) *Orientalism*, Vintage Books, New York

Salamé, G. (1980) *As-Siyassa al-Kharijiyya as-Sa'udiyya Mundhu 1945: Dirasa Fi al-'Alaqāt ad-Duwalyya*, Ma'ahad al-Inma' al-'Arabi, Beirut

Salamé, G. (1982) 'Institutionalisation du pouvoir et affinités tribales dans les pays arabes du Golfe', in *Al-Abhath*, AUB, Beirut, Vol. XXX

Salamé, G. (1984) 'Al-Jami'a wa at-Takattulat al-'Arabiyya', in *Jami'at ad-Duwal al-'Arabiyya bayna al-Waqi' wa at-Tumuh* Centre for Arab Unity Studies, Beirut

Salamé, G. (1986) 'Lebanon's Injured Identities: Who Represents Whom During a Civil War?', The Centre for Lebanese Studies' Papers, Oxford

Salibi, K. (1965) *The Modern History of Lebanon*, Weidenfeld and Nicolson, London

Sani Bey, A. (1924) *Al-Khilafah wa Sultat al-Ummah*

Sant Cassia, P. (1983) 'Patterns of Covert Politics in Post-Independence Cyprus', *Archives Européennes de Sociologie, 24*, 115-35

As-Sayyid, M. (1963) *Takwin al Yaman al-Hadith: al-Yaman wa al-Imam Yahya 1904-1948*, The Arab League, Cairo

As-Sayyid, R. (1984) *Al-Umma wa al-Jama'a wa as-Sulta: Dirasat fi al-Fikr al-Siyasi al-'Arabi al-Islami*, Dar Iqra', Beirut

Scott, J.C. (1976) *The Moral Economy of the Peasant: Rebellion and Subsistence in Southeast Asia*, Yale University Press, New Haven

Seale, P. (1965) *The Struggle for Syria*, Oxford University Press, London

Shabika, M. (1966) *Al-Sudan 'Abra al-Qurun*, Cairo

Sharabi, H. (1966) *Nationalism and Revolution in the Arab World*, D. Van Nostrand, Princeton

Shils, E. (1957) 'Primordial, Personal, Sacred and Civil Ties', *British Journal of Sociology*, pp. 130-45

Sivan, E. (1983) 'Ibn Taymiyya: Father of the Islamic Revolution', *Encounter*, vol. *60*, no. 5, 41-50

Skocpol, T. (1982) 'Rentier State and Shi'a Islam in the Iranian Revolution', *Theory and Society, 11*, pp. 265-83

Spagnolo, J. (1977) *France and Ottoman Lebanon, 1861-1914*, Ithaca Press, London

Spinoza, B. (1981 edn) *Tractatus Theologico-Politicus*

Staniland, M. (1985) *What is Political Economy?*, Yale University Press, New Haven and London

Stavrianos, L.S. (1981) *Global Rift*, William Morrow and Company, New York

Stinchcombe, A. (1968) *Constructing Social Theories*, Harcourt, Brace and World, New York

Stivers, W. (1982) *Supremacy and Oil: Iraq, Turkey and the Anglo-*

American World Order 1918-1930, Cornell University Press, Ithaca, N.Y.

Strange, S. (ed.) (1985) *Paths to International Political Economy*, George Allen and Unwin, London

At-Tahtawi, R. (1973) *Al-A'māl al-Kamila*, Al-Mu'assasa al-'Arabiyya, Beirut

At-Tahtawi, R. (1982) 'Fatherland and Patriotism', in John Donohue and John L. Esposito (eds), *Islam in Transition: Muslim Perspectives*, Oxford University Press, New York, pp. 11-15

Tibi, B. (1981) *Arab Nationalism*, Macmillan, London

Tignor, R. (1966) *Modernization and British Colonial Rule in Egypt, 1882-1914*, Princeton University Press, Princeton

Tignor, R. (1984) *State, Private Enterprise and Economic Change in Egypt, 1918-1914*, Princeton University Press, Princeton

Townsend, J. (1977) *Oman: The Making of a Modern State*, St. Martin's Press, New York

Troeller, G. (1976) *The Birth of Saudi Arabia: Britain and the Rise of the House of Sa'ud*, Frank Cass, London

Turner, B. (1984) 'Orientalism and the Problem of Civil Society in Islam', in Husain, Olson, and Qureshi (eds), *Orientalism, Islam and Islamists*, Amana Books, Brattleboro

Udovitch, A. (ed.) (1980) *The Islamic Middle East, 700-1900*, Darwin Press, Princeton

Vatikiotis, P.J. (1978) *Nasser and His Generation*, St. Martin's Press, New York

Vatikiotis, P.J. (1980) *The History of Egypt*, Johns Hopkins University Press, Baltimore

Vaucher, G. (1962) *Sous les Cèdres d'Ifrane*, Juillard, Paris

Waterbury, J. (1970) *The Commander of the Faithful: The Moroccan Political Elite*, Columbia University Press, New York

Waterbury, J. (1976) 'Corruption, Political Stability and Development: Comparative Evidence from Egypt and Morocco', *Government and Opposition*, *11*; 426-45

Waterbury, J. (1979) *Hydropolitics of the Nile Valley*, Syracuse University Press, Syracuse

Waterbury, J. (1983) *The Egypt of Nasser and Sadat: The Political Economy of Two Regimes*, Princeton University Press, Princeton

Watt, W.M. (1968) *Islamic Political Thought*, Edinburgh University Press, Edinburgh

Wenner, M. (1967) *Modern Yemen, 1961-1966*, Johns Hopkins University Press, Baltimore

Winder, B. (1965) *Saudi Arabia in the Nineteenth Century*, Macmillan, London

World Bank (1981) 'Assessment of the Manpower Implications of the Second Five-Year Development Plan, Sultanate of Oman', Technical Assistance and Special Studies Division, Washington, D.C.

World Bank (1984) *1984 World Bank Atlas*, The World Bank, Washington D.C.

Yassin, S. (1980) *Tahlil Madmun al-Fikr al-Qawmi al-'Arabi* (Content

Analysis of Arab Nationalist Thought), Center for Arab Unity Studies, Beirut

Zahlan, R. (1979) *The Creation of Qatar,* Croom Helm, London

Zamir, M. (1985) *The Formation of Modern Lebanon,* Croom Helm, London

Zartman, W.I. (1964) *Destiny of a Dynasty,* University of South Carolina, Columbia

Zeine, Z.N. (1958) *Arab-Turkish Relations and the Emergence of Arab Nationalism,* Khayat, Beirut

Zeine, Z.N. (1960) *The Struggle for Arab Independence,* Khayat, Beirut

Ziadeh, N. (1958) *Sanusiyah: A Study of a Revivalist Movement in Islam,* Brill, Leiden

Ziadeh, N. (1962) *Origins of Nationalism in Tunisia,* American University of Beirut, Beirut

Ziadeh, N. (1967) 'Al-Fikr al-'Arabi fi Mi'at 'Am', in Sarruf *et al.* (eds) *Al-Fikr al-'Arabi fi Mi'at 'Am,* American University of Beirut, Beirut

Zureik, E., 'Theoretical Considerations for a Sociological Study of the Arab State', *Arab Studies Quarterly,* Vol. III, No. 3, pp. 229-57

Contributors

Said Bensaid is Head of the Philosophy Department at Mohamed V University, Rabat. He is the author of books and articles in Arabic.

Charles Butterworth is a Professor in the Department of Government and Politics at the University of Maryland. He is co-editor of the critical edition of Averroes' Middle Commentary, and has translated into English works by Averroes and Rousseau. He is the author of numerous articles on Islamic philosophy and political thought.

Dale Eickelman is Professor of Anthropology at New York University. He is the author of *The Middle East: An Anthropological Approach* (Prentice Hall, 1981); *Moroccan Islam* (University of Texas Press, 1976); 'Kings and People: Oman's State Consultative Council', *Middle East Journal*, Vol. 38, No. 1, Winter 1984.

Iliya Harik is Director of the Center for Middle Eastern Studies, Indiana University. His publications include *The Political Mobilisation of Peasants* (Indiana University Press, 1974); *The Arabs and the New International Economic Order*, (ed and co-author), (in Arabic, Beirut, 1983); co-editor and co-author, *Local Politics and Development in the Middle East*, (Westview Press, Boulder, 1984).

Elbaki Hermassi is Professor at the Faculté des Lettres et Sciences Humaines at Tunis University. His publications include: *Leadership and National Development in North Africa*, (University of California Press, 1972); *Third World Reassessed* (University of California Press, 1980); *The Battle for Legitimacy* (forthcoming).

Fahmi Jadaane is Professor of Islamic Philosophy in the Faculty of Arts, University of Jordan, Amman. He is the author of various books in Arabic.

Bahgat Korany is Professor of Political Science at the University of Montreal and Director of its Etudes Arabes. His publications include: 'The Take-Off of Third World Studies', *World Politics*, Vol. XXXV, No. 3, 1983: *The Foreign Policies of Arab States*, with A.E.H. Dessouki *et al.*, (Westview Press, Boulder, 1984).

Ghassan Salamé is Professor of Political Science at the

American University of Beirut. His publications include: *Saudi Arabia's Foreign Policy since 1945*, (in Arabic, 1981); *State and Society in the Arab Levant States*, (in Arabic, 1987); *Le Théâtre politique au Liban: Étude idéologique et esthétique*, (Beirut, 1975).

Index

'Abbas, Ferhat, 76
'Abbasids, 112, 233
'Abd al-Raziq, 'Ali, 13-14,
  114-19, 125, 139, 141,
  145-6
'Abduh, Muhammad, 109, 154,
  172, 234-6
Abu al-Futuh, 'A, 139
Abu Seif, Salah, 234
Al-Afghani, Jamal ad-Din, 14,
  109, 173, 234
'Aflaq, Michel, 154, 165-7
'Alawites, 28
Algeria: pre-colonial, 33-4; and
  colonialism, 36, 41, 43, 62,
  116-17; territory, 69-71;
  mobilization, 79; opposition,
  81-3
Allocation state, 181, 183; see
  also Production state and
  Economy and the state
'Amarah, Muhammad, 143,
  146-7
Amin, Galal, A, 216
Amir, Samir, 232
Arab League, 5, 19, 67, 72
Arab Nationalism, 20, 38, 43-5,
  49, 153-4, 160, 164, 167-8,
  227
Arab Socialist Union (ASU),
  195-7
Arab-Israeli Conflict, 72, 196,
  236, 239
Arabic language, Arabization,
  19-20, 75, 82, 95, 145,
  155-61, 158, 162, 211
Arendt, Hanna, 226-7
Aristotle, 13, 84, 93, 95, 102-3
Aron, Raymond, 205
Arslan, 'Adel, 236
'Asabiyya, 7, 16, 63, 207-9,
  213, 219, 224, 229-30, 237
Al-Assad, Hafez, 237
Atatürk (Mustapha Kemal),
  112, 115, 236

Augustine (Saint), 104
Authenticity, 11, 16, 162, 170
Authoritarianism, 82, 146, 158,
  207
Ayrout, Henry, 234
'Awdah, 'Abd al-Qadir, 14,
  120, 122-6, 128, 130, 132,
  136
Al-'Azm (family), 37
'Azuri, Nagib, 165

Ba'th Party, 167
Al-Baghdadi, 'Abd al-Qadir,
  151-2
Bahrain, 24, 30-1, 37, 67,
  211-12, 217-18, 221, 223
Al-Banna, Hasan, 119-22, 128,
  170-1
Batatu, Hanna, 235
Al-Bazzaz, 140-1
Béji, Hédi, 9
Ben Bella, Ahmed, 235
Berbers, 49, 63, 82-3, 93,
  223-4, 227
Bousaid (dynasty in Oman), 26
British colonialism, 6, 10, 34,
  37, 60-4, 68, 117, 139, 216,
  218-19, 230
Buyides (dynasty), 234

Caliph(ate), 13-14, 25-6, 28,
  49, 97-8, 100, 102, 109,
  112-14, 116-28, 130, 132,
  134-6, 139-42, 145-6,
  152-3, 160, 169, 189,
  209-10, 233-4
Christian Civilization, 12,
  103-4, 140; Arab Christians,
  21, 163, 193; Christians of
  Lebanon, 32, 226-7;
  Christian states, 56, 59;
  relations with Muslims, 161,
  181
Civil society, 12, 17, 149, 237
Classes: emergence of, 39-41; in

the Maghreb, 75-6, 79-81,
83, 91; in Morocco, 208
Colonialism & state formation,
8, 10, 17, 22, 24, 36, 39,
41-3, 49, 61, 76-8, 116-17,
223
Constitution: law, 3-4; &
umma, 21; in Lebanon, 36,
38; Islam in the Arab
constitutions, 52, 113, 119,
121-4, 132, 137, 139-42,
161; in Al-Banna, 170-1; in
Morocco, 184, 189, 194

Democracy: freedoms, 45; in
the Maghreb, 82-5; in
Western/Arab thought,
91-2, 102, 109-10, 119, 122,
125-8; in Islamic thought, 140
Dhufar, 198, 202
Druzes (in Lebanon), 32, 219,
226
Ad-Duri, 'Abd al-'Aziz, 7

Economy: and emergence of
state system, 7, 23; role of
the state, 9, 34, 78-81, 178,
225; impact of imperialism
39-41, 216; crisis and revolt,
83-5; different economic
systems and
complementarities, 45, 86;
and political culture, 228-32
Education(al), 35, 75, 79, 110,
178-9, 182-4, 186-8, 190,
193, 195, 199, 201, 217
Egypt: state formation, 24-5,
29, 33-6, 38, 40-2; and
Sudan, 73; rise of patriotism,
153-5, 159-60; popular
vision of state authority,
195-9; the military, 234-5
Equality: among states, 56-8;
among Muslims, 125, 129,
142, 144

Al-Farabi, 13, 93-4, 97, 151
Al-Fasi, 'Allal, 15, 141, 154,
161-3
Fromm, Erich, 222-3

Geertz, Clifford, 10, 21, 181
Al-Ghazali, 97
Gulf Cooperation Council
(GCC), 66-7

Harbi, Muhammad, 82-3
Hasa (province), 28-30, 211,
215
Hashimite (dynasty), 38, 43,
221
Hassan II, 28, 70, 184
Hawar Islands, 67
Hegel, T.F., 51, 205
Herzl, Theodor, 239-40
Hijaz, 22-3, 27, 29, 36-8, 43,
65, 215, 219
Hobbes, 13, 92, 106-7, 109
Hourani, Albert, 14, 21, 157,
231
Husayn, Ahmad, 140
Husaynid (dynasty), 33
Al-Husri, Sati', 7, 235

Ibadi (sect), 25-6, 40, 42, 186,
197, 199, 200, 211
Ibn 'Abd al-Wahhab,
Muhammad, 28-9, 211-12
Ibn 'Ali, Husayn, 219
Ibn al-'Anbari, 150
Ibn Bajah, 93
Ibn Badis, 13, 116-18
Ibn Hanbal, 29, 130, 214
Ibn Khaldun, 13, 16, 22, 43, 84,
93, 109, 126, 146, 151, 169,
207-10, 213-14, 228
Ibn Manzur, 151-2, 155
Ibn al-Muqaffa', 99-100
Ibn Nabi, Malek, 237
Ibn Rushd (Averroes), 13, 15,
93, 210
Ibn Sa'ud, 'Abd al-Aziz, 29,
63-4
Ibn Sina (Avicenna), 93
Ibn Taymiyyah, 98, 130, 180
Ibn Tufayl, 83
Al-'Iji, 112, 126
Ijtihad, 120, 131, 135, 140,
144, 146-7
Ikhwan (Saudi), 51, 63-5, 220
Imam: as chief, 23-8, 30; in

Islamic thought, 97-8, 112, 121, 123, 125-8, 145-6, 152; in the Ibadi sect, 186, 200; in Saudi Arabia, 221
Independence, 40-1, 76, 78-9, 81, 113, 118, 120, 125, 154, 161, 178, 183-4, 188-91, 216, 224, 226-7
International Court of Justice (ICJ), 69-70
International Monetary Fund (IMF), 83-4
Iran's revolution, 47, 221-2; war with Iraq, 66-8; Arab reactions, 147, 230-1
Iraq: state formation, 6, 21, 24, 28-30, 36-8, 43; territory, 67-8; conflict with Syria, 73; islamism, 133, 140; the military, 235
Ishaq, Adib, 157-9, 163, 173
Islam: in modern politics, 17; panislamism, 20, 26, 44, 49, 153-4, 157, 159-62; in Arab constitutions, 52; as a pol. theory, 57; islamism in the Maghreb, 81-4; Islamic view on authority, 91-111; Muslim Islamic pol. thought, 112-48; Islam & patriotism, 152-9; Islamist views of nation, 168-73; militant Islamism, 201
Islamic Liberation Party, 132, 138
Israel, 4, 9, 48, 52, 54, 72, 160, 168, 174, 182, 196, 224, 230, 236, 239
Issawi, Charles, 40, 238
Istiqlal Party, 141, 190, 203

Al-Jabarti, 'A., 169
Jawish, 'Abd al-'Aziz, 139
Jihad (Holy War), 58, 98, 129, 152
Jordan, 6, 14, 21, 24, 37, 43, 50, 61, 73, 91, 133, 217-19, 221

Kāmel, Mustapha, 162-4

Al-Kaylani, Rashid 'A., 235
Khalafallah, Muhammad A., 14, 143-7, 162
Khalid, Khalid M., 13, 115-16
Khalid (the tribe of Bani), 30
Khalid Ibn al-Walid, 233
Khalifa (Bahrain ruling family), 31
Al-Khatib, 'Abd al-Karim, 128
Al-Khomeini, Ruhollah, 147
Khuri, Ra'if, 157
Kurds, 49, 63, 227
Kuwait: 4, 206, 215; pol. system, 24, 29-31, 91, 221; & colonization, 36-8, 218; national identity, 44; state territory, 49, 65-8, 72; pol. economy, 229

Labour Unions in the Maghreb, 80-1, 84-5, 88
Laroui, 'Abdallah, 75, 217, 239
League of Nations, 10, 37, 60, 219, 231
Lebanon: state formation, 6, 16, 31-2, 205, 219; under the mandate, 36-8, 61-3; Lebanese identity, 44; territory, 72; pol. system, 91; sectarianism, 222-6
Legitimacy, 7, 11, 16-17, 20, 22-3, 27, 34-5, 42, 44-5, 75-7, 80, 85, 178, 181, 184, 202, 209, 214, 217-22, 226-7, 235
Libya, 23-4, 29, 43, 49, 52, 69, 86, 88, 91, 216, 223, 236-7
Locke, 13, 92, 107-9
Lord Curzon, 61
Lustick, Ian, 10, 224-5

Machiavelli, 92-3, 102, 106-7, 109
Al-Mahdiyya, 216
Mahfouz, Nagib, 101
Mamluks, 31, 34, 234, 237
Ma'nid (dynasty in Lebanon), 31
Maronites, 6, 16, 32, 219, 224-7

Mauritania, 19; territory, 62, 66, 69-71, 88
Al-Mawad, 13, 97, 122, 130, 151
Al-Mawdudi, Abu al-A'la, 109, 129
Migrant workers, 185, 188
Migration, to the city, 203
Military (the): & the state, 16, 207, 232-7; military oligarchy, 23-4, 33-7; Ottoman, 58; & patriotism, 166; Moroccan, 183, 188; dissidence, 201; in Oman, 203
Modernization, 21, 179, 182, 187, 216, 222
Morocco: state formation, 7, 10, 16, 20, 23, 27-8, 30, 38, 41; territory & territorial conflicts, 63, 66, 69, 70; pol. & social movements, 76, 78, 82-4, 87-8; social conditions, 182-4; elections, 188-94
Al-Mubarak, Muhammad, 128-33
Muhammad 'Ali, 29, 34-5, 60, 155, 215-16
Muslim Brotherhood, 119-20, 122, 132-3, 160, 170-1, 185
Al-Mutwalli, M., 141-2
Al-Muti'i, 119

An-Nabahani, Taqiuddine, 14, 128, 132-8, 227
An-Nadim, 'Abdallah, 160-1
Nasser, Gamal 'Abd an-, 14, 20, 53, 154, 165-6, 168, 185, 195, 197, 232
Nassur, Adib, 160
National state or Nation-state, 3, 8-9, 11, 15, 20-1, 35, 47, 49-51, 53, 55-6, 60, 76-7, 80, 156, 171, 205, 207, 211, 220, 222-3
Nation: Maronite, 6; Syrian, 7, 152; Arab, 50-5, 77, 87, 140, 159; in the Maghreb, 75; Islamic, 117, 126-8; and the Caliph, 112, 119, 126-8,

135-7; in al-Banna, 120-2; in al-Mubarak, 130-1; in Khalafallah, 143-6; French, 155; in S. Arabia, 211; see also Umma and Watan
Nationalisation(s), 4, 229, 231
Nationalism, 6, 9-10, 14, 16, 20, 38-41, 43-5, 61, 76, 153-4, 157-60, 162-4, 168, 200-11, 218, 226-7, 231
Nizam al-Mulk, 13, 99-101

OAU (Organization for African Unity), 69, 71
Oil, 4, 6, 19, 45, 48, 68, 72, 181, 186-7, 202, 221, 229-30
Oman, 7, 16, 19, 23, 25-7, 29-30, 37-8, 40-2, 68-9, 177-8, 186-7, 197-203
Ottoman Empire, 8, 24, 48, 57, 58, 60, 67, 68, 218, 237
Oumlil, 'Ali, 169, 171

Palestine, 5, 24, 37-8, 60-1, 72, 133, 165, 226
Palestinians, 4, 14, 45, 50, 132, 225
Pan-Germanism, 226
Pan-Slavism, 226
Party(ies), 71, 76, 78-9, 81, 85, 120, 121, 122, 132-3, 137-8, 141, 167, 170, 181, 190-7, 203, 208, 214, 232
Plato, 13, 84-5, 99, 102-3
Polisario, 13, 84, 93, 95, 99, 102-3
Production states, 181, 183; see also Allocation states
Public sector, 4, 183, 229; see also Economy and the role of the state
Pye, Lucian, 222

Qabous, Sultan of Oman, 26, 178, 187
Al-Qadhafi, 9, 86-7, 237
Al-Qaradawi, Youssef, 120, 128, 139
Qasim, 'Abd al-Karim, 67, 235

Quraysh, 126, 209
Qutb, Sayyid, 120, 133, 138, 159, 171-2, 227

Representative government, 33, 38, 70, 91, 98, 122-4, 126, 128, 161, 184, 188-9, 193-5, 200-1, 225, 235
Revolution, 40, 61, 68, 73, 78, 108, 112, 147, 149, 154-5, 157-8, 163, 166, 178-9, 184-5, 187, 195-6, 231, 234-5
Rida, Rashid, 119-20, 159, 169
Al-Rihani, Amin, 53, 212
Riots, 83-5, 155, 183, 203
Rousseau, Jean-Jacques, 13, 92, 108-9, 155, 163

Sabbah (dynasty in Kuwait), 30-1
Sadat, Anwar, 185
Sadian (dynasty in Morocco), 28
Sahara: 6, 34; West Saharian conflict, 69-71, 73, 87, 162, 203
As-Sanhuri, 139-40
As-Sanusiyya, 216
Saudi Arabia: 6, 7; state foundation, 28-30, 210-19; territory, 63-4; pol. regime, 91, 220-2; pol. economy, 229-30
As-Sayyid, Ahmad Lutfi, 231
Secular regimes, secularization, 7, 24, 30-1, 52, 56, 64, 113, 155
Self-determination, 61-2, 70, 92, 109
Seurat, Michel, 229
Ash-Shahbandar, 'A., 152
Shari'ah, 29, 34-5, 42, 52, 96, 98, 184
Shari'ati, 'Ali, 109
Shi'a: 10, 42; in Yemen, 26; in Lebanon, 32, 223-5, 227; Shi'i Fiqf, 146-7; in the Gulf, 211
Shihab, Fuad, 225

Shihab (dynasty in Lebanon), 31
Shroener, 226
Shura, 120, 122-8, 130, 135-6, 140-4, 178, 186, 199-200
Sidqi, Bakr, 235-6
Socialism, 166, 185, 195
Somalia, 19, 60, 236
Stinchcombe, 219
Strike(s), 79-80, 88, 201, 214
Sudan, 10, 19, 43, 49, 73, 109, 216, 227, 237
Sunni, 10, 26-7, 29, 32, 152, 186, 211, 223, 226
Surur, 128
Skyes-Picot Agreement, 60
Syria: 6-7, 21, 24, 28-9, 31, 34, 36-8, 44, 49, 61-2, 73, 91, 133, 152-3, 159, 206, 216, 219, 223-4, 226-7, 229, 235-7

De Tocqueville, 108
Taba (enclave), 72
At-Tahtawi, 14, 155-9, 169, 173, 177
Tax(es), 23, 152, 188, 214, 228
Territorial definition, 7-8, 48
Territory(ies), 11, 19, 23, 29, 32, 35, 37-8, 43, 50-2, 59, 61, 66, 68, 70-3, 130-1, 137, 151, 158, 165-6, 172, 209-10, 226, 239
Terrorism, 5, 7-9, 11, 32, 36, 47-50, 53, 55, 60, 62-74, 76-7, 174, 221
Thomas Aquinas St., 104
Thousand & One Nights, 99, 101
Tizi Ouzou, 82
Trade barriers, 40
Treaty of Ifrane, 69
Troeller, Gary, 6, 218
Tunisia, 22, 33-4, 36, 38, 40-1, 62, 76-84, 86-8, 91, 153, 223
At-Tunsi, Khayr Ad-Din, 157

UN Security Council, 67, 73
USSR, 73, 238
Al-'Umar, Dhahir, 37

Al-'Urayssi, 'A., 165
Umayyads, 112, 144, 233
'Umda, 185
Umma, 7, 14, 20-1, 49, 53, 94,
    101, 149-54, 158-60, 164,
    166-8, 171, 203, 226; *see
    also Nation and Watan*
Union Socialiste de Forces
    Populaires (USFP)-Morocco,
    190-4, 203
United Arab Emirates, 6, 19,
    24, 29, 68, 91
United Arab Republic (UAR),
    74
Unity, 6, 16-17, 20, 52-5, 57,
    69, 82, 85, 121-2, 140, 160,
    165-6, 168, 196, 211, 221,
    226-7, 236
Universal suffrage, 86
'Uqair Convention, 66, 68

Wealth distribution: in Islamic
    thought, 138, 201; in
    capitalism, 50, 79; in the
    Maghreb, 80-5; & reforms,
    185, 196

Wahhabis, 20, 25, 34, 65,
    212-16, 220
Watan, 14, 149-66, 168, 170-3;
    see also Nation and Umma
Water, 48, 51, 66-7, 72-3, 150,
    191, 214
Weber, Max, 44, 46, 51, 81,
    185, 205, 232
Wilson, 61

Yemen Arab Republic (North),
    7, 19, 23, 25-9, 36, 42, 68-9,
    91, 203, 206, 211-12, 216
Yemen, People's Democratic
    Republic of (South), 19-20,
    24, 25-7, 29, 36, 42, 62,
    68-9, 91, 203, 206, 211-12,
    215, 216
Youth, or the young, 38, 44,
    80-1, 85-8, 179, 186, 190-4,
    196, 199-201, 217

Az-Za'im, Husni, 235-6
Az-Zahrawi, 165
Zaydis, 26-7, 211
Zuraiq, Constantine, 235